Praise for *Electric Katieland*

"Madame Electric has wowed the mind, stilled the body, and opened my heart. Plants come in all shapes and sizes, and it's incredible to learn of how Katie found her medicine. This book will be yet another drop in the ocean of wisdom, present, past, and future."

— Chris Cole, MA, LPC, *Mind The Center*

"This book is a firsthand account of spiritual awakening and healing Trauma with integrative methods, including the use of sacred sacraments — psychedelics. Katie traverses her soul's human experience of suffering, duality, and separation with courage, humor, and radical honesty. Her book takes you on a page-turning winding journey that highlights the persistent and patient path of a Spiritual Warrior having a traumatic human experience. Katie's life story proves that healing from Trauma is non-linear, confusing, and often-times messy. And this is okay, because this is the reality of what the collective experiences when healing from Trauma. With each page, Katie earns more trust credits with herself as she trust falls into her SELF. As her awakening unfolds, Katie gives you permission to do healing your own way — you absolutely cannot get your healing wrong. Katie truly embodies the Way-shower archetype and teaches you that it is okay to find your own unique path to healing yourSelf. Through her life story, may you find permission to meet your own Inner Healer within your curiosity, courage, creativity, connection, and compassion — and to begin to trust that your soul's song will sing you Home."

— Shannon Myers, M.S., CRC, CIMHP, Founder of *The Integrative Counselor*

"A blistering depiction, generously peppered with jest and levity, of the shackles of patriarchal dominance experienced by one feminine embodied being and her journey breaking free, finding healing, and claiming her truth with the help of psychedelics in a world afraid. From her unrelentingly expressive and passionate youth, to the depression from suppression, and on to rediscovering her own genius, Katie paints a captivating mosaic of the heartbreak and freedom in challenging unhealthy systems while rediscovering her wild heart in the modern world."

— James Eshleman, Psychedelic Guide, *The Center of All Directions*

"A viscerally powerful description of the deep, confusing, and soul depleting wounds created by the invisible hand of an ancestral patriarchal system. Katie's story reveals the depths of will and courage needed to reclaim one's sovereignty and soul from the grip of deeply felt forces of selfestrangement. She shows us that motherhood and earth medicines are powerful initiatory tools that can free women from the illusion that they are powerless, unworthy, and undeserving of living in harmony with their deepest selves. If we are to change the world, we need more women healing and redefining motherhood, womanhood, and the sacred task of embodying the divine feminine in our families, our work, and our relationships."

– Michaela Carlin, *The Psychedelic Mom Podcast Host*

Electric Katieland

A Journey of Awakening

KATIE MOSELEY

ISBN: 979-8-9888541-2-8 (Paperback)
ISBN: 979-8-9888541-3-5 (Digital)

Library of Congress Control Number: 2023914632

Any references to historical events, people, or places are from the author's memory and perspective. Certain names, places, identifying characteristics, and events have been changed to protect the identities of those involved.

The author of this book does not dispense medical advice or prescribe the use of any technique as a form of treatment for physical, emotional, or medical problems without the advice of a physician, either directly or indirectly. The intent of the author is only of offer information of a general nature to share her personal story of healing. In the event you use any information in this book for yourself, the author and the publisher assume no responsibility for your actions.

Front cover image by Pulp Studio.
Interior design by Laura Jones.

Printed in the United States of America.

Denver, Colorado

www.electrickatieland.com

DISCLAIMER

~Everything here is true, but may not be entirely factual. Certain names and identifying characteristics have been changed, whether or not noted in the text, and certain characters and events have been compressed or reordered. There are as many perspectives as there are people in the world. Thus, out of more than 8 billion filters, this one is a reflection of mine, and it is my truth expressed in words. ~

AUTHOR'S NOTE

The intention of this book is to tell a story of healing trauma, which is a collective trauma playing out behind the closed doors of many homes around the world. It is also a trauma being played out in front of us in everyday life. It is a story that speaks of healing on the micro and macro level. It is the healing of one family, healing ancestral trauma for generational lines, and healing the collective through a massive shift in consciousness. Healing is a spiral of awakening. At times it seems more trauma is created in the attempt to heal. This story is told to show what it is to live in truth. To speak outside the script. My way of speaking may not be true through the lens and filter of another's space time dimension of the human experience. In a quantum reality, every event that could happen, has happened, and is happening. There is no blame. There is only the experience. There is only the expression. There is only creation. There is only Light and Dark. There are feelings, an infinite range of feelings. Being human is being a spectrum. This is the spectrum as I experienced it. I offer gratitude to all who danced in this experience with me. The characters from my life who played both hero and villain are a reflection of humanity. There is some of this in all of us. This is the mirror effect and I acknowledge it. When the mirror is cleared to a single zero point, there is only Love. I love all the people, characters, lessons, and experiences described in this book. My intention is to honor and allow all aspects of each human to be seen, loved, and accepted, especially the shadows, so they can transcend into light. There is no judgement. Through every window of pain, there is a greater capacity for love. As consciousness expands, my intention is to see the shadow and release it for myself and all involved for the greatest good of all. Infinite love and blessings to all who walk the path in the Age of Aquarius. There is only love here.

DEDICATION

This book is dedicated to my two amazing, precious daughters. They are miracles. They are the bravest souls I have ever met, and I am forever grateful for them. I am blessed to be their mother. They inspire me every day and have been the light to keep the kindle burning to spark this into creation. I honor their full range of emotions and the gift they are to this world. Their wisdom, innocence, joy, empathy, unconditional love, and laughter is pure magic. Thank you for choosing me. I choose you both for eternity with infinite love from my heart.

THANK YOU

I extend deep love and gratitude to the wisdom of the plants. The spirit of Ayahuasca, Psilocybin, and Kambo have been Guides, showing me how to reconnect with God–Source Consciousness. I remain in awe of their expansive nature and infinite love.

Introduction

"What is inside that you are holding onto? Is it guilt? Is it blame? What is it? Look deeper, Katie..." She floated away from me, as her soft voice, with its Eastern European accent, echoed in the halls of my mind. Her voice. I knew it from eons ago. Through the stars, the galaxies, the infinite string of eternities. Like waking from a fainting, her voice, my teacher, guiding my soul back to Self, as I wake up out of the dream.

When you call her in...she appears.

Ayahuasca, ayahuasca, ayahuasca.

The medicine is in you. She is conscious.

Wake up.

The story of my Earth journey is told in a triad. This journey is not linear, and neither is the book. It can be read front to back, back to front, and middle to the outer expansion points. Each chapter is a moment in time woven while past, present, and future are happening simultaneously. As within, so without. If you wish to start at my entry point, that is Triptych I. If you wish to dive into the Underworld with the spirit of the plants, that is Triptych III. If you wish for every tunnel of light in-between, including the entry points of my daughters, those are Triptych II.

No artist tolerates reality.

~Nietzsche

Contents

Triptych I: Paradise Lost

Triptych II: The Garden of Light and Dark

Triptych III: Dreamscape

Triptych I:

Paradise Lost

Lipstick Shoes

I smeared the clammy red rouge from the crown of my forehead, crushing it over the bridge of my nose, pouting my sacred soft lips, and landing on the dimple in my chin. My four- year-old soul peered into the mirror with Braveheart blue eyes and thought, *this feels right.*`

I attempt to trace my sanity, and it's as easy as writing cursive in reverse. I know for certain I have at times leapt right over the edge. I've willingly taken a swan dive with a blissful smile on my face. The smile of freedom. At other moments, I was most desperate, waking up to a mid-falling-off-a-cliff feeling, like a dream that leaves you with a caved stomach, gasping for air. *Oh shit! How much longer till I hit the ground? Just let me bounce. I need relief from the g-force.*

Even during desperate times, everything appeared right as rain, just before it turned into a burning house. I know the drill: numerous friends, full bank account, steady work, and then whoosh, up in flames it goes with one mistake. Some people walk on coals. I walked on eggshells. I used the "house on fire" analogy for my husband, Kane, one sweat-logged Texas afternoon. He needed instruction and I volunteered to be the in-your-face-teacher.

I grew frustrated from his lack of engagement. The blood began to sizzle on my neck. "Here. This is how it works," I snipped, as I drew him a picture and labeled each stage. Sometimes it was over house chores, paying bills, the wish to plan a vacation, or because most days he was stoned. He told white lies to disappear for hours fishing, instead of connecting. I heard the voices of my parents, "you have to work at a marriage." A man being a project was normalized for me. Whether I was trying to persuade him how to act or convince him I was worthy of love, I thought this type of "effort" was ordinary.

My fingers shook with agitation as I hastily taped the paper to the fridge door, knocking off several ticky-tacky souvenir magnets, one from Arizona with a cactus and roadrunner, and one from that mind-blowing trip to Oklahoma. The magnet was a blank yellow shape of the state. Yep. That's Oklahoma. Kane had a butterfly land on his finger as he held a machete. I remember the look of enchantment on his face. Those looks were deceiving, because they were fleeting.

"You're abrasive, darlin'. That's why no one likes you," he consoled. My prince charming, how did I ever find him. He thinks all "Northernerns" are blunt. In Texas culture, people talk around the subject instead of getting straight to the point. At times it could be considered a more fanciful way to converse, at others it left a person wide open for manipulation. I got swirled up in the stories, like a cattle dog spinning me round and round until I was dizzy. Yes, now the cattle dog is in control, and I didn't even know I was being herded.

I'm sure I made a delightful impression on Kane's friends and family. "Oh my, this must be how Northerners do things," they surely thought to themselves, with cocked heads and pursed lips. "She needs some Jesus in her life."

Burning house phase 1: cherry red stick of dynamite; phase 2: innocent match; phase 3: house fully engulfed in flames. The trick is to prevent the match from ever meeting the dynamite, despite the fact they were made for each other. What would he care anyways? He said himself that he wished he came home to find the house burned down. Daily.

We lived in his grandparent's dilapidated ranch house in cow-poke land. He inherited it. "Yup, this whole thing has bum wiring from Pops," he said as he gazed at the ceiling, scraping his mouth with a toothpick, while sucking the spit through his teeth. I hated that sound. It made my skin crawl. How did I wind up with this hillbilly? His dating profile said he was into techno and sci-fi movies, but this was like someone put *Deliverance* on repeat.

"You can polish a turd, but it would be easier if it just burnt to the ground. One of these days…" he sighed, lost in a dream of arson. He was a bit outlandish, and that's what kept my attention. Was Kane a real person, or was he a conglomerate of all the movies he'd ever watched, alone as a child. I couldn't decide. If my soul signed up to learn how to transform from victim to victor, his signed up to be the villain. He added a few embellishments. Villains are raised by watching their daddy do lines of coke on the front porch and prying their eyes open during horror movies to "make them a man." The villain always has a parent that was murdered. Yes, Kane drank deep from the family cup of trauma, just like me.

I jabbed my finger, pointing to the paper on the fridge as he turned his back to me. He used to look at me in the eyes when we first met, now I never get to see them. Where were the flowers? What happened to *Someone should tell you you're beautiful every day, sweetheart?* Those days were already gone. He was the first one to say 'I love you' when we started dating, but not anymore. That was the love part, and this was the bomb.

"Do you get it now? Why aren't you paying attention?" I asked with the condescendence of a 1940s schoolmarm who had been walked over one too many times.

"Real nice, Katie. I'm fixin' to go," Kane grumbled. "You know...you sound like one of those uppity carpetbaggers. Better watch that."

What is he...the headmaster? Worse, the slave master. I forgot I was in the South. Epigenetically, he had a sadistic side.

"Go where?" I asked as he turned his back to me again. No response. This was typical, right from the beginning.

I'm from near Chicago. A dating website landed me in rural Texas. While I was running from something—being publicly shamed from a sexual assault case at work, to be specific—I fell into a big black hole. It sucked me up completely. Kane was from the deep South. The son of a drug-dealing father that had a shoot-out in the middle of town. It took place a few blocks from where we now lived. It was as if they stole a page from a movie script. Our script. And we were deep in the middle of a scene.

Kane didn't like to talk about family ancestry. "Jesus, Katie. You don't talk about that stuff in the South," he snipped. "You ask too many questions. People don't want to know." There were a lot of things about Southern culture that took me years to decode. Family origins was one of the taboos.

As I made my way to Texas, I snuck the dynamite in on the U-Haul, along with my asshole cat. But Kane had dynamite too. A stack of it, and he loved to hold the match.

My exit strategies were limited. Is it possible to extinguish a smoldering stick? Nah, I'm pretty sure I'm stuck watching the fireworks and waiting to see what the collateral damage looks like. Though they all involve fire, not one explosion is exactly the same. I'd be lying if I claimed it wasn't entertaining and even at its best, electrifying.

Explosion to the laymen. To a habitual self-destructor? Expansion.

Cut to typical, beginning of life, rosy montage. What kind of chromosomal double helix dance was taking place when I entered this confusing world anyways? What possessed me to cross over from the limitless ecstasy on the other side of the universe? Birth…it just happens.

Truth be told, being a baby is a bit foggy, but my husband recalls his own infancy with questionable detail. He won't laugh. He'll say it without any doubt, his Southern drawl as certain and as unapologetic as when he states it'll be 115 degrees out today, and I should water the dogs.

Like a Vietnam Vet having a flashback, he'll declare, "I recall coming out of the womb. It was a rude awakening into a cold, noisy room." He'll continue with the dignified air of a Confederate commander, "I was unaccustomed to the confines of my body." *Is this guy for real?* Apparently, the process was traumatic in nature, and yet he delivered himself, unfazed.

My mother-in-law, a devout Southern Baptist, lovingly scoffs at his reincarnation stories. Her words swirl with Texas twang, "Bless his heart. I taught him better than thayt."

As I gazed at Kane, he assured me with a dry nod, "I never took to all that Baptist programming. It's more likely we were seeded here by extraterrestrials." He was eccentric, and that's what I liked about him. True to art student coding, I wasn't interested in suburban Bob. I felt like life was some kind of pseudo movie, where people were assigned parts. I think I was the flakey unwanted girl, cast by my father. Kane was playing some kind of lead character. He was amusing, charming, and switched up the tone enough to keep the movie suspenseful. Like a movie you can't look away from, he had me hooked. It took me awhile to know if he was the villain or the hero. I couldn't see much in a house filled with smoke.

In lieu of a womb memory, I inherited a thoughtfully attended baby book, inscribed with dates and details noted beneath the photos. I studied the cover of the album from the 1970s, its caricatures displaying freakishly huge heads and eyes. Not an ounce of cute painted into that horrifying artwork. They may as well have put the child from Rosemary's Baby on there. "Oh, she looks like an angel! You must be so proud," the ladies at the Christening would ooh and ahh.

Mom used her 1960s typewriter to document sentimental events from my babyhood. I picture her, solemn, sitting alone in a dimly lit house, contemplating what she should detail about her baby. "Hmm, I suppose they will want to know the basics." Mother struggled to make decisions for herself—I imagine because she was rarely given the opportunity. I'm not sure what original use she had intended for her typewriter. She was the first in her family to go to college. She became a preschool teacher in the late 70s, when women were expected to giggle and act ditzy—got herself hired by some macho principal who thought of the faculty as his flock of little girls. And that worked for her, because due to her childhood trauma, she was emotionally stunted. That's what poverty and patriarchy do.

She noted developmental characteristics, stating, "Katie is alert, active, and curious," along with a short story about me spilling a gallon of cherry Kool-Aid all over the kitchen floor. Nothing too out of the ordinary. I can see she wanted to embrace her children—she loved children. But she didn't always know how. It's like the wires of empathy and objectification got crossed.

My grandmother said she hated breastfeeding. "It was painful!" she shared, clearly resentful. No one appreciated it, so why do it? But she had to do it, to keep the baby alive…but no one was appreciating that either. Because children cost money, they were seen as a burden, especially if you were recovering from the Depression or got pregnant out of wedlock, like my grandmother did. You weren't just unappreciated, you were shamed, ostracized—and you passed that trauma along to your children.

Much like most babies of the late 70s, I was nurtured by being dumped off to 'cry it out' alone in my crib for hours on end, smacked on the hand, spanked on the butt by age one, and treated like an adorable doll who was an incredible chore. People were being fed the image of love in magazines, but not shown *how* to love. They were taught "tough love," which is rejection, withholding, and punishment. Other "love" came from external validation. The connection to the heart got lost on the boat while immigrating from Poland. It got swallowed up by the American Dream. It was image, not energy. It was a glossy picture of a hug, not an actual skin-to-skin, breaths-in-sync, hearts-touching hug.

Mom assured me I was cherished from the start, "Oh yes, we were so happy when we got to view you through the window of the nursery in the hospital!"

"Did anyone hold me?" I questioned in bewilderment.

"Well, the nurses did, but newborns mostly sleep. Babies cry when they are hungry, tired, or need a diaper change. They helped with that. They started sleep training you so I could rest. Back then they gave mothers medicine to dry up their milk so we wouldn't leak all over our nice clothes when we went home. And of course I held you! You rode in the front seat of the car with me when Daddy drove us home, sweetie," she placated.

"Don't babies cry to communicate? Like to communicate an emotional need…like to be held and comforted after being held for nine months next to your heartbeat?" I would challenge her to ponder. But I could feel the block. She would stare off and change the subject. The only training taking place in that hospital was training a mother's instinct to go offline, to emotionally disconnect from her baby.

They sold her the 1970s version of the Twilight Sleep birthing method. Mom was taught by her pediatrician that breastfeeding was for poor people. This was a stigma she desperately wanted to shed. The luxury of a new kind of motherhood was being bottle fed to her on the boob tube. This was the status shift she was longing for. Her happiness banked on it.

"Oh, you liked to be alone," Mom suggested, when I asked her what I was like as an infant. *What?* Mind you, I am the middle child, with two male siblings. I suspect I was *left* alone, without much of a choice. Despite my disbelief, she insisted, "Oh yes, you wanted to lie by yourself in your crib. You liked that."

It sounds strange. Maybe I had already given up. Was I a super goth baby? No, a loner baby. *She needs space,* Mom thinks. It was easier for her to look away.

"Mom, babies don't learn to self-soothe. They learn no one is coming to help them, so after minutes or hours of crying, day after day, they give up," I told her.

"That's ridiculous, Katie. You can't spoil the baby, or she'll never let you put her down. She'll be sleeping in your bed until she's ten!" Mom declared. Half the married couples I knew weren't having sex anyways, so what did it matter.

"Some therapists think the baby adapts a foundational core belief about life, like "*I am alone, and no matter how much I cry, no one is coming to help me,*" I informed her.

"Well, I guess I just screwed up everything. I guess I'm a horrible mother," she reacted.

She continued with justifications, "Babies have to learn how to sleep. Adults have to work in the morning."

"The baby can die from failure to thrive if you don't hold it, Mom," I said with concern. "I'm going to co-sleep."

"I held you, Katie. Please stop criticizing me," she pleaded. Maybe I didn't die, but it kick-started a fight or flight response in my nervous system, that I'm still untethering.

This concept of "work." It wasn't the same as mine, but they were encouraged to sleep train—shamed into it. I know, because people tried to shame me into doing it when I became a mother, but I declined. Every bone in my body refused to ignore my baby. How did we get so disconnected with being human? It's a collective sickness, and we are paying the price in in-utero trauma. Mother dumped gallons of cortisol into my developing nervous system during those first nine months. She didn't have a doula or midwife. She had the feminist movement that told her she should do it all-on her own. She had the bitterness and judgement of previous mothers. The culture monopolized on her fear. They not only threw the baby out with the bathwater, they threw the mother out too. Then she got ridiculed for being a martyr. But what else could she be? Feminism said she could regain her power by acting like a man. Get a corporate job. Then they could tax her and the baby in daycare. Give her birth control pills, ignore her thirty-day cycle, make hormones an illness. There were multiple "formulas" being introduced in the 70s.

"Women used to die in childbirth. You're lucky we have doctors now," Dad would boast, but I wasn't convinced. What did he know about giving birth.

"Women used to have to rely on having wide hip bones that could bear children. Now they have procedures and women are allowed to get jobs. Heck, they could even be the boss someday. A lot has changed!" Dad cheered. "They don't have babies with midwives out in the woods like a bunch of animals. Things are more sophisticated." Why is this man talking to me about childbirth? I wanted to be guided through the birthing rite of passage by female elders, not drugged and strapped to a birthing table for someone to extract a baby. Yes, that was terrifying. Mom had every right to be afraid. A nightlight with a smiling moon wasn't going to be enough.

Though my babyhood is a hazy memory, my recollection of early childhood is as vivid as a burning orange flame. I piece the time together and discover these glowing memories were taking form when I was three or four years old. Dad is trying to curb me, "You only *think* you remember things from looking at pictures," he tells me, "babies don't remember anything until they are around 4 years old. Most of them don't even feel pain as infants. The doctors will tell ya." But I know that medieval myth isn't true. I won't give him the current studies. He won't hear me anyways. He's been culturally conditioned to do hurtful things to children. No one wants to wake up to that. He had to be right, and therefore I had to be wrong.

I recollect events where no photographs were taken to immortalize them. As inconvenient as it may have been, I was acutely aware from a very early age. My awareness was at its peak before the ego was fully developed. At that stage, I could still remember the prior world. The one my soul came from.

When I was three, we moved to South Dakota. The land of cornfield queens. A yearly opportunity to be crowned the Queen of the Corn Festival. Spoiler alert—it wasn't me…ever. Our kitchen flaunted cheap linoleum tile and the typical dark and gloomy style of the decade.

"I love it! It's beautiful!" Mom cheered as Dad showed her his sack-lunch colored castle.

Perhaps I'm prone to depression as a result of that décor. It imprinted me with unwavering apathy. No baby likes to crawl on puke green carpet and mustard yellow plastic flooring. A design palette suspect for spiraling the psyche of millions of people.

As a toddler I hobbled from the orange and brown marbleized shaggy carpet to the decorative black iron railing in the kitchen. I clutched the bars. "Wow! A playpen for adults!" thought my quick, pre-verbal mind.

I visualize a domestic-products catalog advertisement boasting its message: "Here's a miniature prison in your kitchen so your wife will know her place!" A boardroom full of pea-green plaid suits muck it up over Rob Roys. That's how I imagine life being as a woman in the 1970s, not much different than the 1950s. Barf. At least my adulthood has been spared the essence of that era. *Seriously? You think you dodged that bullet? The extra strength Dawn and concentrated formula Tide fumes must be getting to your head.*

We lived in the Great Plains for two years. I chummed around with my older brother, Jason, while my mom storked my younger brother, Jon. We celebrated a couple Halloweens there, with Jason's face paint always looking better than mine.

"Well, if you would learn to sit still, Katie," Mom would scold. Ugh, Jason was forever the golden example of perfection, not a wiggle in his bones. The only squirm he let squeeze out was a smitten grin on the side of his lip as he was patted on the head.

"Now wiggle your nose like a cute little mouse, Jason!" she instructed him, as she finished his makeup.

"Like this, Mommy?" he grinned, and then shot a smarmy glare at me.

"Oh, my goodness, you are adorable! Those whiskers turned out perfect," she doted, as she admired her artistry. Our animal costumes were sewn

by her, from the patterns she bought at the local Sears store. She was a sanc-
timonious Pinterest mom before the internet was invented. "You know, you
can put little raisins with peanut butter on the celery sticks and pretend they
are ants. The kids love it," I would overhear her telling random stay-at-home
moms at the pool. She wanted to be seen too. But I think she was largely
faced with chauvinism, which resulted in passive aggressive tendencies. It
was so passive, I didn't pick up on it until my twenties.

Mom turned to me to study my presentability. "Oh, Katie, you've already
smeared your cheetah spots," she said, frowning with disappointment. She
wanted me to look perfect, so she could look perfect. Her worthiness was
tied up in us kids. She was groomed into the family code of dysfunction.

I looked up at her like a kitten who had licked clean an open container of tuna left abandoned on the countertop. I was mildly feral, as a
cheetah should be. The tuna was pushed into the corner of the floor by
now. I smeared my face with it, whiskers and all. *Don't even look at Jason.*
You know he's got that smug mouse smile plastered on his face, like he
coyly snatched the cheese out of the trap. He was master of the game and
was always "doing the right thing." It worked for him, but not for me.
I couldn't sell it like he did. I was the junkyard pit bull to his pompous
pedigree.

My toddler teammate was a girl named Beth. She had platinum blonde
hair. It was thin and wispy, like a baby's first locks that haven't yet been cut.
She must have been great fun to hang out with, because one day, at age four,
I decided to walk to her house. I didn't tell anyone. I just left. As it turns out,
this is kind of my style.

"You were trying to run away!" Mom panicked as she told the original
version of the story. Then it deflated to, "You were trying to go to Beth's
house." Something tells me it was a combination of the two, but who wants
to repeat a story about their four-year-old already wanting to run away. I bet
I was searching for a walking stick, that woody insect that captivated us as
children. *That stick is alive! It has eyes…and antennae!* It wasn't as colorful as a
ladybug tickling our arm hairs, but its microscopic universe was fascinating
to behold.

In our neighborhood there was a spacious open area of grass in the shape
of a half circle. A sidewalk rounded the corner, but I chose to walk in the
cool garden of jade. I was hypnotized by the smell of fresh cut summer grass.
It summoned me to lie in its crisp yet soft embrace for one dizzying minute.
At that age, the plants still had sparkles around them. It was like a hazy silver

mist that went around each green leaf…and it wiggled. I loved watching it. I wondered if that was the glitter the fairies used. I looked for them too, but I never saw one. In the picture books, they were always by the blue bells. I'll have to find some of those.

That day, it was dusk and the sky was overcast. The air hung as if a storm was coming in; calm, yet intense—a little scary, but I liked it. It felt both powerful and peaceful. A storm *was* coming in. I had no idea it would last for the next forty years.

A while later, my parents found me wandering around, chasing butterflies of bliss in the vacant yard. A memory trapped in my senses like a favorite song. It breathes with freedom and excludes being scolded. However, I'm sure I was. No poor deed went unnoticed in our house.

On weekdays, Mom took us to Beth's house so she could gossip with her mother over exchanged casserole recipes. "King Chicken Ranch, Greg loves this one. Puts him right to sleep in the recliner," she says, with her wine-colored lips gleaming, content with her results. "You have to use almost the whole container of Velveeta, but it's worth it." The gelatinized yellow cube had as many chemicals as rat poison, but was a little more discreet. Beth fancied her mother's makeup, and so did I. We locked ourselves in her mother's bathroom and tested out her beauty supplies. Black mascara, blue eye shadow, ruddy blush, and bright magenta lipstick. Beth was my kind of gal: brave, theatrical, and resourceful. The doorknob was missing a lock. We improvised by pulling out one drawer until it blocked the door.

"Girls…you better not be getting into the make-up!" Beth's mom called upstairs.

Beth reached out and smeared her mother's lipstick in a bloody slash across the mirror, as if to mark her territory. She's so bold. I think I have a crush on her.

We squished ourselves onto the countertop, straddling the sink to see in the mirror, as we tried on different faces. My shin pressed against the sharp faucet opening, as I balanced my body with one big toe on the mirror. I examined my altered appearance and allowed the feeling of this new person to rise within me like a blazing Phoenix. It was instinctive at age four. As fearless as a kid from *Lord of the Flies*. "I'll do what I have to do…to survive," I told myself, as I stared at my reflection.

"We made Ritz crackers with Jiffy and grape jelly for you girls! Come and get some!" Mom shouted down the hall. Yess, I love snacks. Especially the sweet and savory kind.

I wonder what Beth is doing these days. Is she still a daring creative soul? Surely she's a theatre actress on Broadway. Perchance she's a housewife who has blended in with the rest of society, hating her life like I hate mine. Possibly she's working an esteemed position in a distinguished career. Must be nice, or would it..

Whatever she's doing, I wonder, "Does she feel different, like she's separate?" Neither of us were peculiar in the eyes of the other back then. We were two of a kind, partners in harmless made up, makeup crime. At four, we didn't settle for someone else's definition of life. We were explorers. We glowed with a light of unified curiosity.

Occasionally, I see a fledgling girl or boy in the grocery store, with a hot-ironed stained face a mother has tried desperately to wash off. I transmit the message, "I see you, little one. You are part of my tribe." I am convinced our "secret handshake" is the bashful grin we exchange and luminous sparks in our eyes.

South Dakota was stale bread and soured milk overall. I was happy when Dad was transferred back to Indiana. I will later have an acupuncturist named Courtney, steeped in Shamanism, tell me I encountered a mysterious negative entity during my time in South Dakota. Supposedly it has been clinging to me my whole life. As if. I thought she was nuts, until another intuitive touched on the subject, without any hinting around. But I'll get to that rabbit hole a little later.

There was a spiraling void in the Prairie Land, and as a child, I sensed it. Lightning ionized the air, and clouds cloaked the sky with grey for two years straight. Thank God we were leaving this vapid wasteland. I felt another Dust Bowl setting in. I needed to get back to safety, back to my Grandmother living in the tiny mint-green house, whom I had a kindred connection to.

My love for make-up as a medium continued as I grew into a 5-year-old artist, unfurling like a seed. In the late morning, my mother would gracefully stand in the bathroom with the door open, fully immersed in her cosmetic routine. Mom doesn't get out of bed before 9:00AM. "I'm just not a morning person," she'll pacify her challengers.

This was her Zen time. She was oblivious to a wee hand reaching in and snagging a few bullet-sized cartridges of red. She was transforming herself for the day, bathed in a glowing yellow that emanated from our disco decade lavatory. In those moments my mother was shining. She was calm—a side to her I rarely saw.

The thick brown carpet in my bedroom felt like scratchy burlap underneath my feet. My room consisted of two dressers painted burnt orange. It looked like that crap color you get when you mixed all the leftover gallons.

"It's peach!" Mom pounced, with impermeable optimism.

Their interest in my taste maxed out in the clearance section. I think they found the color sample labeled "prison food" or "Aldi canned beans." In one of the bottom drawers was a stack of crisp white drawing paper, a starchy and hygienic contrast to my bedroom furniture.

Grandpa had built nine toy boxes, one for each of his grandkids. The wood shop in his basement stayed as busy as an elf's workshop during the height of late-November commercialism. Oodles of toys were constructed in the lower level of the house he had assembled. Legend has it, he picked workers off the local train rail and housed them for a few days as they laid beams.

Grandma hand-painted details on the knick knacks. Crayon carriers shaped like cats, turtle foot stools, and wooden ducks with flapping rubber feet. Jason got to sit on the work bench. Of course he did. While *I* got to help the females make upside-down pineapple cake. And then got told, "You better not eat it, or you'll get fat!" *Who ARE these people?*

My toy box was painted that disgraceful charred orange to match the dressers. Inside was a pair of black leather high heeled shoes with chunky wooden platforms. They must have been my mother's, but I couldn't imagine her wearing them. She was petite, and those pumps were straight out of "I'm Gonna Git You, Sucka." The shiny brass buckles drew me in like a moth and I got a charge out of trying them on. It is nearly impossible for a tenderfoot girl to walk in leather boots with wooden scaffolding, but I tried. The early stages of a shoe fetish, one of a few kinks I'd walk into.

The soles were made of a tire treaded rubber. In an instant, I was carried away by an artistic brainstorm, which inspired me to smear ruby red lipstick onto the underside of my dress up sandals and walk on the paper. Lipstick emits shades of crimson with the velvety creamed texture of an oil pastel. It was a scarlet relief. A waxy print on my immaculate white paper. I stood in awe of my glorious masterpiece.

Then my feet ripped the paper and sunk it into the spongy carpet. It was hindering my artwork. As I lost my balance, I stepped onto the floor. Yes, I fumbled onto that priceless poop brown carpet and made footsteps all over it—an extreme foul in my father's house.

"Oh. My. God. Katie! What are we gonna do?!" Mom gasped, as she stood in shock. There wasn't enough Resolve to cover me. She was mortified and started cramming my artwork into the bottom drawer of the dresser. We were *both* in trouble. She scrambled for a bucket of water and soap. I watched her get on her hands and knees, gripping the scrubber with determination as she dug it into the carpet, frantically using her elbow grease in an attempt to erase my failure. When she was done, there were patches of lightened sopping wet carpet in my room. "Now, go get some work towels and help me dry this floor."

Dad got home at 4:45PM sharp every day. Dinner on the table at 5:15PM.

"Where are all the garage towels?" Dad asked, as he killed time before dinner was ready. "I need to wipe some oil off of the floor out here."

"Oh, I need to wash those. I was doing a lot of cleaning today," Mom said, trying to cover up. She flashed me the stank eye, like a best friend who got suckered into your mischief during school recess. She was going to be "put on the wall" at Center School, for all to see. No more jump rope today. Oh well, we both kinda sucked at One-Legged Duck anyways.

Unable to make practical use of his time, by completing his garage floor task, Dad stomped down the hallway in his usual flat-footed march. Fee Fi Fo Fum, I smell the blood of an—oh crap, he's coming. It sounded like he weighed one-thousand pounds. He had a disability. No arch. Even his foot resisted bending the rules.

"What in the God. Damn. Hell…happened in this room?!" he hollered, as his eyeballs bugged out of their sockets, like Sy Sty from Garbage Pail Kids. I shifted my peepers to the wall, as I pretended to look for what he was pissing about. He wasn't falling for it.

"Get in the family room," he ordered, in a monotone cloud that hung in my room as we left.

I weaved down our hallway as it grew into the Great Wall of China. A lump in my throat formed while my brothers sat playing blocks on the carpet. As Dad stomped in behind me, they froze, mid block stacking.

"Pull your pants down and bend over my knee," he instructed with solemn detachment, "your underwear too." With the pride-swallowing reluctance of a witch being walked to the stake, I cinched them down to my knees. I could feel the hairs on my legs brush against his jeans, and goose-bumps form from the air touching the bare skin on the back of my thighs.

My face flushed with humiliation as my brothers stood silent. Dad knew the shaming was more potent when it was on display. I braced myself for the sting, as I stared down at that shit brown carpet. It turned into a teary

blur of muddy water as I counted in my head. One…two…three…four…
five.. A generous whack for each glorious circulation around the sun. My
spirit of innocence wondered, *why are these my parents, and why do they hate
me so much?*

"You boys want a bare butt spanking, too?" Blank stares. "No? Well then,
stay off the carpet with your messes. You're lucky I don't use a wooden
paddle, like they did when *I* was in school. Now *that* hurts."

I was dismissed. I pulled up my pants and scampered to my bedroom. I
stood in front of the sliding mirrored doors to the closet and lowered my
drawers. Handprints again. I'd be sleeping with my butt propped against a
pillow tonight. My cheeks clenched tight to try and ward off the sting, but
it always ended in throbbing pain. My digestive system responded. I was
gassy and crampy. For the longest time, I thought it was the food. But it was
emotional. I was tightly wound, because it was hard to relax. In fact, I never
really learned. I learned that letting my guard down was dangerous. Physically and emotionally. I learned that love from a man is pain, confusion,
humiliation, and betrayal. And somehow this was "for your own good."

Regardless of my father's lack of Celestine vision, I knew lipstick shoe
prints made for fabulous art. My golden thread as a creator glittered brighter
than my surroundings, and that made me his target. But it didn't take Picasso
to see my miracle was much more appealing than mud colored yarn, sparsely
glued to a thin foamy mat.

Nicknames

J ob interviews. A test of my ability to anthropomorph from painted desert dog shipped in from the Sahara to First World-ready house pet.

"She doesn't breed well." A potential boss strolls in with a puffy chest, like he just got out of the quarterly Supervisor Workshop. He sits with hands together, each fingertip meeting the opposite, creating a skin-toned, ten-digit cage he'd like to place me in. Thinking he's crafty he asks me, "What three words describe you the best?" He pauses and looks at me with a crease between his brow, like he's dropped a real philosophical wonder onto me. "Take a minute." He says, holding up a hand to assure me not to rush.

This can't be the interview. Apparently the position is so lame that a "yay" or "nay" boils down to three subjective words. To this I propose the "Golden Trio": passionate, apathetic, and unpredictable. He nods his head, panting over the first one, like a Golden Retriever salivating at a big yellow tennis ball. He's waiting for me to drop a couple more buzz words like "innovative" or "adaptable." But something tells me I wouldn't make it past the first interview if I was honest about the second two.

Yes, I may passionately devote myself to your prestigious establishment, then I may start feeling uninspired and apathetic, and on a whim decide I need a complete change in career. Here's my letter of resignation: Lorem Ipsum. That's right, doggo, I flashed you the ball, then faked you out with the throw. He ran in circles for a minute and eventually stopped in his tracks with a *"dert"* look on his face. I know, two can play at this game.

"Thank you for your time, Miss Sexton," I'll hear a million versions of, as my resume is tossed into the "reject" pile. It's fine. I didn't want that job anyways.

People love to be labelled as long as the word on the tag sounds like 'beautiful,' 'kind,' 'ambitious,' 'successful' or 'reliable.' I want some labels to stay the same, while I ask permission to grow out of the old ones. Even the positive ones can feel like a lockdown. Beautiful: like a model, but not forever sweetheart. Kind: never allowed to be in a bad mood anymore. Ambitious and successful: enough will never be enough. Reliable: obligated for life.

Of course, the tags on the other side of the pendulum are no better. Mine came cleverly disguised as nicknames. The first one was awarded like a 10th Place sky blue ribbon. I guess that's better than a rainbow colored Participation badge that says on the front "You Tried!" and the back: "but you suck."

"Here comes Hard Way Kate!" Dad blustered as I entered the room. He's so clever. Someone give him a slot on *An Evening at the Improv.*

My throat hollowed with hesitation as I choked out, "Why did you say that?"

"Because you can never leave well enough alone. You have to go and learn the hard way. Not too smart, are ya?" he charged. The message moseyed in like the smoke of an opium den, smelling sweet on the surface, but paralyzing once consumed. I wanted a nickname. Nicknames make you special. But not that one. That one felt like I was Carrie getting pig's blood dumped on her at the Senior Prom.

How about Smart Way Kate, Fucking Genius Way Kate, You're Gonna Be On Star Search And Win Someday Kate? You Are Number One Kate.

"Do we have to put the Dunce cap on ya?" asked Dad.

"No," I slumped.

"You know that's what they did when I was in school. You didn't want to be the one with the Dunce cap on in the corner. It let everyone know what a dummy you were. The kids laughed. It worked. Taught you how to act right," he said with bitterness.

A six-year-old little girl who is confident and assertive? He was gonna shut that shit down right away. No one wants THAT crap. Dad didn't understand that bending to someone else's version of reality *was* the hard way for me. I wasn't cut from the conformity cloth. It felt like my bones were being smashed by a gyrator rock crusher, and it was setting me up for a lifetime of reconstructive surgery. I was inquisitive. Curious. But whenever I tried to engage in conversation, he was offended. I didn't understand it. When I spoke, he was angered. Eventually, I spoke less, and questioned my thoughts. Would this get me in trouble? How could this be interpreted by others? What is everyone else saying that seems agreeable to him? I would try to solve the equation. I developed a racing mind that tried to keep me out of harm's way. Because just being me, upset the big people. Then he was mad I wasn't confident enough. Then I got ridiculed for having low self-esteem. But when I had high self-esteem, I got spanked or slapped in the mouth so hard it made my lips numb. It made no sense.

Jason hammered away, like a construction worker in training, at his rugged block of wood in Dad's garage. I loved pounding nails into his scrap wood on Saturday mornings. It was the same satisfying bang I enjoyed while cracking the bat in softball. The force of connection jolted my hands and vibrated up my forearms, as I felt the smooth solid metal seamlessly pierce and instantaneously slide into the hole it created in the wood.

I. *Bang!* Am. *Bang!* Smart. *Bang!*

"Do you want another nail, Katie?" Jason asked.

Give me the whole box. I thought.

"Now Katie, do like your brother is doing. See how I taught him to put the longer piece on the bottom and balance the shorter piece on top? Do that," Father instructed, as he oversaw our architectural models. There will be a test afterwards. There always was. Were our results a playtime "fail" or a playtime "success"…soon to be determined.

"Okay, but I'm going to balance the longer piece on top and put it cross-ways like a cross. I want to make a new design," I replied.

"Come here, you bossy little shit. Do you wanna whack that nail right through your finger and look like an idiot the rest of your life?" he barked at me, dropping the weight of a lifetime of humiliation. I pictured myself with a nail stuck through my index finger as I tried to write my name on my paper in Mrs. Larson's class. *It would only be my left hand, and I'm right-handed, so I guess I could live with that.*

I leaned towards my brother, "Can't they just take the nail out?" I asked.

"No, you dummy…you can't take out an object from a puncture wound or you'll bleed to death," replied Jason, in his best G.I. Joe deliverance of tactical survival.

I cowered on the slick concrete floor. It was cold to the touch, and spotless other than the sawdust we would be enlisted to sweep before going inside for lunch. Dad rearranged my blocks like a disgruntled high school shop teacher.

"Here. This is how it's done. For God's sake Katie, quit trying to use your big brain." He rubbernecked my brother's structure. "Ah! Now that looks good! Perfect, Jason, you may go inside and clean up for lunch."

Jason lifted his brows and flashed me one of his smiles that said, "You should have done what Dad said!"

"Get the broom and dust pan. I don't want this mess blowing around while we are eating," Dad said. I stacked the blocks under his tool bench in the worn-out Seagram's Seven cardboard box purposed for "scrap wood with nails in it." Not to be confused with the deteriorating Bartles & Jaymes Wine Cooler box known for "untainted scrap wood." I lifted the hammer to set it on Dad's work bench, using two hands so I could balance the weight of the metal head. *Clunk.* I felt important when I held the hammer. It was for adults, and men. And they seemed to have all the freedom..and power.

"File that child under Non-Compliant," the boss reported to the secretary, as he barged through the swinging screen door. It had a perpetual squeak. The slow release air cylinder routinely malfunctioned, managing to slam in a mind-snapping *WHACK!* when you least expected it. Dad routinely blew a gasket. His ears needed WD-40.

I made him uncomfortable. Maybe Mom could use her fabric scissors to cut red felt letters "HWK" for his preferred "Hard Way Kate'" label and sew them on my purple wind jacket. That idea would get his stamp of approval. "Sounds like a productive 4-H project for this summer!" he'd say. All I wanted was a new neighbor to play with me for the summer. But Hard Way Kate kept moving in next door. *God I can't stand her.* We need to build a privacy fence.

"You know, I can't stand people who don't allow you to live past your mistakes," Father preached from his Suburban-made soap box on Saturdays.

Head scratch. *Fuck. Did I do something wrong again? Who is he talking to? About what? I'm confused.* Did someone not let *him* live past a mistake? Wait, that would imply *he* made a mistake. Dad never makes mistakes. EVERY-ONE. KNOWS. THAT.

Weekends were full of impromptu speeches. Dad was running for re-election in the family room. If I snuck out the front door and pussy-footed to the right, I could avoid the campaign tour, while skipping to the back yard. Saturdays were great until the sun came up. After The Berenstain Bears was over, things got a bit dodgy. I had to stay quick on my feet, like an acrobat at Barnum and Bailey Circus. I favored sitting on the ropes, peering in through the gaps in the thick canvas and watching the show from a safe distance. This way I could see how things were lining up, catching a glimmer of the performers as they dazzled the audience. I didn't want to be *in* the audience. Someone might call on me. Forget that. I'm not trying to get eaten by a bear.

"It's my way or the highway, get used to it!" Dad chanted, while he hosed down the screened-in porch floor.

"So, he wants the outside floor to be as clean as the inside floor?" I asked Mom, as I looked at the concrete slab in the screened-in porch.

"Yes, dear," she answered, as she fluffed the fruit salad she had doused with Cool Whip.

Okay yeah, that makes perfect sense.

"Learn how to play the game, Katie," Dad harped at me. "Life will be a lot easier once you do." That's the thing about privilege. You are only granted it, if you bow to it. Dad would say, "watching tv is a privilege. You have to earn it, and if you don't follow the rules, that privilege can be taken away." It was our weekly reminder. Privilege was about control. Class privilege. Family privilege. Sitting on the couch privilege. I had to play by his rules. This system is perpetuated by the reward and punishment method used in school. Here's the carrot..not good enough? No carrot. Here's the love..not good enough? No love. But you Sally, you get a golden star. Maybe someday Tommy will get a golden star too, but only if he plays by the rules. My cousin used to say, "don't bite the hand that feeds, Katie." We don't only need food to survive, we need love. And I needed that golden star to receive love, even if it required me to self abandon. Those are the rules.

My ten year old jaw dropped like a piano. This game is insulting.

How could he reduce my life to a meaningless game? I wondered, flabbergasted, as I paged through the *'Teen* magazine on my bed. That cannot be the purpose of life. I had feelings. What part of the game had room for feelings? None, unless they were being used for manipulation. Games were filled with competition and gloating. There were winners and losers. You can gloat-we'll call that "pride," but don't be a sore loser. I didn't care for the games, especially board games or card games. I had no desire for them. I wasn't motivated by things that moved other kids. Sometimes I wished I was. They seemed to be having more fun. I tried, but it all seemed pretty boring. I had to sit at the dining room table, in the uncomfortable wooden chairs, through the never-ending game, and act like I was as excited as they were. If I didn't, I was accused of not liking my own family. Love was motivating. But if the consequence to non-compliance was a spanking, then I was more likely to muster a "it didn't hurt."

The game my father spoke of, was his version of a game. It was one-sided, imposing the rules as he understood them, without room for anyone else's interpretation. His proposal was a simple math equation with concise Algebraic finality. He was talking about the matrix. He wanted that gold star, the biggest boat, and I imagine he wanted love. But I defy simple math. I wanted to do card tricks with the game, and create a new equation, using the infinity of pi.

Dad wasn't letting me live past my shortcomings. Every time I boasted my ideas with vigorous passion, *bam*, shot down. Hard Way Kate, getting benched again. There was only one lens, his lens.

When I was four it sounded like, "Doh, di, doh. That's a funny fireman's hat you got on there. What are you going to do, fight a fire?" he delivered with a dopey voice sprinkled with sarcasm. He was mocking me, but I was blinded by innocence. I thought this uncomfortable feeling in my body was love. Allowing those I loved to tease and demean me became normalized. Arguing my worth, or performing as an attempt to receive love became a foundational connection wired in my early childhood.

As I learned to fight back, I complained, "He's laughing at me!"

"Oh don't be such sore loser. I was just joking," he contended, as his foot kicked me in my rear, with a force that pushed me to stumble on the way out the door. This was one of Dad's favorite moves. I shared the brunt of it with the dog.

On other occasions, "Wow, did you put your eyeshadow on in the dark, Katie? Looks like you got a black eye with all that purple," he teased. "Look Jason, your sister's got her war paint on again." Why couldn't they tell me I looked pretty? That's what make-up was for. I knew that much.

"No, I did it this way on purpose," I muttered as they laughed. *See, you're not pretty. You look like a clown. It's embarrassing you even try.* Some girls were put up on a pedestal like a princess, but I was the butt of the joke. I can hear him, *that's because you weren't acting like a princess. Figure it out, smarty pants.*

"Get with the program, Katie." I was pressured on a regular basis, like I was being trained for the Olympic sport of Obedience. I liked to compete against myself. I didn't want to get *with* the program. I wanted to get *beyond* the program. Something he never did. I wonder what programs he was forced to swallow at my age. How much resistance did he throw up, before he bought into the story he was now forcefully redistributing to me.

"Here she is…Abby-Normal!" Oh god, he's really outdoing himself. So this is how it's going to be. He couldn't connect any more efficiently than any of us could make the buzzers go off on the Electric Project Kit that sat gathering dust in the basement five months after Christmas. My chest caved into a pit of nothingness. He was oblivious. I think my soul accidentally passed through the wrong portal.

"Katie Mi' Lady!" I heard from across the street. My best friend Sarah's dad hooted with an Appalachian flair and a boisterous smile whenever he saw me. His jubilation hit my palate like a juicy plum. I felt loved. That kind of nickname I could embrace. Jerry was a Veteran who spoke with a Kentucky accent and wore his heart on his sleeve. He was lively—one night, during a sleepover, as Sarah and I were listening to the crickets chirping a symphony outside, he jumped out of the closet to scare us. The following morning he woke us up by blasting "Pretty Woman" by Roy Orbison and singing from the hallway. Then Sarah and I took a shower together to save water. We hurried because Jerry dumped cold water on us if we went too long. There was an element of freedom and chaos that occurred at her house. I liked it. People were messy there, and it wasn't hidden.

"Come over! Jerry is dressing up as Freddie Kruger tonight and we are having a fright night for my birthday," Sarah said, trying to entice me to hurry. Her dad had duct-taped plastic knives to his hands and was scraping them on the vents in the pitch dark of their basement. He was likely a few Southern Comforts in, but drinking among adults while watching kids was socially acceptable. Being intoxicated around kids was acceptable, smoking in cars with closed windows, and laying in the back of a car without a seatbelt was acceptable too.

In middle school, Jerry kept us doing chores as long as he could, to keep us away from the boys. "Sure, you and Sarah can go out…just after you defrost this freezer here," he'd say on a Friday night. We would be held up for hours, chatting with him the whole while in the kitchen. He would give us tedious steps about how they would have done a chore like this in the military. Ten o'clock would roll around and he'd say, "awe shucks, looks like it got too late. Maybe next weekend." I wrote him little notes on napkins and he saved them. He tucked them away next to the poems he wrote for her mom. Jerry was sentimental, a trait I was not familiar with in other men. He swooned over Sarah's mother, and I was enthralled with their display of romance.

By the time we reached our senior year of high school, Sarah's parents turned into the type to buy a case of beer or a flask of Mad Dog 50/50, and inconspicuously leave it in the garage. "Don't get drunk tonight," her mom warned as she headed out the door to waitress. She was an Italian who mowed her lawn in a banana-colored string bikini. Their baby blue house was across the street from our busy neighborhood pool. She knew the chain-link fence was lined with onlookers, happily judging her. But she didn't give a shit because she had a toasty-brown tan and rock hard abs.

"Oh screw Nancy. She's such a prude," Sarah's mom voiced as she applied baby oil with her Palmolive hands, adorned with bright purple polish.

"Dude, you totally missed it last night. Jerry poured gasoline on the driveway and lit it on fire! Then he let us climb onto the roof," Sarah filled me in. "But someone called the cops. Probably goody-two-shoes Nancy across the street."

Sarah and I crouched like deviants around 1:00AM on a fourth-grade sleepover. "Shhh! Get down here by the vent and listen," Sarah would hiss, motioning me over.

As I leaned in, I could hear her mom moaning loudly as she made love with her dad.

"Oh Jerry! My pussy hurts for you!" her mom cried out.

"Lay down. I'm gonna put my snake in your grass," Jerry grunted.

Our eyes bulged as we giggled under our breath.

Her parents had a collection of *Hustler* magazines on top of their dresser, as well as "The Book of Making Love." It was published circa 1975—the hairy edition. It was stacked on the bookshelf in their family room, its binding staring at us, as we ate our mac and cheese fancied up with chopped hot dogs. Sarah and I simply referred to it as "The Book." One page was filled with black and white images of boobs—all different shapes and sizes. The next was butts. And then, penises. Wow.

Jerry's passion meter went overboard at times. "Watch out for the broken glass," Sarah cautioned as we tip-toed by the tawny 1970s Cadillac in her parent's garage. "Jerry is having trouble with work." Self-regulation isn't an innate skill. Then again, I'm not sure what the appropriate response is to unemployment. I gave her dad a pass. At least he was the type to cry, buy her mom flowers, and try to make up for it. Some say it's a red flag. But I think it takes courage to live life with emotion, to screw up, to let people talk shit, and to keep trying again despite all the naysayers. It takes courage to keep your heart open. I'll take an apology over no apology any day. If he meant it, even for a moment, I felt he had a moral compass. Portions of it may have gotten lost in his military jacket overseas, but that took courage too. As a child, my dad never apologized, and this made Jerry's behavior seem better. More human. More open to the possibility of change. Jerry was a little wild, but I liked it. I identified with it. When it came to life, he was all-in, with an extra shake of pepper to spice it up. And when the chips were down, he'd say, "well, if life was fair, horses would ride half the time!" There was an air of unattachment to the setbacks, and that is necessary for the risk-taker.

Morning Procedure: No sleeping in allowed at Sarah's house or mine. I was nestled inside the soft womb of my blankets, slowly letting my brain wake up, when the Fire Guard yanked the sheets off me and dumped cold water on my bare skin.

"Time to get up! You're gonna be late!" Dad shouted. "This one was born late," he laughed. So much for entering the day calm and centered. This house served revenge with a side of resentment for breakfast.

"There's some scrambled eggs in the microwave for you. They are probably cold by now, but that shouldn't matter because you don't like them anyways," Mom served with the repressed anger of June Cleaver.

"We're headed to Grandma's! Put on shorts! It's hot in her yard!" Mom called down the hallway. We were headed to Grandma Peterson's house. The reward would be dinner at Grandma Kowalski's later, where we were allowed to sneak salami and Black Cherry sodas out of the fridge in her basement. The only thing Grandma Peterson had going for her were Nilla wafers.

Dad pledged his allegiance to his mother every weekend and worked in her yard like a schoolboy. He liked gardening, but I question the root of his dutiful compliance. The 1950s propaganda went far beyond "Duck and Cover" for him. He internalized the program to serve his parents with unwavering sacrifice, specifically his mother. I wondered, "what kind of Norman Bates bullshit was going on in that house?"

"Quit asking questions. Go watch TV," I hear my parents dictate.

Architecture and Design magazine was poppin' in the 50s, but the nuclear family model needed to detonate. It was as disturbing as the three-armed Cabbage Patch Kid Mr. Lawson had on display in his classroom during sophomore year Social Studies class. He loved the A-Bomb era. We watched clips on VHS as he sat in the back of the room talking to himself.

"Watch out, little Timmy! The giant ball of fire is coming! Hurry up and get under that desk!" he reenacted. "Do you think he's gonna make it? Oh...oh...awwwe! Turned to a poof of dust. Gosh, I really thought that textbook on his head was gonna save him." Then he disappeared into the hallway, only to be spotted through the window smoking a cigarette it the teacher's parking lot. I squinted one eye as I peeked through the screen door of Grandma Peterson's house.

"Do we have to go inside?" I whined to Mom. It was as icy as a funeral home in there. My brothers were already out back, choring away at the cornfield patch that was under yearly attack by a raccoon. Dad had a varmint vendetta and intended to fry it with an electric fence.

Grandma sat at the red formica and chrome kitchen table sipping a cold Hamms. The Virginia Slims of beer. Anything that rhymes with Spam, the canned puke they sell in stores, cannot taste good, but she seemed to like it. She was a frail, but stern woman with a smoker's rasp. Her Keds were scrubbed white and she wore cornflower blue polyester slacks with an elastic waistband.

"But I thought nurses were healthy?" I questioned Mom.

"Not in the 50s, honey. Back then doctors smoked in the patient's rooms, even if you were dying of pneumonia," Mother educated me. Grandma was the type of little old lady who would take you to Dairy Queen for ice cream, and then blow smoke in your face the whole time.

"Smoke follows beauty," she would cough out. Wow. I must be a fucking super model. She would roll up in her Buick decked out with velvety maroon interior. Each crease in the seats was mortared with ashes. Grandma was a little rough around the edges, but being gifted a Strawberry Sunday brain freeze was her redeeming quality, and worth the pollution.

I quietly swirled side to side on Grandma's malt shop barstools, sneaking in a full turn when no one was looking. I ate my wafers with a glass of orange juice as I pondered my father's black and white childhood photo in the 3x4 frame, carefully displayed in the dining room. He was of average build, pale complexion, and, at that time, sported short curly hair. He wore black glasses, very *Stand By Me*. One lens was much thicker, to correct his lazy eye. It was hard for me to imagine him as a child, but there he was staring at me, past the glare of the glass encased photo, about my size.

As an adult, he tried using contacts to mask his inadequacy, but the lenses were too irritating. "I don't see how anyone can wear these things! They feel like razors in my eyes! I have work to do. I can't be putting up with this crap!" he threw a tantrum as he stormed into the bathroom. "This is age discrimination, I know it," he would say on other occasions.

During my entire childhood, I never once noticed his eyes weren't perfectly symmetrical. I observed that he towered over me, and his ears got bright red when he was angry. He had a bushy mustache, and at times his eyes shot daggers straight through me. The lens on his glasses were magnified like a coke bottle on one side, but I never noticed. It never registered until *he* pointed it out.

"I've only seen his baby picture once," Mom confessed. Embarrassed by being born cross-eyed, a condition that corrected itself and resulted in a slight lazy eye, he kept all evidence of his imperfections under lock and key. I wonder what kind of shame his mother felt as she tried to gaze into her baby's eyes and connect. The disconnect. One society doesn't allow for. The pressure for a picture perfect baby is high now, I can't imagine what it was during the 50s. Parents attaching worth to a perfect infant image demonstrates our dysfunction. There's no baby book that says, "in order for your baby to thrive, dress it up and take a picture of it. This will help it while it's with a stranger all day while you go to work. If you feel a little down at first, post a picture on social media. That will engage your dopamine while the baby is sleep training."

However, I could relate to cringing at your baby photos, because I despised mine too. Mom dropped off a set of *my* newborn pictures slightly after I gave birth to my first child. It was a blur of yellow gingham, ghostly skin, and lacy bonnets. I was horrified. That can't be me. I felt an instant rejection of my photo. Just the sight of the lace made my body hurt.

"Ugh, you were an ugly baby!" my husband confirmed. Maybe it was the hormones from recently giving birth, or knowing I was a hideous baby, but I washed over with shame and bawled my eyes out standing in the center of the kitchen. I thought, how could someone love such a pasty-white, unsightly baby? How pitiful I was born that way. I wanted the image to have never existed. *How dare that baby look so ugly.* No wonder she left me in my crib all the time. In a sobbing panic, I ripped up the photos and dumped them in the garbage can. They landed on top of the five gallons of Chicken Alfredo someone brought me during maternity leave. By that time I knew how strong the urge was to hold your baby when you hear its cries. My whole body tightened with discomfort. Nature made sure I tended to her every time she made a sound. This made me wonder, how could my mother ignore these massive cues inside a woman's body to protect and nurture her child? I hold my baby to emotionally regulate her. I didn't even know the term yet, but I did it, because instinct taught me to, and I listened to that powerful intuition. But she didn't. Some women didn't, and I wanted to know why.

Courtney, my acupuncturist, shared her opinion, "Don't worry, all newborns are ugly. They look like aliens."

Was this consoling? I suppose we are in fact plopped down from another dimension. "On some level your mom knew your baby photo would upset you. I think she was subconsciously trying to hurt you," she shared. She was probably right. Even after I lost the baby fat, Mom posted pictures of me at my heaviest, after I asked her not to. There was some kind of strange jealousy I detected. A venom seeping out.

Oh great, another mind-fuck for me to obsess over while I'm alone nursing at 3:00AM

"That's possible, but she held me, fed me, and changed my diapers. I don't think she's like that," I defended. Having a baby opened a pandora's box of bitterness for my mother. I didn't want to look inside it. I wanted support and this was getting too twisted. I am having so many feelings I can't even name them at this point. Especially not during the sleep deprivation stage, which lasted about four years. Acute for two. Okay let's be honest, it's going on nine.

"Yeah, she may have seen past it then, but as an adult she knew you wouldn't like it. Don't you think?" Courtney added.

Great, everyone concurs I was an ugly baby. It's a miracle I wasn't dropped off at the Fire Station.

I was only a couple of weeks old in the photos, sitting on a dark velour photographer's blanket, in a scratchy white dress with elastic pinching my tender newborn skin. I gazed off into the distance, unfocused baby eyeballs straining to make sense of shapes and textures that didn't have any relevance. I looked afraid and vulnerable, with no one at my side. Helpless. Lost in the sounds of clicking cameras and echoing voices. I could feel this baby's sadness through the photo, and I didn't want to, because she was me.

Under every bully lives a coward that hates their baby picture. That was my father, and I could relate. New Meetup Group: People who feel rage towards their infant photos. I felt sad for that oafish cherub. As impossible as it seemed, I would have to learn to love that strange alien baby carefully posed like a marionette for Olan Mills Photography.

Bored Games

"No Katie, we are *upper* middle-class," taught Jason. "Sarah's family is *lower* middle-class, doctors and lawyers are upper class, and the garbage man is lower class. Get it straight."

"But why does it matter?" I questioned with innocence.

"It matters because you don't want to be poor. I'm going to be a tycoon, so I can do whatever I want," he said ear to ear with pride. We were introduced to a belief system that defined worth as being "better than" someone else. It's a system aligned with opposition, climbing the ladder, status-chasing, separation, and judgement, in order to secure our "worth" in the world. If "class" had to be taught, then surely a world could exist where class was de-valued, and worth redefined.

"But Dad said not to talk about how much money everyone makes, so you can't tell anyone what class we're in," Jason warned.

Money…even more taboo than sex.

Dad thought humanitarian work was foolish. "You have to work hard to play hard," he repeated from the stone age.

"I can already pulverize you in Monopoly," Jason added with the air of a future Capitalist.

"Yeah that's because you're greedy. You like owning all the railroads just because you can, not because you'd ever enjoy a train ride," I analyzed my brother.

"Duh," he anointed the conversation.

"Well, I'm going to help people," I declared with virtue in my voice.

Dad rumbled a deep disapproving laugh. Like a ruthless banker, he mocked me. "What, you want to be a social worker or something?"

"What's wrong? What's a social worker?" I queried, half afraid of his reply.

"Do you want to be poor for the rest of your life?" he examined my stance.

"No. Why?" I wondered with hesitation.

He proclaimed, "Social workers are fools who go running around trying to help people, and never actually get anything done. They waste their time, and wind up as poor as the people they are trying to help. That's not a job. That's a charity."

"Maybe I'll be a teacher like Mom," I defended.

"It's almost the same thing, Katrina," Dad confirmed.

My tender ten-year old heart sunk into my stomach.

The Bumper Sticker

"**D**on't pop the clutch! You're killing the engine!" Dad panicked as the navy blue Chevy S10 hurled us forward on the car seat. "Do you know how much a new clutch costs?!" He was five seconds pre-aneurysm.

I mastered the stick shift in two lessons. There was no other option.

Operating a manual, no power steering junker lent itself to cultivating good driving skills. After I learned to crank the wheel and parallel park in a rust bucket, reminiscent of the stone age, it was smooth sailing in any other vehicle. I was a pretty decent driver, minus the DUI at eighteen. I was swerving on that particular evening. Not stick shift related. It caused a bit of a glitch when they kicked me off the National Honors Society a few weeks before graduation.

Mom stood aghast, like the judge just ripped the crown off *her* head, center-stage at the Homemakers of America Pageant. "But...but..."

Dad lined the shelf below the dashboard of the truck with cheap brown carpet. This was his go-to design preference. It transcended decades. I found it as necessary as pom-poms in a Cheech and Chong van. An accessory that left me thinking, *but why? Why does everything have to be turd brown?* The seat was ripping, exposing chunks of crumbling foam, so he duct taped it together and hid the evidence under a woven Navajo print cover. It was unsightly, even for the 1990's. The hand-me-down pick-up was intended for my brother, but when he graduated high school I got to drive the denim chariot.

"Yeah, Samantha, you gotta ride 'bitch' because you're the shortest. Sorry about your luck," I said to my high school friend.

"Well I don't have any money for gas, so sorry about *your* luck," she would one-up me. We exercised our independence by taking secret joyrides into Chicago. I scribbled I90-94 onto a scrap piece of paper and stopped at gas stations for help when needed. Who needs GPS when you're trying to get lost. Lake Michigan is to the upper right on the paper map folded in the glove compartment. We'll find it. The cobalt blue pick-up helped me escape the stale, privileged box I lived in. I took advantage, as much as I could, like most high schoolers do. My method was working at Eagle Foods, a family-owned grocery store where they *"care so much we carry your bags out to your car!"* It was open 24 hours, which gave it a nice balance of grit.

During the day, I baked in the summer sun at Chapin Woods Pool. Our house was directly next door, about 20 paces through the back yard.

"I'm going to the pool to lay out! I need to memorize the codes to the produce," I reminded Mom. I had a lined piece of notebook paper with columns of numbers hand-written in different colored pens, next to every fruit and vegetable known to the Midwest. My oily hands smeared the notes together as I touched each line, trying to think of a rhyme to make the sequence stick in my head. Studying the codes was like a Mala Bead meditation. When at work, it put me in a relaxed trance, accentuated by the repetitive beeping of the scanner. I typed in each code. 287. Green Apples. 525. Iceberg Lettuce. 106. Red Onions. Like becoming fluid in a new language, the number had to become the food. The number now had a taste, color, and texture in my mind's eye.

"I'm headed to work!" I shouted to whoever was keeping tabs on me these days.

"I hope you put some Aloe on! You're letting your skin get too fried in that sun! Just wait till you get old. You'll wish you had worn a sun visor!" jingled Mom. I pictured myself wearing her visor with the green see-through plastic, like that of a mafia poker player. Do they sell those anymore? I think hers was from a 1981 trip to Daytona Beach.

I scooted into my station with crisp tan lines and cut off jeans. I was supposed to be wearing khaki shorts that went past my fingertips, but I thought they made me look like a boy. I had already been shamed for looking too "masculine" when I was in softball. They called me a "dike" and "lesbian" for having muscles and playing sports. But I wasn't pretty enough to be a cheerleader, and there was some code of conduct I did not comprehend. Apparently I did not know how to "act like a girl."

"Umm...you're gonna get in trouble!" taunted Mike, my favorite bag boy who stole NoDoze to get himself hyped up for his shift. He gossiped a mile a minute, and I listened as I kicked up my Vans and twirled my sun-bleached hair.

"It's Monday night. No one's going to notice what I'm wearing," I assured him.

"Rick came in last night and bought shampoo. He was dressed as a woman, but I know it was him. His rough hands from roofing houses are unmistakable. Can you believe that?! He's a total cross-dresser!!" Mike ping-ponged with his mouth agape.

"Oh my God yes, I know him! He lives across the street from my Grandma Kowalski on the East side of town."

"NO. WAY."

"Ya, and get this, he called her one day and asked her to come over because he wanted to show her something. So my grandma went across the street and knocked on his door. She said she could see the silhouette of a person in a night gown through the window, so she thought he had a woman over. Maybe he wanted to introduce her—"

"Who was it?! Was it him??? It was totally him, wasn't it?" he pressed, like an eager gambler, throwing in bets before the horses rounded the finish line at the local tracks.

"Yep. It was Rick," I confirmed.

"Oh. My. God. I knew it! Okay, I'm going to aisle 10 to get hair gel and dental floss. I swear I'll let you ring it up before I leave. I won't forget this time." Mike was so full of it. I knew he was going to give himself another five finger discount. Last time it was a tube of Nivea and a pack of fruity Mentos. He couldn't help himself. The Sunday shift was devoted to making any excuse to travel to the back of the store.

"I'll price check that! I can restock that!" I offered, creating a reason to wander down the aisles, accidentally rounding the corner of the produce section each and every time.

There he was. The "older boy." I developed a disorienting crush on the college dropout with the hippie vibe, fashioning a chestnut ponytail. On my lunch break I nonchalantly crossed the threshold of swinging doors, into the warehouse in the back of the store. He was busy chucking spent lettuce into the air. Basketballs of green, shredding apart into a soft bed of wilted potential.

He flashed a sparkly grin at me—the kind only a twenty-something boy can exchange with a teenaged girl—and I meekly recoiled to the safety of the break table. As I stared at the worn out wooden planks of an old picnic table, etched with artifacts from all the employees that came before me, I thought, "If only he would make the first move, I could be doing more than unpacking this soggy turkey sandwich." But it never happened. We hardly exchanged a spoken word, let alone a kiss. Unless you count my daydreams.

In that case we had mad make-out sessions every. single. Sunday.

Best of all, my neighbor Roger worked at Eagle Foods as a butcher. He was as close as family.

"Don't go back there today, little honey," he'd say, "it's bloody, and the cow is still giving me the evil eye."

"Thanks for the heads up!" I'd chirp, feeling bashful as the circle of white-aproned meat men chuckled at my neighbor's joke.

The meat department hung carcasses just past the frigid plastic flap doors. It was a modern shield to a medieval display of beasts, strung up as raw as my desires for the salad master.

"I'll take the bags out this time!" I volunteered between customers, during the night shift.

I walked to the semi-vacant parking lot, allowing the street lights to beam down on me, adding one thousand watts to my tolerance for confinement. I bent my neck to soak up the full moon, hanging low in the indigo summer sky. The silvery globe illuminated an array of cumulus clouds that painted the endless ceiling. *If I could float up there, I could be free.*

"Katie! I parked by you in the back!" Samantha called out. A few friends gathered in the parking lot as my shift ended. We stood around smoking Camel Lights or Newport Lights, whatever someone managed to gank at the local gas station.

I leaned against Samantha's black Buick Century and immersed myself in the sea of concrete stillness. The rows of empty parking spots, lined with yellow paint, welcomed me like a giant maze of balance beams, which I traced with my mind. As my back pressed on her car, I felt the vibrating bass, pulsing through the aluminum doors, seducing me further with an air of freedom. She blasted House or Drum and Base mix tapes our amateur DJ friends made us. Terry Mullen was her favorite, along with DJ Shadow and Danny the Wildchild. The supermarket paved a place to breathe in and breathe out.

"Oh darn, did they schedule me during Saturday night mass, as well as Sunday morning?" Or did I repeatedly switch shifts to make that happen—yes I did. My many years of Catholic indoctrination, taught me to religiously miss church as a teenager. I had questions, and they weren't being answered in the echoing chamber beneath the steeple.

I still loved the ambiance of an empty church. I snuck into quite a few magnificent cathedrals with brilliant stained glass windows, and sat there…waiting. I hoped to be touched by a message of Grace, only to leave with a sense that whatever I was seeking was on the other side of a two-way mirror. It could see me, but for some reason, I couldn't see "it." God was over there eating a ham sandwich with his blessed hand. I just knew it.

Our red brick church stood for over 100 years. It was adorned with marvelous vaulted ceilings and archaic images bestowing both wisdom and judgment, all at once. I could hear the whispers of angelic mysteries to be tapped into, while the organ played, breathing life into the lungs of the church.

It burned down. My home town chapel. I'd rather die of smoke inhalation than go to a church in a new building. Romanticizing religion required its ancient attributes for me. I wanted to osmose insights through crumbling brick walls, hanging onto imprints of knowledge, waiting for me to grasp their tangibility. New churches don't have that. I thought new churches were creepy, like Joel Osteen creepy.

I was working at the grocery store to lift my obligation to attend mass. It was one of those bitter cold nights common to a Midwestern winter, where Lake Michigan rides a vaporous cloud over your back and stabs you with a shiv it picked up from the Joliet State Prison. My door lock was frozen and the key wouldn't work, so I ran back into the store.

"What aisle is that de-icer stuff in?" I asked the midnight shift cashier.

"Aisle 11. We over-price it, but it works like a charm!" she said, as she straightened the boxes of Double Mint gum. "Sweet! Thanks!" After she checked me out, I hurried back to my truck and emptied half the 2 oz. container of de-icer into the key hole. I wasn't sure the ingredients of the chemical mist would do anything, but it worked in seconds. My key was able to turn to the left, and reward me with a comforting *click*.

My parents were on one of their weekly movie dates, that usually ended with a night cap at the local bar. I had a small window of time, just long enough to pop in, raid the liquor cabinet, and slide back out to see what kind of excitement I could find for the evening. My trusty pick-up fish-tailed up an ice-slicked road to our house. I ran in, downed two stiff whiskey and cokes, just like my dad does, and then chomped a piece of gum. Easy peasy, instant head change on the go. *Now, where do I find my people?*

I cruised over to the local truck stop, and its adjoining restaurant, infamous for harboring many-a-bored teenager on a weekend night. I recognized the 1980s Shelby of my good friend, and secret crush, Tido. Who could resist a boy who drove a vintage powder blue Dodge Shelby with white racing stripes? I knew my fellow Beastie Boy fan turned part-time raver was inside. I acted like I was making a call at the pay phone, then wandered around until I was noticed. My mega crush, dipshit friend was playing games at the video arcade, fashioning himself an expert against some ten-year-old kid. He was still wearing his busboy getup when he noticed me.

"What's up, city slicker! Cold weather got you seeking the warmth of the truck stop oasis?" he said in his fake Bronx accent.

"Just looking for a cure to my boredom," I spat back at him, as I tucked my gloves into my pockets. My fingers were still numb, but I wasn't about to show any signs of weakness. Tido lived with his dad off Third Avenue. He had a long dark mustache and always sat next to his two greyhounds. He drank Harveys Bristol Creme Sherry, and looked like he was on the cover of a Burt Bacharach album. Tido was usually gone on the weekends…who knows where he went? He was a mystery, and he was mysteriously available to me this Saturday night. I wasn't going to let *that* slip out of my hands.

"Then seek no farther. I'm on my way to a rave in Chicago. You can ride bitch if you like," he snarked at me. How could I resist such a smooth talker? I have a weakness for tall skinny morons wearing Gazelles.

Tido was famous for local antics, like breakdancing on the downtown sidewalk or performing mediocre adlib rap songs. We waited outside for his best friend Sam who worked as an usher at the twin cinema built in 1930s. He was closing out the register with the ticket lady who sat in the window box every night. She was a sallow, gaunt woman with short hair. No one could guess her age.

Tido started rhyming like he was Run DMC making a video for MTV.

"Skel-e-tor, Skel-e-tor…she co-llects your tickets at the mo-vie door. She stares at your dick, with a spooky gaze, but don't lick that pus-sy…cuz she's been dead for days." We broke into tears of laughter as he scratched his imaginary turntable, and belted out five more verses.

A few minutes later Sam busted through the double doors, under the marquee. "Dude! I could hear every word of that song as I was closing out for the night! Loretta heard you and your stupid Skeletor song! You're such a dick, man. That old lady is going to go home and kill herself now," Sam said with his teeth clenched, eyes bugging out in a hissy.

"Oh shit. I didn't know you could hear us. Let's get outta here." Tido came clean, as he ducked his head behind his Adidas jacket.

It was pushing midnight, but I suspected if I called home on this freezing balls night, I might be met with indifference. At any other time, a lame excuse with a request to stay overnight at a friend's house would have been shot down. Highly suspicious, especially if it was made on short notice, late in the evening. However, on a night when my dad would not want to get bundled up and endure the stabbing cold of single digits, I decided to roll the dice.

I had one quarter and one dime left for the pay phone. *Please let this work.*

"Ehrm. Hello?" Dad cleared his throat into the phone. My call wrestled him out of the deep sleep he fell into as soon as his eyes shut after his fourth whiskey and water.

"Hey Dad, um, I'm sorry to call so late, but the locks are frozen shut on my truck. I've tried everything, even that de-icer stuff, but it's not working. It's super freezing cold out. Everything's ice. I'm over at Lisa's. My car's out front. Can I just stay here tonight? I promise I'll be home in time for church," I pitched at him, like a series of hurling fast balls, too many to fit in the catcher's mitt at once.

"What? Yeah, okay. Is her Dad home? That's fine. Just come home in the morning. ASAP." *Click.* Dial tone. Success. I was free to roam the city with my Saturday night side-kick. Yesss.

Tido and I drank a couple beers on the ride up. A drive through the darkness of a stinging Siberian night, into the bright lights of the third largest city in the United States, became a blur of sensations. First the lights, then the speed and sounds, add some liquid to dissolve your mental box, and it rushes over and through you like an urban wave of controlled chaos.

Our friend Paulie would call the cityscape a cheap thrill he craved. "It gets my rocks off every time!" he bragged.

"Oh course it does, One-Ball-Paul. You only need half the foreplay!" Tido would joke. Paulie got kicked in the nuts during fifth grade recess and one of his testicles retreated into his pelvis. Tido wouldn't let him live it down. As a young girl we were taught if a boy is bothering you, it's because he likes you. And if it becomes too much, just kick him in the balls to get him away. I think that's what happened to Paulie. I'm not sure. He shot himself years later, after he got back from the military. Tido didn't even make it back. A sniper got him.

My Italian escort parked in front of a record store on Belmont, and I rushed to follow him inside. He flashed a guy behind the counter a flyer for the rave, and the clerk tossed him a new flyer with the actual location of the party. We hopped back in the Shelby and drove to the destination. I have no idea where we were. Tido seemed to know the city better than I, so I trusted his judgment.

It was another abandoned bowling alley. A raver's paradise. This one wasn't on Martin Luther King Jr. Drive. We had been avoiding that area ever since Paulie had a beer bottle thrown at his car last year. I knew to stay away from Cabrini-Green, but I didn't fully understand what housing projects were until much later. The grown-ups said it was for poor people too lazy to work. The WGN news seemed to agree, but documentaries didn't. The ask for reparations for slavery from the African-American community didn't come into fully understood focus, until I desired reparations from patriarchy in the years after my divorce. Oppression isn't easy to explain to cognitive dissonance.

"Toss him twenty bucks, Katie. Never mind. I gotchu," Tido said in a low voice, as we passed by the door guy. An oversized girl in black Jncos, a platinum blonde buzz cut, and a choker, did a quick pat down on me to make sure I didn't have a gun.

The light show was beaming in streams of green and purple overhead, and the music was booming so loud every cell in my body was quaking with pleasure. It was an instant shift. I loved it. The music almost negated any need for drugs. *Almost.* We got there around 2:00AM, and Tido took off to chat with some people he knew. I met a circle of young ravers, they must have been 13 or 14 years old, who embraced me with an offering of a hit of LSD. Did I want one? *Yes, yes I did.* Is 3:00AM a good time to drop acid? Hmm...I would peak around 6:00AM, and still be tripping around noon when I went home. Yeah sure. Let's do it.

"You dosed just now? Ohh shit! Have fun with that. I have to drive, so I'm not down for that kind of ride tonight," Tido remarked making a gesture to his hand, "just herb for me."

The sonic beats whirred over my skin and percolated my nervous system, as I lost myself in uninhibited grinding to a flow of Chicago Deep House. I wasn't Katie—I was an anonymous girl devoted to the dance of an electronic tribe. This was my Sufi trance. I could lose myself for hours doing this. It was absolute bliss. I wanted to move my body and dance like this all the time. With or without the L. The boy next to met shook his head and sweat sprayed down my arm in a shower of pings. There it was...sparkles. The higher frequency was setting in. This is the place I already knew. The one with rainbows. Where everything is just vibrating energy.

"Hey, the sun's about to come up. I gotta get back," I heard in my ear, as someone tapped my shoulder. The gatekeeper was here to lead me out.

"Are people going to an after party?" I asked.

"Nah, they're gonna be shooting up in that neighborhood. I'm not going over there. Not our scene," Tido informed.

As we walked into the parking lot, I realized I was not quite myself. We wedged into the icebox, both in a sleep-deprived daze, and headed homeward. It was gloomy in Chicago. Winter lasted forever, hanging with dark murky clouds. LSD turned the icicles into prisms. I needed the prisms. Color helped my mood. The ride was smooth until all the alcohol and water expanded in our bladders and we needed to stop. We pulled over at a diner with a blinking *Breakfast Buffet Here* sign. This almost topped the bizarre meter of tripping in a gas station.

The first time I did LSD, I was in the ladies room of a Chevron station on the corner of 125 and Washington. A fluorescent ceiling flickered with a static buzz as I took a piss in their bathroom. *This is normal. People pee. Nothing weird going on here.*

"Hit the fucking ground!" I'm sure I heard someone shout outside the door. Feet scuffled and voices grunted and whispered to one another. A cash register screamed with the spillage of coins. I was afraid to come out because I could hear the terror and pandemonium of the place being robbed. I sat on the toilet and held my breath as a rack of chips got dumped over into a crinkly mess. *It's a shit show out there. See what happens when you start fucking with the program? You're in for it now, Katie. No place to hide. Better pull your pants up.*

After it got quiet I edged towards the door and slowly turned the knob, making sure it didn't click. I peeked around the edge and was shocked to see undisturbed rows of merchandise and a lack of dudes in black ski caps holding the cashier at gun point. The elevator music flipped on just in time to stroll me out the front door and into a white windowless van. With a big exhale, I joined my fellow volunteers in the sugar cube test panel.

I've had some practice since then. The diner was straight out of the 1970s. Dark and geometric. This is a perplexing combination to the person peaking on acid. A somber lack of sound stood on the outside of the doors, but once through, I was hit with the rush of clinking dishes and clambering conversations. Murky brown. Tinted orange. Mirrored walls with gold leaf cracks. Red carpet cut from the Stanley Hotel led me to the bathroom in a pulsating hexagon ripple. I played a little game of, *the carpet is hot lava…step on the moving pyramid to cross the river.* I made it.

Every drip of water in the bathroom pipes was connected to the single drops of water circulating through Earth. Wow, this water closet is filled with oneness. I sat as the strange sensation of peeing wrapped my vulva in waves of wetness. Were my intestines falling into the toilet? If that happened it would really take some thinking to fix and I wasn't in the head space for logical gut retrieval. I tried to relax and focus on the visual of the palms of my hands. My skin was breathing and my veins wiggled as they pushed the blood to its circulatory station. The skin suit is very strange.

I thought to myself, "The peeing is done. Now I must pat my crotch dry with this bendable paper." Done. "Okay, how does this flusher work? Do you push it up…or do you push it down? Fuck, I hope I don't break the handle." I washed my hands and tried not to get distracted for an hour. "Tido is waiting for me. Go outside."

"Dude, do you realize you're going to be tripping all day? You're fucking crazy, Katie," said my stating-the-obvious genius of a friend. He dropped me off at my pick-up that was still in the parking lot of the truck stop. Swerving to avoid every enhanced bump in the waving road ahead of me, I drove across town and over to Lisa's, where Dad thought I had spent the night playing spin the bottle and having pillow fights. No, he didn't think that. I only wish he thought that. He would wake up sober and cranky, and I would have to spend the day dodging bullets.

As Sunday morning established itself in the sky, I thanked God Lisa and her dad never went to church. She looked me up and down as I stood freezing at her back door. "What the heck are you on?" She inquired.

"I'm tripping. I need to call my parents and let them know I'll be home soon to go to church." I tried to assure her of my having it under control. "It's no biggie. It will be easy as pie after that." She didn't look convinced.

I dialed my house and Dad picked up, "Hello, it's me, Katie, I'm calling your house, home…where I live."

My father paused with a nervous chuckle, "Uh yeah, I can see that."

"So I'm good. I'm just really sleepy because I woke up, but now I'm super awake and I'm going to go to church, but I'll come home first," I offered.

"Okay Katie, great plan. So did you get your car doors working this morning?" He baited me.

"Oh, yeah, they're all de-thawed now. The sun is super bright and I think it melted everything. Good thing I stayed here. It was cold, but that's okay. I can drive it now. It's no problem. I'll just wear my sunglasses because I didn't bring any spare clothes or whatever." I tried desperately to string together sensible responses.

"Okaay. So we will see you in a bit? When you come home to get dressed for church?" He asked.

"Yep. Just gonna eat this cake first. Thanks!"

I held the phone out to Lisa so she could help me hang it up. The cord had wrapped around my legs like an octopus headed for my mouth to shut me up. My friend fed me some yellow birthday cake with chocolate frosting that stuck to my mouth like a piece of foam. As a reflex, I let it fall out of my mouth like a child reluctantly learning to eat solids. It splattered on her dad's Harley Davidson rug in the kitchen and I rubbed it in with my foot so he'd never know.

On my drive home, I gave myself a pep talk. "Okay, we're gonna knock this church thing off the list, then go home and listen to the Beatles. It's gonna be totally chill."

I parked my truck in its usual spot by the curb, did about twenty-five spatial checks on its location, and then decided, *yeah, I'm cool.* I walked in the front door the way a snake enters a rabbit hole and did what would seem normal. I scurried to my bedroom, stripped, and rushed into the shower. I could bide some time at this location, wash the sin off me, and most importantly, lock the door.

Nudity, water, and hallucinogens. This was a very earthy combination, and yet I felt like a chemical rod had been lodged up my spine. I must spread the soapy lather all over my human body. Is this what "clean" smells like? It's strong, like someone sprayed air freshener up my nose. What could have been a sensual experience was actually quite weird. Am I pressing too hard? Am I going to damage an organ while I bathe? I felt detached from my body, like I was a thought trying to operate a large, droopy, squishy, heavy wet suit. My hair was loosening with every lather, rinse repeat. Dear Lord, it's a tangly mess strangling my face and choking my neck! *Rinse, rinse, rinse.* Hey, the water is a translucent lavender. Did anyone notice that? It's like someone squirted the shower with grape-flavored Kool-Aid. I watched it run in amethyst streams down the beige bowl I stood in. Wet, dry, dressed—ready for church.

My peak was mellowing into a nice zippery stream of mild colors, and my face relaxing from its multiple hours of perma-grin. Make-up was an exercise in zero-gravity, space-age application. I relied on memory of my usual routine, so I wouldn't leave the house looking like a goof.

Wrapped in the safety of my soft winter coat, I headed out for my next venture. I drove across town, where the Catholic Church stood, watching my late arrival with its all-knowing glass. My perception cracked open, waiting for the heavens to jump in and fill it with celestial secrets. On my way up to the building, I walked over a split, bumpy sidewalk, its concrete aging beyond fifty years. The roots of friendly trees pushed up, creating hills and crevices, reminding the slab who would reside here longer. The snow was melting in spots where the rich hummus soil breathed premonitions of green grass seeds pushing towards spring. I reveled in the textures of Mother Earth.

Getting the hang of navigating each footstep while tilted, I walked up the steps to the church, opened the towering oak doors, and entered the womb of God. It was packed and I was left standing in a crowd in the back. I couldn't see the service being performed at the altar, so I focused on standing still and refraining from talking to myself out loud. The congregation was full of human warmth, which was broken up by shocks of cold every time the back doors were opened. To my right stood an old man, who must have been in his eighties. His wrinkles were wavering over his face, like a slow pulsing of energy, gearing down in voltage. I watched his aging process unfold before my eyes. Was he really here?

The little girl in front of me acknowledged his presence, so he must be real. Her energy was bubbling with the brightness of a new creation. Her voice reverberated with variants of high pitches, laughing, giggling, shimmering. She sent waves to the old man who met her youthful presence with a smile. The veil of reality was peeling back, showing me the orchestration behind the performance curtain. The God of my knowing showed me a peek into the cycle of life, in a way I had not witnessed before. The little girl was a beam of light on her way in, shooting unbridled rays of brilliance in all directions, and he had been reduced to a soft flame, a well-established ember, steady, yet at risk of being snuffed out if not cared for properly. These were two sparks, exchanging a twinkling wink of cosmic existence within the confines of the human experience. I observed the continuous path of their souls. That felt pretty substantial. Time to cut out before Communion.

I arrived home and decided to play it cool and lay in bed for a while. I snuggled up with my black cat Tinker Bell, and got lost in my mind. *I have a few minutes, maybe I can figure out "LIFE."* I petted her soft black fur, as she sat like an Egyptian Goddess on my chest. Her purrs vibrated any acid anxiety away. I gazed at the color sprinkling off the ends of her whiskers. Her eyes slanted with pleasure and poise. I'm in the zone. The trippy feline zone. Cats are part LSD. I'm sure of it. Cats are tripping balls all the time.

"Katie, can you come here for a minute?" someone bellowed down the hallway.

Ah crap...*you will not break my zone...you will not break my zone*, I recited to myself.

"Sure, coming!" I responded. I heard whispering outside my doorway, or did I? A wave of paranoia was setting in. How to have a bad trip 101: dose at your parent's house.

Father was sitting on the love seat, and Mother the far end of the couch. That left me on the couch, facing an extremely bright five panel bow window. All of the lamps were on. Really? Do we need this much light? It's like a damn interrogation room. *Yes, that is the plan, Katie.* I held my hand to my forehead and morphed into the thinking statue, beginning a History Channel-worthy, in-depth-contemplation of the fabric structure of my pants.

He started in on his rant. "So I woke up in the wee hours of the morning today, you know, because I didn't sleep well after someone called and woke me up at midnight last night. And I got to thinking how it was interesting that the locks froze so fast. Then I thought, wow! What an astounding display of physics! I should go see this in person! Then I thought, hmm, maybe Katie needs some help with her chemistry-defying truck. So I took a little drive by your friend Lisa's house. Funny thing is, I didn't see your truck anywhere." Busted.

"Her dad lives on Illinois Avenue, but you can park in the alley," I shrugged.

"The thing is, I drove down Illinois Avenue, and the alley, and the side streets, and Washington Street, and Canal Street, and all the streets, Katie. I even drove by the Illinois River, but I didn't see your truck parked anywhere, which is strange, because you specifically told me you parked it in front of her house and couldn't move it all night long, due to those pesky frozen locks."

"Yeah that's weird," I murmured as I deliberated if my eyelids were a quarter of the way, half way, or three quarters of the way open. What is a normal amount for your eyelids to be open? Would it be odd if I sat with my hands over my eyeballs? Seems like that would be way more comfortable.

"So whose parent's should I call next? Because I already talked to Lisa's dad and he doesn't know anything about you staying at his house last night."

"Uh, no one's?" I answered him.

"Are you ready to get serious, Katie?! Because I don't get mad, I get even!" Oh shit, he was gettin' all Chuck Norris on me. "Who were you with?!"

"I was out…with people."

"God damn it Katie! Your smart ass shit is going to get you in worse trouble! You just can't seem to learn, can you?!" His veins were bulging out of his forehead and I'm pretty sure one of his arteries was waving a finger at me.

My lack of compliance was making him lose. his. shit. Insubordination was the worst poison known to my father's ego. Example: When you are planting marigolds in the flower garden with your mother on a pleasant spring afternoon, watch what you let escape. If you happen to make the mistake of releasing some spontaneous laughter at a joke he doesn't find funny, and then further your blunder by telling him "Hey, you should lighten up," you might get a broom thrown at the side of your head. Broom incident lesson 101: don't laugh in front of Dad. In fact, per his request, don't even smile. "You look foolish," he'll tell you.

As his ears went past red and began taking on purple, I feared they would fall off. My father's rage escalated and he began talking with his entire arm, moving it in a downward axing motion. All I could think was, "Wow, look at the trails. How do they do that?"

He was livid. "What the hell are you on anyways, Katie? You don't look drunk or hung over. Your eyes are wide awake looking. Are you taking cocaine?"

I burst out laughing. I couldn't help it. Any slight misuse of a drug reference was a major faux pas to a high schooler. Personally, I didn't know anyone who did cocaine. In my mind, it was a leftover token from 1980s movie legends. As I pictured a scene from *Coming to America,* a baffled look rolled over my face.

"Oh, you think this is funny?" he condescendingly questioned me. *Oh Dad, you're so classic.* "I'll give you a reality check, little missy, and I will get the truth out of you, eventually. Until then, you're grounded for a month. No truck. In fact, I've got a little adjustment to make on it. There won't be any stickers placed on MY truck anymore. Now go to your room," he lectured.

I quickly scuttered down the hallway and into my room. Safe. I peered through the venetian blinds and watched him as he stomped his way across the front yard, in his stark white Nikes. He crouched down behind the rustic truck, where a carefully placed bumper sticker was located. It was the color violet, the flame of the crown chakra. Bold white words simply said, "Question Reality." It was my motto, and he was peeling it away.

The Piece of Lint

I'm seeing a new therapist. A client-practitioner relationship, of course, nothing more. I prefer to dump my most intimate thoughts onto complete strangers. Less risk. I build a taboo friendship. One that ends the moment someone stops paying. Transactional relationships are familiar...familial.

"Here's your early dismissal slip, Ms. Sexton," the high school secretary says as she delivers me a side eye. "I hope everything works out." I can read her mind. *There goes another one of our honor roll students...hope she can get back on track.* Evidently she heard about my parents reporting me missing last week. It was only *one* night after two days of fighting. I didn't see what the big deal was. The first night Dad got mad about the phone and threw it at me, accidentally hitting Mom in the face with it instead. The second night he put me in a choke hold when I tried to leave the house. When you can't overpower the toddler by picking them up, it escalates to wrestling moves on a teenager.

I was stoked that the newly scheduled therapy appointments were getting me out of school thirty minutes early for the next few weeks. After driving 20 minutes to the next town over, I shuffled into a small Family Counseling office, expecting to hear about my overnight delinquency for the next hour. I was sorrily mistaken. Instead, I sat with a white-haired woman named Miss Higgins, who wore a smart Carnation Pink plaid suit, and listened to my father deliver a persuasive speech on the importance of Prom Night. The dance was a priority—a demonstration to the world of my impeccable normality. A display of their irreproachable parenting.

The goal of this 45 minute time slice was to prove I needed to go to a school dance in exchange for all they have done for me. Their life-sized doll was malfunctioning. "Can you give us a new chip? This one is defective," my father would say if he could.

"I see Katie is in the Art Club, on the Diving Team, and just got her Life-guarding Certification," the therapist related with the warmth of a home-room mom.

"That's nice, but I'm talking about Prom," Dad replied with the cocki-ness of a 5 o'clock news anchor. I was birthed solely for their entertainment. Jackie Kennedy wasn't catching the drift.

We had three appointments, until Dad pulled the plug. "Whose side are you on, lady??" he bickered at the therapist.

"Well, Mr. Sexton, this isn't about choosing sides. It's about understand-ing where everyone is coming from and supporting needs, so you can grow as a family." Obviously she was not on board with his vision.

"Excuse me?" he stuttered. *How dare that therapist suggest something incon-gruent with his agenda. And in front of everyone.*

Miss Higgins looked at me with a helpless shrug in her eyes that said, "My hands are tied," a close resemblance to the "Your dad's a dick" look. I had seen that one a few times. Her neck flushed while contending with my father, though she remained calm, neutral, and logical. This made his blood boil into an erupting volcano in each ear. "What the hell am I paying you for?" he snarled. Miss Higgins knew we would never be back. "Your mother wants to see her daughter dressed up. You're shattering her dreams. Just go to the Prom. How hard is it?" he guilted me. *Didn't they already go to high school?*

"Well, I haven't been asked," I admitted with shame.

"Well, do boys know you are available? If you've been going around saying you don't want to go to the dance, then maybe they don't think they should ask you," he schooled me.

Oh, so I should make myself more "available"? I imagine this was not the stance of most fathers of high school daughters. "So, I should let them know I'll have sex with them?" I asked with a tinge of cynicism.

"Excuse me? What did you just say? Not all guys want that, Katie. I'm talking about Prom," he responded, about ready to short circuit.

"But I thought you told me that's literally all boys want. That it's all they think about and they keep score cards or something," I stated, recalling a previous educational lesson with him.

"What? Just go to the dance. I'm talking about Prom, not all that MTV crap," he sputtered in a flurry. Dad had a loathing for MTV ever since their Safe Sex campaign brought the word "condom" into our living room. He got up and left the room.

"I ran into Anne's mother this morning. I guess *she* is going to the Prom,"

Mom chimed in as she began folding clothes.

"Anne is on birth control, Mom," I answered.

"You don't know that," she said, flustered I had extended the conversation to a truth bomb. "You could go with a group of friends. They have post-prom activities for teens to do."

"Yes, I do know that. Anne and her boyfriend have sex in her bedroom at her parent's house. Do you want to do that so I can go to the Prom for you?" I delivered.

"Katie, stop," she said as she threw the shirt back into the basket and stomped out of the room.

I wasn't about to have sex with any boys though. I had been scared of waking up pregnant since I was about six years old. The Catholic Church taught us the Virgin Mary woke up pregnant with the Messiah, and that she was lucky because other women who got pregnant out of wedlock were called a whore and stoned to death by the townspeople.

Mom went to the Prom herself that year. She volunteered to help with the post-prom decorations. I guess she liked those teens better than me. That was fine.

I yearned for Dad's protection, but that's not how it was going to pan out. When spoken therapy didn't produce results, he began writing dissertations. His first thesis: Prom. Followed by: Look What You're Doing To Your Mother. And my personal favorite: If You Hang Out With Losers, You're Gonna Wind Up Being A Loser. I arrived home from school to a ransom note of subtle harassment in the form of overbearing penmanship that continued through my twenties. I crammed the shoebox of hate mail into my closet where it sat like a giant brick of disapproval.

After I notched my last high school summer with a suspended license, I headed off to college. Meh, I won't need a car for a couple years anyways. Escaping my hometown will make me feel happy! Wrong. My thought became a dull echo as I crept up the stairs to a school psychiatrist on the third floor of the medical clinic a few semesters later. I bulldozed through a few psychologists doing nothing more than talk therapy. Then someone decided, "Just put her on meds."

I had zero clue what I wanted to study. That was the first problem. If anything, I wanted to take a year off to think about things. Heck, if I took a few years off I could travel and then quality for grants rather than take out massive loans. But my dad said one way or the other, kids had to move out at 18. If I didn't go to college, then I was to get a job and a rental of some sort.

I didn't receive any input on how to do this, just a delivery of the needed outcome. Much like the directive, "If you get pregnant, you are kicked out," I started receiving at age 13. Their version of sex education. I wanted to go to a college in Arizona because it was so warm and sunny. My aunt lived there and I liked the desert. But Dad wasn't okay with that. If you want to go out of state, I'm not helping with any living expenses. You can figure it out yourself. Besides, your mother would be devastated.

The last counselor I vented to, recommended a book, of which I read about one chapter of. It was so hard to concentrate. I didn't like the disorganization of the dorms. The food was gross, and the whole structure didn't make sense to me. It seemed like everyone was merely concerned with check things off a list. I thought the point of higher education was to expand intelligence. This depressed me too, just like when I learned corporations dumped toxic waste into waterways through loopholes. It seemed everyone was completely okay with a system that operated like a dystopian nightmare adorned with plastic flowers. A lightbulb quivered in my now dimly lit grey matter.

The chapter was entitled: Self-Talk. It suggested "it's hard to be happy when you are internally bad-mouthing yourself." *What kind of ass-backwards rhetoric is THIS?* Dad definitely did not write this one. He wrote the opposite term paper, referencing "how to influence and persuade people," accompanied by "don't be a wuss."

"You have to push yourself," Dad always said. He was highly supportive of my talent at softball, and trained with me to no end. "If you're gonna be great, you have to go a step beyond everyone else. This applies to everything in life."

"So why don't you practice with Jason this much?" I asked with the naivety of a child who would take two pennies over one dime.

"Because your brother sucks at baseball. Come on, you can tell. And I know you're a girl, but you're actually REALLY good. You're all muscle. Now get out there and pitch me that bucket. Your arm is on fire!" he said like he was molding the next pitcher for the White Sox. I was a sucker for the praise.

Years of clients had worn a butt dent in the doctor's goldenrod yellow sofa chair. It was complete with balding velour on the arms, where nervous hands had rubbed away the soft fibers. Why splurge on a new one when you're pushing retirement age? She peered at me from behind a stack of messy papers on her desk, with a look that told me she was bored to death with her job. After years of listening to people's problems, I might be too.

As I proceeded to tell her my deepest insecurities, "I feel like a novelty, like people don't really like me," she dazed away and focused on the sleeve of her periwinkle sweater. She sluggishly began to pick the tiny pieces of fuzzy lint off her winter attire. *Is she really doing that?*

From *my* seat, I was experiencing an internal Congratulations Party, adorned with a banner, glitter confetti, and Queen playing *We Are The Champions*, you know…because I made it to the appointment. I had been having a series of mini heart attacks on my way to class. This was putting a slight damper on my collegiate performance. *Maybe I should mention that to her.*

My general state of being was that of being drugged on Special K, that horse tranquilizer shit. I'm saying I was tired. Debilitatingly fatigued. Why? I had no clue. I was doing the same diet of coffee, alcohol, coffee everyone else was doing. I wanted to know why my system was ringing like a five alarm fire, ten minutes before I had to leave my apartment for class. I attempted to douse it by fulfilling endless "one last things" to make myself feel "right." It made me late, which added to the constricting pressure in my chest.

After a panicked, brisk walk onto campus, I arrived outside my classroom, anywhere from three to thirty-three minutes late. With palms sweaty, I stood in the university hall as a woozy rolled over me. Blotchy vision—I'm getting used to it. Nausea socked me in the stomach as it called me a loser. My mouth lost its ability to salivate. I felt the judging eyes of my classmates, along with a perturbed glare from my professor, as my panoramic view turned into a swirling blur of neutrals. My chest continued to squeeze the oxygen out. I couldn't function. In a state of disorientation, I blinked a few times to get my vision back, paced two laps up and down the hall, then did a 180 and headed home to lie in bed until my pulse returned to normal. Sometimes it took a couple hours. Afterwards I was exhausted and slept like a narcoleptic. I was failing two classes due to this dilemma.

"What drugs do you do? Alcohol? Marijuana?" the psychiatrist probed.

"None, really. Well, I drink sometimes, but I don't like the way marijuana makes me feel. I get paranoid," I told her.

"I understand. You're the people that wind up in here instead," she assured me, "Describe the paranoia for me." "Well, it makes me question my decisions and the road they have taken me down. I feel like I'm lost and wasting my life. It feels like I'm in a bad dream, rather than reflecting on actual events. It's like I'm stuck in a foggy dimension, separate from others, like I don't really know anyone, and I'm playing out a game where I go through the motions of life, but am trapped suffering this fake existence on the wrong plane, until I die, or..."

"Hrmm, yes, that sounds like a pretty hefty dose of paranoia," she noted.

Sheesh, she cut me off before I could finish. When I smoked weed, I felt confused and unable to form sentences, much like I would feel on the smorgasbord of psych meds I was about to get put on and off over the next ten years. Being high, whether it was on weed or prescription pills, made me feel like I woke up in the wrong reality and now I was stuck here. Afraid to move. Afraid to talk. Afraid to be. Of course that was also the way I felt when I was sober, so I wasn't exactly making a breakthrough. Neither option felt normal, whatever that was.

"I'm giving you a prescription for three Xanax. It's normal to feel nervous about public speaking. *Oh good, I'm normal.* These will get you through the three speeches you have for class. As for the depression, I'm prescribing you Celexa," she informed me. I conveniently forgot to tell her about the heart attack sensation. Bringing that up was way too anxiety-inducing. Plus I was ashamed to admit I was missing class and my grades were plummeting. *I'll bring it up next time.*

"The anti-depressant won't fix things for you, but it will foster a state of mind where you can make improvements or cope with your circumstances for the time being," she said. "Do you understand what I'm saying? This pill will not make you happy, or help you choose your degree, but it can help you be more receptive to options."

She dealt a mid-line first impression of medication. I would have gone with the "it will numb you into a stupor, which a potential suitor may prefer, but will leave you feeling like you have swallowed your own soul down with the pill and shit it into the toilet, to be flushed, sent through the community filtering system, and fed back to you in the we–all–know–this–is–shit–water status." What is the mental health industry anyways, but a board of men describing how to behave "normally" in a capitalist, patriarchal society. "Normal" and "mental illness" are bias constructs at their core.

I took the pharmaceuticals for a few months, then started to feel suspicious. I still had no direction or grip on life, yet somehow I was content. No passion or creative energy, which is a problem if you're an art student. It toned down the drinking, but I didn't trust the overall results. Who was this watered-down Frankenkatie? If she picked a degree to focus on in this state of mind, is it even her? Will she still want the same goals when she is off the pharmaceuticals? I wondered those things.

"Which meds are you on?" My roommate's friend asked.

"Celexa and Xanax," I replied.

"Oh nice, they won't prescribe me Xanax anymore. It works too good I guess. But I did get this new drug they have called Adderall. It's the best speed I've ever had," he shared. "I'm gonna ace my Business Statistics class this semester.

Who was this guy? Business majors did not hang out not the east side of campus.

That was it; I committed to drinking for a week straight, as I went off the pills. I figured that would stave off any withdrawal. Sometimes I'd have a night of binge drinking to get "it" out of my system or to sober up from day drinking. Seems counter-intuitive, but that was the method everyone else was doing, so I gave it a try. I began my research. I was not impressed with the direction the anxiety and depression were going. After suffering 21 years of asthma and a poor immune system, I was skeptical of pharmaceuticals. Western medicine told me I would grow out of asthma. They had no answer for the immune challenges. I was tired of dumping money into medications that created side effects that required more medications. It was never ending, and I kept getting sicker and sicker. I went through this with steroids for asthma. They made me bloated, irritable, jittery, and sick. Mom took me to numerous specialists when I was a child. They had me blow into tubes and try to measure what I could feel more accurately from the inside. I asked the specialist, "isn't taking steroids bad for you?" He told me it was bad in the long run, but I needed to breathe now. So this was the choice. He was grey, overweight, and sweaty. The doctor wasn't the picture of health I had expected to get advice from.

The local naturopath store sold homeopathic remedies. I wanted to learn more. I was getting colds or strep throat every three months. I was on a rotation of antibiotics and yeast infections. I bought a couple books on natural cures. One for asthma and one for anxiety. I found some very unexpected topics in these publications. The resounding culprit for both was inflammation, and there was a whole chapter on vaccines. Apparently there was a whole world of information I wasn't aware of in that department. I dove in search of the root cause. I wanted to find out how and why it started, and what could I do to make it vanish? I wanted to forget what a nebulizer was. This interested me more than design class, algebra, or poly-sci 101.

The more I read about wellness, it seemed an entire shift in lifestyle was required. But my world would't allow that. I was taught I could only buy food from the dollar store while I was in college. One item at the co-op, where "organic" food and toiletries were, cost as much as my entire month's budget. I didn't know how I was going to make this switch. And would it be worth it? None of the holistic remedies were covered by my health insurance, not even a massage. If the things in these books were true, and the testimonials authentic, then I was learning about yet another uphill battle with the current systems that be.

I remember Dad's words, "you can't fight the man, Katie." He was in a Halliburton rabbit hole last summer. The plant eliminated his job. He claimed business was changing for the worse and entered into a 5-year lawsuit with his company over discrimination. He represented himself.

"I'm never gonna win. Not with these assholes. The company has more legal money than me, and that's how this game works. But I'm pissing them off, making them come to all these court dates," he boasted. Revenge was his fuel, and Mom was lost in the mix.

I only spoke with Dad a couple times a year at that point. Mom was the go-between, and her messages always got crossed with opposing agendas. Toxic families think manipulation will bring people closer together, but it's a house of cards that comes crashing down eventually. That's why they need a scapegoat.

I didn't know what the term organic really meant. They didn't use that term when I was a kid shopping with Mom. This was a new term. A lot of my classmates in Biology were talking about it. Monsanto had a branch in our college town. They were responsible for the genetic engineering of all the corn grown in Illinois, and people seemed to be pretty mad about it.

As I took myself off pharmaceuticals, I knew I had things to purge. All the chemicals I had been ingesting, and emotions I had been stuffing. I thought alcohol was the only way to achieve this. Poison in, poison out… wait, poison back in. *You're a damn genius.* As my hangover cleared, I felt like me again. Not exactly happy, but with a familiar pulse electrifying my mind. Unfortunately, the current eventually zapped me back to my hometown.

I managed to drag myself through college, graduating with a BFA in Sculpture and a Minor in Art History. My parents were so proud they took a vacation to Florida the week of my graduation ceremony…without me. So I didn't go either, although this was the prom I wanted them to attend.

I attempted to slide back into the nest for a short stint as I entered the adult world. But a faulty child lock on a bottle of bleach made certain to prevent that. I borrowed Dad's 15 year old beige Astro van to drive to an interview. As my laundry bounced, the bleach bottle fell over and rolled around the cab, weaving a white web along the carpet that spelled, "you will be kicked out before you move in."

"You have no respect! You screw up everything! Didn't college teach you how to twist a cap shut?" Dad shouted, as I packed my bags once again.

I gave downtown Chicago a valiant effort instead, arriving back in my hometown a year later, where I began working as a teacher's assistant. I tried again to move home, but Dad wanted to control what jobs I applied for. Being a teacher's assistant for the special education department wasn't good enough for him. But I had such a hard time getting through undergrad, I wanted to explore working in the field before I invested more money in education. I rented an apartment with my cousin's friend instead.

"Katie, your mom has to stop coming into my work and asking about you," Danica informed. She was my new roommate.

"Oh, God. What are you talking about?" I asked, apprehensive of where this tale may lead.

"I dunno, I was trying to do hair and she came in like you were a kid on the back of a milk carton," she dropped on me, while making herself a Strawberry-Hibiscus tea.

"I'm twenty-seven years old for God's sake. I'll take care of it. I'm so sorry. I hope you didn't get in trouble," I said, as I set down my groceries. I was grateful Danica was a health nut, like me. Salad never went bad in our fridge.

"It's okay, but I can't be having that stuff at my work. I'm sorry I had to bring it up, but you know…" her voice trailed off as she went to her room to listen to Common and stare at her crystals while she got into "Dani" mode.

My new roomie was a societal ninja. The high school counselor had a fit when her IQ tested off the charts and yet she chose to go to Cosmetology school.

"I want to make people feel happy, because that makes *me* feel happy," she told them. "I can bust out some Sudoku, but I'd rather have hair be my main gig," she offered like an angel with a wand. I knew the issue with Mom was getting out of hand. She was coming into my after school art teaching job too. She would bring leftover food or things that seemed harmless. But

I felt suffocated. I wanted some boundaries. I knew we were in the same small town, but I was trying to be an adult. It was distracting, and I needed a nice way to tell her.

I drove to my parent's house early that evening to politely, yet clearly, address the milk carton issue. I was relieved Dad was at a golf tournament. No need for this to get all dramatic. I could quickly speak to Mom in private, and then jet out outta there.

"Oh hi, honey! What are you up to today? I saw your new roommate Danica this morning. She's so nice," Mom wafted my way.

I sat down at the dining room table. "Yeah, I heard. Can we talk about that?" I gently suggested.

"Well I'm cooking dinner in the kitchen, but sure. What's up?" She asked.

"So, Danica almost got in trouble for talking to you while she was working on a client. Her boss doesn't like people loitering. I think it made her feel uneasy. Were you asking her questions about me or something?" I pried for clarification.

"Well, I'm sorry if she was upset. I just wanted to say hello," Mom refuted, her voice cutting off, like an electrician hacking the line, the day your bill is past due.

"Yeah, but were you asking her where I was? I mean, you could call me, or else assume I'm busy if you don't hear back from me right away. I feel like it's kind of embarrassing to have your mom poking around as to your whereabouts when you're in your mid-twenties," I confessed with frankness.

"Well I'm *so* sorry you don't want your mother around. I guess I should just disappear off the face of the planet if you're so embarrassed of me. Is that what you want?" She began to cry.

Oh fuck. This is not going as planned. *Abort mission, you fool!!*

"All I'm saying is that maybe it's not appropriate to go into my roommate's place of employment and start asking her where I am…like, it's not the time or place, don't you think? It's not like I live in a crack house. I'm fine. You don't need to check on me," I said.

"Why do you hate me?! Is *nothing* I do right?!" she yelped out as she began shaking like a rocket booster at lift off. The proximity to the thrust caused my body to tremble. This is not what I expected. I fell for the ambush. Time to launch.

I followed Mom as she steamed into the kitchen, and began to plead with her, "Calm down! What are you doing?"

She grabbed a steak knife. *What the fuck is happening.* She lifted the knife and I froze like a drop of spit in an Alaskan winter. For a split second I thought she was going to come at me. *A cortisol dump is what's happening.* Instead, she motioned to stab herself. It was a flimsy steak knife, weakened from decades of going through a dish washer, but it cut through meat and that terrified me. My head started to ring and I was hit with racing thoughts. This was way worse than testing as a lifeguard.

"Is this what you want?!" she yelled as she pierced the knitting on the chest of her sweater. *Holy fuck!* I'm getting water boarded with buckets of emotions. It took me a few years of sloshing, but eventually I realized, *this isn't mine.* This stuff she is throwing at me isn't mine.

"What are you doing?!? Mom, stop it! What the fuck!" I yelled at her.

I was becoming as numb to these incidents as a teenager being forced to attend a spaghetti dinner at the local church Youth Group. Can you hand me that steak knife you were using? No? Okay, I'll just use this plastic fork to poke about a thousand holes through this styrofoam plate.

Her outbursts started when I hit puberty. Doesn't everyone's mother fall into a weeping mess on the floor, gasp for air, declare their failure, accuse their family of not loving them, then get up and finish baking a chicken and rice casserole, like someone flipped the breaker? As I learned later in life, it's pretty common. Women aren't happy. Mothers aren't happy. Things are fucked up. But the steak knife threw me off. She upped the ante.

"Mom, put it down. Stop. I promise. Everything is fine," I said in my most base-line voice. She was crying. Sobbing. I had no idea why she was so unhappy. At 27, I didn't have the perspective yet. I knew there was something wrong with our family. I knew there was something wrong with the big picture too. But I was so "in it" I couldn't see the forest for the trees.

Once her tension released she set the utensil down. I walked out the front door like a hostage who had just been released, muttering, "This is what I do. Juggle crisis situations, any time I speak up for myself." I needed to distance myself from them. I began seeing my parents as children, acting out insecurities and hurt feelings, like a holographic glitch being replayed in a state of utter unawareness. I couldn't help them. I could only help myself. But I barely knew how to walk away. My whole system was infused with their patterns.

I called my father and my mom's best friend when I got home. I asked them to check on Mom, because she was not acting like herself. I told them about the argument. Movies always showed mothers having "nervous breakdowns." But what was that anyways. They depicted women as mentally weak and prone to these "episodes". Is that what I was witnessing? Men were starting to treat me that way too, but I wasn't having a breakdown. I wanted to be treated with intelligence and respect. I wanted my feelings acknowledged and reciprocated. I was frustrated. After 4-5 decades of this frustration, is that what they are calling a breakdown? It doesn't seem like an accurate term.

"Okay, I'll make sure she gets some rest. She's very sensitive. You know how much she worries. She might need a glass of warm milk," Dad spoke like the head nurse at an old people's home working the Alzheimer's unit.

I went to my apartment and cracked a drink with my roomie. But I was so exhausted, I crashed before I could even finish it. I thought the situation had been diffused. Sunday went by without a word. Monday I went back to work. Just before my day of assisting special needs students got started, I received a cell phone call from a belligerent man. It was Dad. I should not have answered.

"I talked to your mother about the incident you described to me, and she has quite a different version," he led on, like a jaded, small town detective. On Sunday, there had been an investigative undertaking, at which I was found guilty. Private Investigator Dad responded to his findings by calling and yelling at me at 8:00AM, Monday morning.

"What are you talking about? I'm about to start work, like I'm already in the classroom," I informed him, as I sensed the impending doom of the conversation.

"Excuse me! I wasn't finished talking, Katie! You are so rude! You have no manners and you could give a shit about anyone but yourself," he laid into me.

My hands started to tremble, then went numb, like they always did when his words started to slit my throat. My lips stiffened as I tried to speak through the rapid pulse pounding past my vocal box. I opened my mouth to speak, but at first nothing came out but a gasp for air. "I was trying to help her by telling you what happened. How can you be mad at me?"

"Help her?! You're a bully, Katie! You treat people like shit and then I have to pick up the mess! How can you treat your mother like this?!" Dad bellowed.

My eyes welled up with tears, turning the room into a blurry window. I knew the other teachers were staring at me. I couldn't detect the walls anymore...they were a thousand miles away, but the floor was about to meet the ceiling. Incidents like this made me dizzy and disoriented. I excused myself from the room full of teachers who could hear him scolding his daughter. No wonder I was only a teacher's aide. According to him, I was still an incompetent child.

I rushed past the students, who were moving in the opposite direction as me down the hallway. I made it out the side door in time to hear the last half of his speech. "She would have never threatened to harm herself if you hadn't bullied her into a corner!! She told me how you belittled her and told her she was a horrible mother! How would you feel if you were her?! Oh, but you don't think that way, do you! You just think about poor Katie and how everyone needs to bend over backwards to please you. It's all about you. When is it ever going to stop with you?" He laid into me.

"But, Dad, I never said that! She was going into my roommate's work during her work hours while she was with clients, asking her where I was and what I was doing. She could have gotten my roommate fired! All I told her was to call me first. I was setting a boundary! Not just for me, but for my roommate at her place of employment," I defended.

"Your mother worries. You know that, Katie. How hard is it to answer the phone, or call her back? How hard is it to come over when she asks? How hard is it after all she's done for you. And give me a break, your room-mate is a hairstylist. No one cares if someone's mom comes into a ladies salon," he dished out.

"It's not professional, and the owner was annoyed. I was trying to have a calm discussion with mom about it at the dining room table, but she kept standing up and then she went into the kitchen, and started getting hyster-ical," I said.

"You are so full of shit. Listen to you. Oh you're just the sweet angel trying to help everyone. Well I know better than to buy that bullshit. You instigated the whole thing and then pushed her over the edge. You like to fight and you pick on your mother, who is barely able to stand up she is so upset today. She's resting on the couch right now. If I were her I would never forgive you. But you know your mother, she'll fall for your shit because she is such a nice person," he dealt me.

"Dad, I have to get inside to work. I don't want to get in trouble. The students are already in the classroom. I have to go," I said, feeling the numb-ness coming on.

"They'll wait…" he kept on, but I hung up the phone. There was noth-ing I could say to convince him of my honest intentions. I had to bear this shaking adrenaline and ringing siren in my head. I hated feeling like this.

Try to act normal, Katie. You can't think about this right now. You have to work. My body buzzed but my face went limp and eyes glazed over. I would stay in this trance to get through the day. I would hold my skin-shell up, and occasionally let the puppet strings pull the corners of my lips up to smile, while I turned to rubble inside. *You can do whatever you need to do to escape this madness when you get home. Just stay calm and leave at the normal time, so you don't get fired. No one likes someone with personal problems.* This was also weird to me. Work places were always saying things like, "we're a family!" If that is true, why is it taboo to talk about a problem I'm having with my family? If work is an extension of my family, can I get some assistance? Because it affects everything. But that is a show too. They only want the nice pictures and the positive feedback. If shit hits the fan, work and personal have to be separate. Work is only fair-weather family. That's part of the sales pitch.

"Fuck this. I'm not answering the phone anymore," I told myself. But it didn't prevent his sly words from burrowing deep into my head and heart. A few months later, letters started arriving in the mail at my next place of residence.

"Katie, you've got more fan mail today! I'll just leave it here on the counter, next to the others," my new roommate, Scottie, cheered as he cracked a Miller Lite.

"Well, Hells Bells, I've finally hit the A-list, and gotten myself a stalker," I joshed, as I walked into the kitchen, setting down my purse. It was Thursday and I had 30 minutes to change from teacher to waitress. My head filled with pressure and I dizzied upon viewing the long envelopes stacked on the kitchen counter. *Should I even bother?*

One after the other, scorching pieces of paper had been arriving. Each with poison strung together into sentences that accused and berated, practically calling me a murderer. The lined paper quivered as I held it just far enough away from me so it couldn't get a complete sucker punch in, as I read it. The shaking began in my hands and pinged up my arm like a case of "the bends" popping up my appendages. Paralysis took over as I read his essay on what a shit human being I was, an abysmal disappointment, and the cause of my mother's pink cardigan suicide attempt.

I rarely took advice from anyone, but I let Scottie read the letter while his sidekick, Kai, loafed in our living room. Scottie was a childhood friend from my neighborhood and stood with me at the bus stop through our grade school years. We both knew of the erratic, behind-closed-doors behaviors our parents displayed. Walking the tightrope was an unspoken understanding. Scottie knew that I hated wearing bows in my hair, would rather catch frogs than play tea party, and that my older brother cried when he lost his shoe in the creek…but he didn't tell anyone, and so I knew I could trust him.

Scottie looked up at me with a cocked head and watery eyes and said, "This is garbage, Katie. Throw it out and never read it again. Let's have a drink after you get off work."

I was grateful for someone to acknowledge another option. I didn't know a different choice existed until then. Throw it away? I thought I was supposed to come up with retorts to prove myself, to explain the truth. But Scottie knew, there was no use explaining. It was time to cheer up.

Kai tilted his head from the edge of the sofa and gave me a wink. "Lighten up, Starshine. He ain't worth it."

Shift engaged. Instead of adding the letter to the little black box of hate, I dropped it in the garbage. I tried this unsuccessfully in previous years. I'd sob as I read the harsh words, slowly convinced of their insidious truths. When my eyes were too hazy to read them anymore, I would encase them back into their box, like a dirty little secret. I didn't want anyone to know of this darkness and rejection. Defeated, I would put them back into my closet. Like an addiction, I had been poisoning and programming my mind with the disease of his words. Nope. Not this time.

I dumped the whole shoebox full of letters into the garbage. I tied the kitchen bag and walked it to the street side as I headed out to waitress. Thank goodness it was garbage day the next morning, or else I might have dug through yesterday's dinner scraps to read those despicable words one last time.

The dump truck came, and at first I felt guilty. That's what the mind fucking does, but it wasn't long before I felt relieved. I allowed myself a freedom I hadn't experienced in 27 years. I gave myself permission to reject his words.

A couple of months later, I moved again. This time to Grandma's house. Thinking time had smoothed things over, I tried to join my parents for a Friday night fish fry at the local Fraternal Order of Eagles. We sat at a table and had a few drinks. Dad usually drank whiskey, mixed with water or Coca Cola, and occasionally on the rocks. I popped into the kitchen to hang with one of my cousins for a minute. I preferred the back of the house where I could sit on the countertops and cuss with the cooks. Dirty aprons and cigarettes hanging off lips. Those foul-mouthed hooligans were my people.

Exercising questionable logic, I thought, this is a great time to pull Dad aside and tell him I'm sorry about the whole Mom stabbing herself thing. He usually lightened up after a few drinks, usually. It was still a form of Russian Roulette. *Just do it. Things will be better if you get the truth off your chest.* Just beyond the dinner crowd, up a few smoky stairs, and into the hallway where the bathrooms were located, I decided to bring it up.

"Hey, I'm glad you came out. See, we can have some fun," Dad said with the confidence of a second whiskey wetting his tongue.

"Yeah, I'm glad I came. You know I feel bad about that misunderstanding with mom. You know I would never want to hurt her. I've felt really distant from the family and it feels good to meet up," I dropped like a casual jacket.

His face shifted, and he got that I'm-drinking-it-on-the-rocks-tonight squint in his eye, as he pointed his finger at me. "You know Katie, it's your own fault you're distant from the family. You can hide away at your grandma's house and tell everyone your sob story, but I know the truth."

"I listen to advice from my elders and sometimes Roger tells it to me straight. I know I'm not perfect," I said, trying to soften the defense, but the spin was already setting in.

"Roger isn't your father, and if you were anything like his daughter Janet, I would have been grateful," Dad delivered.

"Whoa, what is *that* supposed to mean? She's not perfect either. You know what? He's been more of a father to me lately than you have, anyways," I snapped back at him.

That was enough to do it. Holyfield just stepped into the ring. It was too quick for me to see it coming. The whip in my neck and the instant sting and pounding to my temple let me know I had crossed a line. *What did you think was going to happen, you fuck up? You're too big for a spanking. You've graduated to getting bitch slapped in the back end of the bar. Nice job. I'll send you a congratulations card in the mail.*

By the time I gained my senses back, he had left the hallway. I was scared and embarrassed. I didn't feel angry when I got hit, I felt shame. Why doesn't someone love me enough to treat me better. Then I arrived at the conclusion: I must be worthless. Even to my own parents. I looked around to see if anyone was watching. But no one seemed to notice. They were off in a distant room, or down the stairs. The bathroom was next to the back door. I snuck out to the street, instead of rejoining the dinner party. I popped into a few other local bars, and continued to drink. I felt like a degenerate, so I slept in my car. Not just because I was too drunk to drive, but because that is what losers do. They get stuck.

I felt the bruise the next morning as I put on my hard hat to start my new job. "You're a loser" wasn't a mere thought, it was a throbbing reminder on my forehead. "Fuck this. Next time I'm gonna go Mike Tyson on him," I thought. But it didn't matter. My new job in construction paid well. I could finally make some real money and get myself further away from this place. I didn't like having student loans, and I felt powerless to make any real shifts. I had a hard time juggling too many things at once. How can anyone think about goals when they have so many bills? People kept calling it "adulting," but they all seemed unraveled. Why was this considered being an "adult." Adulthood equates misery and receiving bills was the only rite of passage? Everyone seemed to cope through drinking, pills, sex, or marriage and making babies. The last one was rewarded the most. But why was working all day in exchange for only a few hours of enjoyment the accepted model? I wasn't sold. However, my new job didn't require me to think about what clothes I had to wear, make up application, or even talk to people. I would be flagging for the road crew. I would be alone, twirling a wooden flagger stick, and maybe that's what I needed for awhile.

The Glass Slipper

"Fuck labels," responded my fiery Pamela Anderson-look-alike cousin when asked if she was straight, lesbian, or bisexual. "Who knows, and who cares?" Madeline said. But people do care. It's human nature to want to understand things. I knew.

When I wanted to play with frogs and muddy up my pink dresses, people had an issue with it. They had to classify my behavior with nature.

"She's just not a girly girl. She's a tomboy," Mom said with disappointment in her tone. A "tomboy," insinuating I was "less than a girl." I became aware of gender implications at age seven, and it followed me, disrupting my balance between feminine and masculine. For some reason, girls couldn't be pretty AND play in the dirt, unless they were planting flowers. Only then was it acceptable. The phrase, "you are pretty" was only spoken by Dad on occasions when I was forced to wear a frilly dress for church, usually on Christmas or Easter..holidays when the most pronounced idealism of patriarchal femininity was demanded. His strongest offering of validation and love was when I was being the least authentic version of myself.

It's a challenge to step into your womanhood, especially when your childhood is drenched with gender norms and rejection. I found other ways to relate to being female. Madeline and I went to the Glass Slipper on Friday nights and tossed singles at the smoking hot girls, sliding down tall shiny poles like they were auditioning to be Baroque painting models.

"It's the only bar open past closing time out here in the sticks," Madeline brushed it off. But I didn't need convincing. Attractive girls owning all the men in the room. What isn't fun about that? Meh, forget the men. Hyper sexual women breaking the rules. Here's my I.D.

"I hope I don't run into my dad here," I confessed to her. "That would be a major buzz kill." *Not to mention a turn off,* I thought to myself. Something about girls, all oiled up and smelling like Passionfruit Paradise lotion from the tanning salon, made me feel good about life. Being *around* sexy made me *feel* sexy. Besides, this wasn't too far from my norm. I was used to strutting around half naked as a lifeguard. I liked being naked. Instead of a pole, I climbed up and down the guard station, twirling a silver whistle to command attention. I was used to men watching me rub myself with Hawaiian Tropic SPF 0. We had something in common.

"Do you think he'd drive out here?" Madeline grilled as we got out of her grey sedan.

"Yeah, he's a freaking alcoholic. He knows every bar in a 50 mile radius."

"They're *all* alcoholics," she said, with a look resembling the one a mom gives you when she's tired of your bullshit. Madeline was born with that look.

"Get this, he drove me home from the bar the other night, then went back out to some other party with my mom. The next morning he asked me how I got home! I was like, uh, *you* gave me a ride. He had no clue. And *I'm* the one with a DUI?"

"Holy shit. Classic," Madeline laughed.

"And I suspect he's an old horn dog like his cousin Steve, who has been seen with high end escorts in downtown Chicago lately."

"No shit?!" she gawked, as she re-applied her lip gloss while we walked through the parking lot.

"Ya. I guess he has a thing for black ladies." I shrugged. "My mom told me a couple weeks ago."

"Wow. Must be nice to be sixty and single…and loaded," she said.

I laughed, "No doubt. Although I prefer my hook-ups to be free."

"Of course! But we all know that's not happening for old white dudes with grey hair…or no hair! They're all a bunch of pricks anyways," she laughed as she turned her attention to the door person.

"Hi, Madeline! Good to see you back! Who you got with you this time?" the security guard asked her. I guess she's a regular or something. Who knows what my cousin has been up to. She flies under the radar with her scandals. Except for the night we both got arrested. Everyone heard about that one.

"Are you supposed to give money to every girl who performs, or just the ones you like best?" I asked her, needing to know proper strip club etiquette.

"I give singles to every girl who comes on stage. Do you know how much it takes to get up there half naked? They have to be confident, even if they're not feeling it on the inside. I give it up for these ladies," Madeline shared.

Duly noted. Everyone gets a single. Maybe more.

The lights were bright as hell to make sure no one was jerking off under the table. I was kinda glad about that. There were female patrons, but most of them were the only girl in a crowd of four sweaty men in either business suits or football jerseys. I seemed to be the only one paired up like a kissing cousin. Girls did lap dances upstairs, and God knows what out back.

I was no stranger to sex shops, but strip clubs were a new luxury. The quaint college town I went to had a dirty magazine shop right on the main strip. It was in-between the Thai restaurant and the mom and pop jewelry store. The local mom and Christian group protested it every year. The store could be entered from the alley in the back, but I wasn't a politician, so I didn't need to use that entrance.

Instead, I roller-bladed right in the blacked-out front door on a Sunday morning. My friend James and I had been blading around town to sweat off our hangover and thought it would be fun to check out some Sunday morning smut. I usually knew a friend of a friend who was working the counter.

"Hey Carl! I didn't know you were working today! Is it okay if we blade through here?" I smiled.

"Indeed, my dear. Blade away, and feel free to treat yourself to something!" He replied with a wink.

I browsed the counter where all the profane trinkets were, tickled my friend with the feather teasing wand as he rolled away from me, then made my way to the back to browse. They had magazines, videos, and some kind of booth in the back that I never went in. Pretty sure it involved a TV screen and a wall with jizz all over it.

"Hey! Is that you, Allen?! How are you? Have you seen Ben and Margo lately?" I sang loudly to a tall gentlemen I remembered meeting at a party a few weeks earlier. He was a local and a friend of some people I hung out with regularly while smoking weed and watching South Park. It didn't occur to me that he was ten years older, alone, and probably didn't want attention drawn to him, as he perused the sex shop on a Sunday morning, while the rest of the town was at church. No, it didn't occur to me at all.

"Oh hey," he forced an awkward smile without fully raising his head. *He must be really interested in that video he's holding.*

"I think I'm going to get this X-rated comic book. It looks pretty cool.

It's done all 50s vintage-like, and it looks kind of hilarious," I said as I held up a copy of *Ramba*, featuring *Say Goodnight, Gracie*.

"Neat. Nice rollerblades," he said out of the side of his lips, as his body grew stiff.

"Thanks! Good to see ya. I gotta get going though, I think my friend is already outside. Later!" I shouted as I rolled up to the counter to make my purchase. Carl rung me up and threw in a rubber dick that fit on my pinky like a puppet. Why *wouldn't* I want one of those?

I wasn't interested in the men at the strip club. Not because I wasn't into men, but because they were acting so weird. In a regular bar scene, men hit on me, to no avail. However here, there was a different feel. I think half of them were doing blow before they came in the door. Bug-eyed and sweaty. Or maybe they were just uncomfortable from trying to hide their hard-ons. I'm glad I don't have that issue. They were fixated on the stage, like a moth to a buzzing neon light.

"Here, you girls take these seats," a guy near the stage offered. He noticed my cousin and I were together, and predicted we wanted to sit side by side. He was right. "I can sit in the seat on the other side."

"Thank you!" my cousin and I chimed at the same time.

"NEXT on the stage is LOLITA!!! Give it up for LOLITA!!" The announcer called into his microphone, then turned up the booty music as Lolita walked up three steps in her lime green lace thong, matching bra, red thigh-high fishnets, and black leather knee-high stiletto boots. She looked like a Christmas present that was going to tie Jesus and Santa together, and whip them into submission.

"Dude, she's hot," my cousin whispered to me. "If I had her body I'd be up there too."

Lolita whipped her long auburn hair in a circle, and began her routine, which involved climbing up the pole and sliding, upside down in a slow, ballerina-like motion. If ballerinas did the splits while pressing their crotch on a shiny, two story pole, that is. She did a few more moves, then made her way like a slithering cobra, to each person sitting around the stage. Most dancers shook their tits a little and let the men stick a dollar bill in their bra strap.

When Lolita came to me, she slid backwards on her knees, until her ass was almost right in my face. Then she flipped over and stuck her big sleek boot over my shoulder. Natural instinct took over. I grabbed the ball of her boot, turned my head to my right shoulder, and licked her hooker heel from mid arch to mid calf. I stopped with a smile out of the corner of my mouth and locked eyes with her, as I stuck a dollar in the top of her boot.

"Well, thank you, sweetie," she said as she bit her lip and gave me a wink.

Oh…so this is what they mean by "make it rain," I thought, as I watched crumpled up bills being tossed in streams above, over, and around me, making their way onto the stage, for Lolita.

"Holy fuck. That was hot," I heard a man say to himself out loud, as he stood next to me. Lolita crawled to pick up her singles, then sauntered like a cat over to the adjacent stage.

Yeah, I feel like that was worth the cover charge. This is my kind of Cinderella ball.

Cookie Cutter

"I'd never do that," I said to myself, while listening to a man share details of his drinking benders, at an AA meeting.

Every person has made this statement. People brag about the crazy stuff they've done while intoxicated, then disclaimer it by setting the bar of insanity slightly higher than they ever crossed. Justifications. Proof they weren't *all* bad, or hadn't lost *all* control. Proof to themselves and hopefully others that they weren't a complete lost cause, a loser, or worse yet, broken.

During college, I was waitressing in an Italian bistro with checkered tablecloths and a lofty attitude. It was owned and operated by a couple lacking an emotional thermostat. If they had one, it was only calibrated for two settings. Subzero and Inferno. The wife appeared to be twenty years older than the husband. He had dark hair and yellow, crooked teeth. At the time I thought, "He must have a granny fetish."

"I don't think it's burning," I said as I wafted the odor coming from the dessert machine. "I know what burnt fucking chocolate smells like! You kids are morons," he yelped. Whoa, man, sorry to insult your chocolate temperature radar. I tried to stay clear of his tantrums, but this led to crossing paths with the ice queen. When I noticed her blonde Clairol grey coverage hair parading around the corner, I knew a belittling was about to take place. Traditionally, it was in front of customers, on a busy Friday night. I never understood how places like that stayed in business. Their delectable pasta dishes must have served as their redemption.

I quit after they got robbed. The owners called me repeatedly because they were convinced it was an inside job. Their number one suspect was the Indian girl who worked as the receptionist, and was thus in charge of the moneybag at the end of the night. I happened to give her a ride home on the night the money went missing.

On my next shift, I was pulled into a back room and questioned by my boss. "Do you see this broken window? I know this robbery was staged. A real break-in doesn't look like this. What do you know?"

"Uh, nothing? I haven't heard anything," I told him, as I re-adjusted the strings on my black apron.

"Didn't you give Nisha a ride home last night? Did she have a bag with her, like stuffed in her coat?" he pried, leaning forward and eyeballing my body language.

"I didn't see anything. She didn't have a bag, and she seemed like her normal self. I'm sorry I can't help you," I confided. He didn't look convinced, and put me back on the floor. A few days later I called in sick because I still had a hangover at 4:00 PM. The alcohol poisoning type of hangover. I determined it wasn't safe to drive, because I had blurred vision. This caused me to be three hours late picking up Samantha from the train station, in the dead of a Midwest winter. She's still pissed.

After I called in sick, the wife called me back, and I picked up the phone.

"Hello? No, this is Katie's roommate. She's sleeping," I attempted save myself from having to be further questioned.

"Are you sure this isn't Katie, because you sound just like her." She didn't believe me for one second. I was mortified, so I quit the next day. I'm sure this only added to their suspicion, causing them to prematurely decide the receptionist and I were in cahoots. For all I know, the husband robbed his own place.

My other coworker was a waitress with a mousy disposition. She was a Psychology student with an intellectual mind. Despite her long-sleeved shirts, I began noticing her wrists were often bandaged. I asked her about it, but she blew it off. "I twisted it playing racket ball the other night," she chucked at me.

I met her ex-boyfriend at the bar one night. "She's a cutter," he slurred, "yeah I finally got her pants off, and she had razor blade cuts all over her thighs. It was weird as hell. That shit's not a turn on."

The next time I worked with her, I knew why she had tape on her wrists. She didn't sprain them playing tennis, she was self-harming. This was a new phenomenon to me. How could someone do that to themselves? And what was the purpose? Then I remembered, I had done something similar in eighth grade.

I had bandaged my wrists at one point in my life. Just once. I was melting away in tears, like a stranded jellyfish on the bathroom floor of my parent's house. It was the only place I could lock the door and be safe from the taunting. We were only allowed to relax at certain times of the day. It made no sense to me, and my nervous system was always on high alert because of it. The bathroom was a practical escape from forced conversations. I spent plenty of time there, usually after coming home tipsy in the later years of high school.

School was easy, somewhat boring. I read everything of interest my freshman and sophomore year. To Kill a Mockingbird, Fahrenheit 451, 1984, Catcher in the Rye, and the Scarlet Letter. I had gotten A's in honor's English since fourth grade, but my parents were always asking for more. Now I needed to be on the National Honor's Society. What was the point? What next? I could see there was no end to it. Reading was getting more challenging for me anyways. I could do it when I was obsessed with the content, but forced reading could take me hours to get through one page. I knew I was smart, but something was shifting for me. It gave me a headache, and it wasn't my glasses. I couldn't concentrate. Any sound was too much sound when I was trying to read. Any movement. Any anything. I tried highlighting passages, writing notes to remember things, and even reading out loud. Those things helped, but it seemed like so much effort. Other people were breezing right through 300 page books. I felt stupid, and I didn't want to be that. I liked getting praised for having straight A's. It's one of the few things they seemed to like about me. I wasn't in honor's Math and that was valued more. I didn't test into it like Samantha did, and that irked me. Honor's English AND Math was the best option. I felt like I could be good at that too, but numbers were like a puzzle. And I didn't understand the way they were teaching the puzzle. The indicator for math seemed to be, if you can do it in your head, you're smart. If you have to write it, you're dumb. Great assessment strategy.

When I was fourteen years old, I began having suicidal ideations. How could I not, after learning about how the world really worked. THAT was depressing. Mom blamed it on hormones. She wasn't far off. No one seemed to have any answers for that either, other than "take a Midol."

"Get your stuff Kate! Let's get going!" Dad called out. "Your little brother is already in the car." His work was having a family day at the plant. Dad was a human resources manager at a chemical plant that made plastics. He was proud of his company.

"Coming!" I replied.

"If you're not early, you're late. Gotta learn that, kids" he taught.

As we walked into the main building, we rounded the front desk. "Women are starting to be able to be more than just the secretaries these days. How about that, Kate!" He commented. His office was dark brown, and smaller than I imagined. He had one small picture of our family on his desk. He had a white board we were allowed to draw on with two colored markers.

Dad lifted a clear plastic bottle filled with white plastic beads. He shook it and said, "Do you see this? This is what all your stuff is contained in. Your laundry detergent, your food- everything. It's plastic. That's what we make here. It provides for the whole world," he said with pride. Making it must be dangerous, because Dad got called out for fires in the middle of the night a lot. That was the year he was also Safety Manager. He also had people make death threats on him. Our code word to answer the front door at our house was, "apple sauce."

I liked the sound of the plastic pebbles as they moved in the container. It was like a rattle or sand. I tried to imagine how they melted it and formed it into jugs. My neighbor said they didn't even use the recycling plant. Most of it got shipped to the main dump regardless of people's efforts. It was all some kind of a show. The boy at the bus stop called it "propaganda."

"There's a magician here today for the kids!" Dad boasted. I was excited about that. I loved magicians.

"Is it going to be scary?" My little brother asked.

"No little buddy, just card tricks and stuff. It's supposed to be silly. You'll like it," he consoled. But first we have to go pick up trash along the highway. It's called volunteering. It's the right thing to do."

"Is is our trash?" I asked Dad.

"Kinda. The trash we are picking up has blown in from the road. It's mostly people littering. But we clean it up as our way to chip in," he shared.

"What about the plant? Does it litter?" I inquired.

"Well, that gets complicated, Katrina. The plant has some waste. It has to. It's a chemical plant, and the chemical waste has to go somewhere. So they give us special permission to dump certain amounts into the river. And then we have to do some stuff like this in exchange for it. It's like taking turns with the waste and clean up. You understand?" He recited.

"You mean the chemicals go in the water?" I asked for clarification as I sipped the water from my plastic cup.

"Don't worry, Kate. There's a lot of water on this planet. It gets washed away," assured Dad.

I dug deeper than his lesson. The chemicals didn't just get washed away. It seeped through the dirt and made it into the underground reservoirs. Then evaporation and rain carried it everywhere. I was surrounded by chemicals. Soaked in chemicals. But no one seemed concerned. It was as equally disturbing as what I was learning about food and make-up. *Peta* had ads in magazines. I kept coming across them. Some had horrifying pictures of pigs and cattle in cages, bleeding wounds, and ground up sawdust and plastic being mixed with their feed. I was disgusted. I vowed to never eat red meat or pork again. But I would scoot it around my dinner plate and occasionally eat a piece to satisfy my parents. I hated the thought that I was contributing to the torture of the animals I loved. I felt their pain with every bite. Dead, decayed animals on my plate. How was this any different than cannibalism? When I lie awake trying to sleep at night, I saw their images in my mind. I asked the butcher at the grocery store why some raw meat looked grey and some looked red. He said when it's fresh from the butcher it's red. But now most of the meat comes from the factory, so they have to put red dye in it so it will still look appetizing. What's worse than eating dead animals? Eating dead animals with food coloring in it so you can't tell it's spoiling. I think I'm siding with the hunters now. If only they weren't trophy hunters. There's no end to it, I thought.

Like many pre-teens, I enjoyed diving into the artistry of make up. But fashion magazines started including inserts depicting bunnies being held by their necks in machines. The machine had a metal arm that held the mascara and squirted liquid from the make up into their eyes. The bunnies' eyes were watering and red. I could not get the vision of this torture device out of my head. I dreamt about it. They haunted me. All my family could say was, "it doesn't hurt them." Or, "you want to wear make-up don't you? You gotta take the good with the bad. Quit worrying and go find something to do." I wasn't consoled. I was horrified. I was surrounded by sociopaths. *What the hell is this place? Why are people doing things this way? I don't want to be here. This planet is devastating. Send me back.* They didn't care about any of the suffering. They didn't care about the soul and spirit of the earth and the animals. They cared about the image. The pretty one. Not the real one.

Dad became increasingly cold and distant, while Mom began unraveling. She had trouble relating to real conversations about life and the future. Puberty was where her threshold ended. Their dispositions continued to escalate exponentially over the next few decades. When children serve as their parents as extensions of self, puberty is a pivotal point. The doll was becoming outwardly more and more sentient. Therefore, they wanted the doll to move out.

I could feel the pressure from the emotional confinement on every inch of my body. It was making me want to rip my skin off. I'm fairly sure this is what it feels like before people spontaneously combust. I looked it up in an Encyclopedia Britannica once, or was it Ripley's Believe It or Not! Apparently you sit in a wooden chair in the middle of your bedroom one day, and explode into dust. There was a grainy black-and-white picture of the aftermath. It was a bedroom kept as organized as a grandparent who "tidies" five times a day, then *poof*, human confetti.

"I spoke with a therapist about you. She said depression is normal for a girl your age. It's a phase, honey. It will pass. She said to try journaling," Mother assured me. The word neurodiverse was not on anyone's radar. It wasn't a thing. Adhd wasn't a term and neither was sensory processing or overstimulation. But I knew I was highly sensitive.

"Oh you're just so sensitive, Katie. You have to toughen up," Mom and Dad would say. Or "quit being so picky. Those clothes are good enough for everyone else. You need to be grateful for all that we buy you. Stop being so emotional."

As I entered the middle school hallways, I wondered how everyone else was just walking around. Smiling none-the-less. My clothes were constantly distracting me. In gym class we had to wear a certain brand of shorts that scratched like sandpaper. When they got wet with sweat it was absolute torture. My skin felt like it was on fire in polyester. The elastic waistbands and tags on my shirts felt like they were made out of cactus needles. Yoga pants hadn't been invented yet. There were bras, with metal underwires poking me, akin to a medieval breast ripper. The boys didn't even have to wear shirts outside. Why was the world this way? It was twisted and I loathed it. Send me to another planet. Uncomfortable clothes weren't just to fit in, they were the only option. It irritated me. And that irritation built all day. It was hard to think. Combine that with no outlet for my emotions, and I felt trapped in my body. I felt stiff and tight all the time. I wanted to release that horrible tension. Why couldn't I move? Sitting in the desk all day. I felt like a voodoo doll. Lugging around body weight, being poked, scratched, and strangled by necklines. How is anyone else not noticing this? I guess it doesn't bother them. I guess I'm different, and I don't want to be different. Right now, I just want to blend in.

I studied the flimsy pink plastic Bic razor in the bathroom and wondered if I could pierce my skin and be gone, like they did in the movies. I thought I would hang over the side of the tub like Liz Taylor, in one of my grandma's favorite silver screen movies. I'd fashion her powerful "doesn't anyone care?" look, while I fell asleep watching a river of blood stream down the drain. Questions formed to be checked off a list later: How long does it take to bleed out, does it hurt to bleed to death, would anyone notice how long I've been in here?

The suburbs are conducive to this type of fantasizing. At first the cookie-cutter life is cozy, predictable, and safe. Then it turns sterile, stale, and dangerous. It goes from *cookie* to *cutter*. Plagued with a sense of anger, apathy, and sadness, I took the razor to my wrist and made a mark. It hardly bled, so I tried a few more angles. I was not supposed to be doing this. "This stings like a motherfucker!" I thought. Yet it felt like a type of relief. Looking at my swollen red skin, I felt strangely satisfied. This is what internal pain looks like. It didn't result in the bloodbath I had imagined, but it settled my tension. I blotted them dry, put Band-Aids on my wrists, and wore long sleeves. No one would notice what I had done, because it was winter. The stinging sensation wasn't my thing, but there was a head change to it. Physical acts created chemical changes in my brain. I noticed that.

"You and I are going to Arizona!" Mom cheered to me from the kitchen. Oh God, perfect timing. "We are going to visit my sister," she shared.

They had a forced family friendship. Dad sang the "Wicked Witch" song from the Wizard of Oz, whenever Aunt Rita left a family gathering. "Ding dong the witch is dead, the wicked witch is dead!" He would jeer, "There she goes with her broom!"

She was nice to me, a little edgy, but I didn't mind her. Aunt Rita liked to sleep late, chain smoke, and brag about her legs. "Look how long my legs are. I've always had the best legs. They're like cousin Doris's. We didn't wind up short like the others," she boasted while stepping her leg up onto Grandma's coffee table.

It was clear Aunt Rita enjoyed showing off her mannequin-like stilts. One year she wore a short red sequin skirt covered in safety pins for Halloween. "What are you?" I asked as she laughed in her raspy smoker's cackle, that told me she was pulling one over on me.

"Ask your mother," she replied with a smirk.

"What is she?" I asked Mom.

"I don't know, I haven't had a good look at her yet," Mom shared, as she straightened my costume. I was a gypsy. I loved being a gypsy because I got to wear thick black eyeliner, red lipstick, a silk scarf on my head, and could draw a black dot on my cheek. Mom said gypsies had those. Dad said gypsies were liars that tricked people into giving them their money, but I felt mystical.

"I'm a hooker!" Aunt Rita rattled from Grandma's kitchen. I could hear Grandma chuckling too, so it *must* be funny.

"What's that?" I pressed my poised mother.

"It means she likes to snag men with her hooks. Like when you're fishing," Mom forced out her mouth. She was flustered. She thought they were laughing at her, and maybe they were. But I didn't have time to solve that riddle. I needed to figure out why being a hooker was so funny.

"Then why wasn't her skirt covered in fishing hooks?" I wondered to myself as I pictured her hooks snagging onto a gentlemen's brown pant suit on Main Street, creating tears. Seemed odd, but they thought it was hilarious.

Once we arrived in Arizona, Aunt Rita, my cousin, Mom, and I went out for Mexican food. I wore a watch over one wrist, and three bracelets over the other. We sat at a table with blue hand-painted ceramic tiles. I tried to do something natural with my arm positioning, but you could still see the Band-Aids. Aunt Rita noticed. Her eyes went straight to them and paused. I thought she was going to call me out. Then she glanced at my mom, who was oblivious to her inspection, and that was it. Nobody said a thing. Denial was my mother's way. Just ignore it and it won't exist.

After high school, I went to an exhibition at the Museum of Contemporary Art in Chicago. It displayed blown up, post mortem photographs of people's wrists that had been lacerated from suicide. The incisions were deep, to pierce the artery. The cuts were made vertically, not horizontally. Technically, an old fashioned razor was necessary, and it must be sunk into the wrist about an inch. Nope, I didn't have that in me. Too much blood and gore. That shade of crimson wouldn't wash out of the bathroom rug quite as easily as lipstick.

I still had periodic suicidal thoughts by the time I was in college, but I switched to a Marilyn Monroe ideal. I'd wash a bunch of pills down with a few martinis, and fall asleep dramatically, yet peacefully in a marvelous Art Deco era room, like something out of The Great Gatsby. I was so tired of trying to figure out how to act normal. It was exhausting. I wanted to take a very long nap. And if I didn't wake up, then maybe people would finally notice me.

Mourning Birds

No matter how many people surrounded me, I felt alone. Whether I drugged myself or not. Whether I had a successful career or not. Whether I put the ice trays away correctly or not. Whether I reached out to connect or not. The tangibility of love seemed fleeting in my life.

I guess that's why I threw myself onto my knees like a famished drifter and shamelessly begged for more, when I got a taste of it. Maybe other people absorbed a steady stream of well-balanced love throughout life, like an efficiently planned drip system. But that was not my experience. I was a dry desert. I was numb to its soft snuggling. I stood a breathing statue. *Your amour will not penetrate me.* Only on a rare and unannounced occasion would the dense matter of marble separate into a spinning whirlwind of molecules, with love pouring in and mingling in a sparkling atomic magical mist.

My love was unreciprocated. I got my heart lit on fire, only for it to be ripped out and thrown with a blasé shrug out of the bathroom window. Homeless people use it as kindling at the base of a metal garbage can. Where is that fucking heart of mine? Oh there it is, that red pulpy mess on the floor.

The first time my heart was met with a comparably irrational lust for love, I was nineteen and he was twenty-nine. Thank god for fake IDs. In college I lived at the Annex, a local dive bar I made my second home. It was packed with hipsters, before being a hipster was coined a thing. Art, philosophy, music, and theatre students. My perfect pool of lovers. One busy Friday night, a tall glass of water sauntered in to satisfy my thirst. He wasn't a student. He was a local. Fresh out of rehab for heroin, he locked eyes with me before looking me up and down with not an ounce of decency.

"Well, look at you, little girl. Aren't you a tough little tigress of beauty? Who let you out of their cage and up to this bar all by yourself?" His words oozed out like a verbal orgasm. Tall and lanky, pale skin, dark hair, older…I have a type. Ex-heroin addicts seem to talk like they are still mid-shooting up. Their bodies forever holding poses like they are an Egon Schiele painting. I was in a black shirt, jeans and maroon leather shoes, an image of Johnny Cash's femme fatale reflection. I was locked in a gaze with Alex, as I blew the smoke of my Camel Light out of the corner of my lips. I loved smoking, like the pied piper of the bar, orchestrating a hypnotic trail of smoldering haze. I inhaled him with every drag. Alex noticed me and offered to light me up, as if I needed asking.

My love was always of Shakespearean proportions. Anything less and it hardly counted. Puppies are cute, but they don't make me want to hang myself. It must not be true love. My love affair with the Annex Romeo would take hold of my heart for two decades, although in physicality it would only last a few years, on and off. Anything more would be too consistent, and missing that necessary trace of torture.

"I need to see your little girl eyes and soft quivering thighs," Alex would breath into a late night phone call. I drank it up. I must be some kind of pervert too. Alex's fiancé had died of an overdose while he was in rehab. This is why he struggled to get close I assumed. Ah, I see you need love of epic proportions that ends in tragedy as well. It appears my soul already knows you. We are one in the same.

As I opened his unlocked apartment, Alex lured me into his Nag Champa-infused den. I heard bewitching music playing down his candle flickering hallway. He stumbled into a wall, acting like my presence caused him to stagger. Sometimes he would lie in bed acting like he was weakened by his desire for me. I was flattered. I let him slip inside my embrace to summon his life energy back. Which I did, over and over.

"I want you Katie" he purred into the side of my neck, just below my ear, healing my wounded heart with his catlike vibrations. Once you've been in the grip of an ecstasy that convinces your body it is nothing but the electrified dust of exploding stars, everything else is merely child's play. Love, that was my drug of choice. The bar had been set to a cosmic level. Earthly courting would never suffice for this teenaged truth seeker.

There's a scientific explanation for why my limitless bliss must be met with immeasurable pain. Newton's Third Law. Love as I knew it, was filled with passionate extremes and devastating lows. To feel is to know, I thought.

"You know, you were in kindergarten when I was a teenager. What do you think of that?" He asked me.

"I don't know. I don't think about it. I just think about you," I replied.

"You're such a sweetie. Grade school was rough. I bet you were such a doll," he cooed.

"I dunno. I always felt weird to be honest. Not pretty at all, and afraid," I confessed.

"You're safe with me Katie, but I know how you feel. People think boys are safe, but they can be overpowered too. If the guys I grew up with were honest, they would talk about what happened to us as kids," Alex vaguely told.

"What happened?" I asked, concerned.

"Let's just say boys aren't safe from sexual assault either. I spent my teenage years wondering if I was gay because of what happened to me," Alex shared.

"I'm sorry. Who was it?" I asked.

"Another neighborhood boy. Older. Bigger. I don't want to talk about it right now," he closed the conversation. Alex had secrets. There were only parts of himself he shared. Sex was one of them.

In the era of written love letters, I mailed Alex an envelope full of photos. I was on a beach off the Na Pali Coast on one of the Hawaiian Islands. After I printed the photos at a Walgreens in Kauai, I discovered one of the selfies had taken on a hot pink lens glare. I snatched the opportunity to carve in the words "I Burn For You". If you snag my heart, this is the kind of ravenous love that will come bleeding out. The photos arrived while a friend was picking up his mail. They opened the envelope and discovered an array of lustful nudes, professing my desires for him. Kalalau Katie…mostly pictured from the neck down.

Alex insisted my birth control pills were horrible for my body and disapproved of my consumption of them. I was trying to avoid an unwanted pregnancy from the guy who was touch and go, but he was harping on hormone balance. This was new to me. He still smoked weed and drank, but he ate strictly organic food and baked his own bread. He would look at me like I was so naive..how could I not know how important these things were?

The flip side of a love characterized by insatiable passion is madness. At one point, Alex lived a block away from my Victorian rental. He claimed we had an open relationship, and as desperate as I was for the nectar of his attention agreed to anything. When he didn't answer the pre-cellphone-era call, looked down the street from my front yard. I could see his lights on.

Later that sweltering summer night, I walked over to the house that I had been beckoned to so many times before. I weaved up the wooden staircase and propped myself up to reach the spare key above the overhang. I could hear voices laughing inside. I pounded on the door like a cop ready to confiscate her stolen goods. When he didn't answer, I jammed the key into the keyhole, threatening to come inside. My hands were trembling too much to operate the lock. Lucky for him, because I was ready to take the acoustic guitar he'd so eloquently charmed me with, and bust it on the floor like it was a Jimi Hendrix concert.

Like Tweedledum and Tweedledee, he and his company grew silent. It was his brother who was probably un-phased by yet another one of Alex's star-crossed lovers gone stark raving mad. When I was first introduced to him, I got the "here comes another one" look, as Alex doted over me, in his seasonal love fest. The leaves would fall soon, and his love with them, leaving me a hungry badger in the onset of a barren winter.

For now, the wild sweat of the summer heat awaited me outside. I wandered back to my place and sat on the front porch, zoning out in my front yard. I listened to the expanding sound of birds chirping, crying out for the dawn of a new day. My marred heart could soon be distracted by the happenings of the coming interlude.

The High Priced Resort

I'm done. I am as devitalized as a stray dog wandering through the street. Someone else take over. Not forever, just until I get my strength back. Bone-weary from the beat down of my 27 year old life. I could stay home from work and order Chinese food. But no, not me. I need to go full blown AWOL. Then I need to be tucked into bed and told everything is going to be okay. I'm having an infantile relapse. The more I try to prove my worth to my family, the more I corrode in the stress of fight-or-flight.

I woke up in Grandma's attic after a night of drinking at the local bar. It was the only option for socializing in my hometown. I knew my college degree wasn't paying off when I found myself in the attic of a 1950s home, with no HVAC venting upstairs, and an elderly woman in a muumuu downstairs. It's not what I had in mind when I took out student loans. Though I must say, Grandma and I made for spectacular roommates. In her day, she was a bartender, a political volunteer, and welded ships during WWII. A woman ahead of her time, who seemed to understand my unique fiery quirks.

I peeked out the aluminum blinds and saw my Jeep…I must have driven home. When I drank, I tended to experience blacking-out. I sucker-punched myself with flashbacks. My stomach gasped for air as I filled in the blanks with the most horrific, embarrassing scenarios. The visions hit me with waves of nausea as I pictured myself a stumbling drunk: loud, laughing, slurring, crying, undoubtedly spilling drinks. My memories formed like the filming of a carnival ride in fast forward. I was uncertain if these broken images were true or not. What if the truth was worse. I didn't like any of this.

I'm not sure how I got into this habit. Loneliness I guess. I liked people, and all the people were at the bar. It seemed to be the only place adults hung out. It was overstimulating though. The alcohol helped with that-at first. But this was happening more and more. Other people didn't seem to be as affected by alcohol as me. I was small, but it was something more. I was sensitive. Whatever I consumed, amplified in my body, but I didn't know that yet. A woman I met at AA called it an allergy. She had an allergy to alcohol. Well don't we all? I mean, it is literally poison, but it's legal, and pushed at social gatherings. So it's confusing. Am I to blame for not using the poison properly? Here's another "Earth Rule" I'm not quite comprehending.

I dug through my pockets and scrolled through my phone. Mortified, I texted a few people and tried to piece the night together. If I could roughly map out a timeline of events, I could get a sense of grounding, cope with the remorse, and perhaps the panic would subside.

I put myself through the wringer numerous times, but today the after-anxiety was worse than usual. I felt drained, like my spirit was disintegrating, and my soul was detached from my body. I had a desperate feeling of urgency, like I had to fix something NOW. It was nothing short of torture, as if my life was at stake—and I wanted to erase the night before.

It was more than just "wanting." It was the willful denial of the impossible, the yearning to bring back a better life from the dead. I was like a child grieving the loss of a beloved pet puppy who has been smashed by an oncoming car in the darkness of a rainy night. I was both the weeping child and the lifeless dog on the cold, soaking suburban curb.

The panic screamed like a demon trapped inside my body. Waves of shivers shocked through my flesh. I wanted to crawl out of my skin. I've heard alcohol referred to as "spirits" and I was summoning some pretty evil ones. I felt like a walking dead person, except dead people don't feel pain, and this was excruciating. The voice of my inner bully roared and I wanted to finally shut it off.

The ground was frozen solid with a dusting of dirty grey snow, appearing as desolate as my lost soul. Meanwhile, my parents were on a vacation someplace warm. I had a key to their house. I sat on my bed, hung over and still a shade drunk. Shaky. Dizzy. Throw in some meds for anxiety and depression, and it's safe to say I was strung out. Things had not been getting better since I filled the prescriptions, they were getting worse. The pack of Marlboro Lights I chain smoked the night before wasn't helping my dehydration migraine.

Why are you such a fuck up? I couldn't bear the thought of my existence anymore. What a waste, living like an outcast in Grandma's spare room. Surely I was a burden on her. At her age, she shouldn't be worrying about me. I wasn't accomplishing anything I was capable of and I hated myself for it. Why was all of this so hard for me? I knew they were calling me lazy, but I felt like I was trying harder than anyone else..I just wasn't yielding results.

I petted my silky cats, one a stately black with golden eyes and the other a Blue Russian. They purred with unconditional love. Hopefully they would forgive me. The thoughts were surfacing. The way out. I recalled back to one of my last shamings from Dad. He said, "Look at you. You're almost 30. It's pathetic. You should be sitting like a fat cat, making decent money and having a routine down." Was he right? Was I pathetic? I guess that's all people saw. I was so embarrassed, I didn't even want to leave the house anymore. It was so isolating. But then when I went out, it was over-whelming. I guess I should have majored in finance, like my brother. That seems to be the only career that's valued. Heck, he got to move back home to build his foundation in life. The opportunities weren't equitable, so how could the outcomes be equal? Nevertheless, I was forced to navigate them, essentially alone.

On previous occasions, they were fantasies. I had no real plan. Today was different. Suicide had been in the passenger seat for so long, it seemed natural, almost inevitable, to throw her behind the wheel. I could pull my car into my parents' garage and seal it off. I had alcohol and three bottles of psych pills. Our neighbor was watching the cats at the house, so I would be chancing them coming over before the fumes had done their job. The pills and alcohol would have taken irreversible effect pretty quickly, I hoped.

It was a two-fold plan to ensure, in some fashion, I would be gone before someone found me. I would drift off to the sound of a running car, maybe some music, and most likely the echoing of my owns sobs. I would have a small window of time in the garage. With my parents being out of state, this was the most plausible scenario I could think of.

In a slight panic, I threw on some clothes, as if I needed to hop into a getaway car after a robbery. Morose errand attire; a pair of boot cut jeans, a moss green sweater, and a pair of knock-off converse sneakers. They were laceless with strands of metallic silver threaded into a plaid. The air outside barely scraped thirty degrees. I skipped the socks, which probably made me look like a disturbed homeless person inadequately dressed for the weather. But I didn't care, my body was roasting.

I hyperventilated as I forced my trembling hands to shove the necessities into my faux leather purse. I stared blankly at myself through the mirror as I wiped my tears and touched up my make-up. The alcohol sweat was gunk-ing up my powder and stinking through my perfume and stale smoked hair.

Good riddance, you're a train wreck.

I needed to make it out the door, past Grandma. She was resting in her favorite blue velour chair, looking out the window, noticing the finches and their delicate bodies withstanding another fierce winter Mother nature hurled at them. Grandma always knew when something was wrong, but she didn't let on.

"I'm going to stay at my friend's house in Chicago this weekend," I fibbed.

"Oh?" she creaked.

"Yes, I'll be back on Sunday night." I walked up to her full but frail body, leaned over, and gave her a tight hug. "I love you."

"I love you too, sweetie. Be careful and have fun," she said, as she gave me a stern smooch on the cheek.

I stood up, turned away from her, and walked towards the door. Tears poured down in a salty blanket onto my cheeks. My last hug with Grandma. She had been good to me, the only one who accepted me for who I was.

I hopped into my boxy blue-green Jeep with hardly an overnight bag packed. Make-up, a pack of cigarettes, and an extra shirt to make it look legit. I wasn't planning on needing more than a lullaby. After driving past Holly, Pine, and Liberty Street, I broke down… emotionally.

My car doors cranked closer and closer like the walls of a booby trap and the floor board nearly squished me from below. Before they crushed my skull, I swerved to pull the car over. Was I really going to do this? Say good bye…forever? Things are moving too fast. I didn't want to wake up to this intense pain and panic ever again. I wanted to not be a loser. I couldn't deal with the shame any longer. I was tired of being the dunce paraded around a circus of humiliation every day. People could see I was unwanted. I couldn't hide from this massive rejection, no matter how low I tried to fly under the radar. One way or another, everything needed to stop.

I knew a place where I could do that. My parents' house was to the left. But that annoying voice started chiming in again. *Oh, so you're going to kill yourself? That's brilliant, Katie. Go ahead, do what the loser would do.*

"Gah! Shut up," I thought. "Is this prick really going to mock me at a time like this?" I turned the Jeep right instead. There was a facility about an hour away I could check myself into. I dialed my therapist on my cell while driving, and she took the emergency call. Fifty dollars for fifteen minutes. Who cares, she can bill my grave if this doesn't work out.

"Is it really necessary for you to check yourself in somewhere?" she asked. *Seriously?* Obviously she didn't understand the gravity of my desperation. "I want you to pull over your car and do some breathing exercises."

"Not possible," I replied. "It's not gonna slow down." I needed time to sit this out, where I wouldn't be able to axe myself, or even entertain the thought. I needed support.

After I convinced my doctor I couldn't do a breathing exercise, she gave me directions to the hospital. I pulled over to quickly scribe a path of survival, on the back of an envelope. *Click.* Thank you!

I now had a goal. I do good with these. Follow the steps and do not get in an accident. Whispering Willow Oaks, or something like that, was a tri-level red brick building. On that drizzly mid-morning, the foyer lights emitted a dull glow through streak free windows, drawing me in like a stray cat on a stormy night. As I opened the door, I was greeted with the white noise of a lobby. My squeaky rubber soles shuffled up to the oversized front desk. A composed woman with a wide smile addressed me with her eyes.

"Hi. Um, I need to check myself in," I muddled to the front clerk. I stared at her with a lost gaze.

She lowered her chin with concern and asked, "What seems to be the problem?" "I'm depressed. My psychiatrist gave me the directions to this hospital," I murmured. You'd think after a forty-five minute drive I would have calmed down, but I didn't. The adrenaline kept pulsing through my veins.

"What's your name?" she asked with a smile. "And can you spell that for me?"

Her question triggered the one obedient bone in my body. After years of drilling, I snapped into the character of a second grader, as I proudly recited, "S-e-x-t-o-n."

"Please have a seat and fill out this paperwork," she directed.

That's an interesting way to keep someone from killing themselves. Give them a stack of papers to begin dutifully filling out. I briefly considered tossing the deck of papers to the side, allowing them to fly through the air in all directions, as I made a dash for the door. But an imaginary SWAT team formed in my mind and tackled me on my way through the revolving door. "*Get down on the ground!! We know you're depressed!!*"

Never mind. I cinched my way to a floral lounge chair, and humbly slouched into submission. If there was one step on the path to avoid suicide I wouldn't have previously considered, it was digging through one's purse for an insurance card. Are these people serious? I could have had a gun to my head moments ago, and their first step was to have me read legal jargon and record member ID numbers on a paper clipped to a board? Well, it certainly was a buzz kill. Apparently paperwork is the antidote to adrenaline.

After a million years, a slender woman in professional attire approached me. "Katie Sexton? Come with me please. You can bring your paperwork with you." She escorted me through a richly carpeted hallway into a small room with a cream two-seater sofa and a couple of peach occasional chairs. A narrow wooden side table was pushed against the wall. It had the typical cozy lamp and pamphlet display for whatever random affliction might ail you. This one highlighted an elderly man with Parkinson's.

I was seated when another woman entered the room. Her yellow dress suit was much too tight, and it was making me irritable. I envisioned a smiley face on it with the words *Don't Worry, Be Happy*. They exchanged a few notes, then "Smiley Face" sat with me.

"On a scale of 1-10…" she began. Ugh. How about on a scale of *ordering Chinese take-out* to *ingesting toxic fumes and a lethal drug cocktail in your dad's garage*? On that spectrum I'm on the latter end, just around *checking yourself into a psych hospital*.

"Are you currently having suicidal thoughts?" She read down her list.

Uh…I was, that's why I came here. "Not at this exact moment," I said. So should I leave? Should I go home where I can brew about how lost I am and how no one is helping me? Then I can drive back here in a couple hours. Sure, I can keep looping around in the Bermuda Triangle of sadness, if that's what you're suggesting.

Happy Face churned out more questions. "Are you having any hallucinations?" she inquired.

Am I? Oh crap. How would I know? Could this whole thing be a hallucination? *No Katie, chill out. You're not hallucinating, but maybe you have. Think hard. Tell the truth.* "No. Well, when you're walking down the sidewalk and think you see a cat out of the corner of your eye, and then it turns out to be a bush or a black soccer ball, is that a hallucination?" I asked. The lack of sleep, throbbing hangover, adrenaline, fear and inquisitive nurse had me questioning my own sanity.

She responded, "Okaay…I know that phenomenon has a term. I can't remember what they call it, but it's not cause for concern. I stumped her for a second, as she dug deep into her grad school grab bag of facts. A depressed patient was not out of the ordinary for her, but a test of her umpteen hours of schooling was.

As the previous intake nurse re-entered the room, my interviewer asked, "Pam, what's that phenomenon called when you see something out of the corner of your eye but it turns out to be something different?"

"Oh, like when you see a squirrel, but it's a leaf blowing. It's something to do with the axons in the visual cortex misfiring information to the cerebrum. There's a name for that," she confirmed.

"Yes, but what's it called. It's on the tip of my tongue."

"Ask Mary. She remembers all those terms."

Black Cat Anomaly. That's what I call it.

Weirdness confirmed. Insurance confirmed. They moved me to another room to wait. So much waiting. Suicide would definitely have been quicker. I sat quietly and observed the staff zooming around with purpose. I had a blind trust, that they knew better than me. What a strange mental space to be in. Willing to sign over my free will, stating someone else could make decisions for me this weekend, or week, or however long this takes. I wasn't confident enough. I signed those papers a long time ago. Maybe *that* is the root of my problems.

I was secretly striving to be liberated from feeling like I needed help crossing the road. I desperately reached outward for something only accessible by reaching inward.

"We need everything on your person. Two females will assist you in this process," a staff person reported. They mean a strip search. It's time to unveil how numb I am to being degraded. It's a nice-looking facility, one with carpeting and cushioned seats, but a prison nonetheless. And I was okay with that. In a sense, I've been building this prison for years. I'm already there.

I am steered into "the green room." It was a trapezoid shaped room painted deep green, nothing on the walls, and a kelly green vinyl bench. I sat down. Am I in "A Clockwork Orange"? Who designed this cockeyed room? A Clockwork Green.

For a moment, I was alone with a female staff member. She looked to me and quietly said, almost under her breath, "Are you sure you want to do this? This is not a cheap stay. It's going to cost about the same as a weekend at a 5-star hotel resort. You are looking at ten grand, at least."

With blank assuredness, I answered, "My insurance will cover it. I have really good insurance right now."

She was used to people being forced to come here by a spouse, parent, or caretaker. Perhaps she was expecting a feisty person in a state of obvious delusion. As I sat on the clammy plain bench, I noticed a couple of metal hoops attached to the bottom side of it. That is the kind of person she is expecting to see here, one that needs to be handcuffed into compliance.

My cuffs are invisible to her. It's not just my wrists that are bound. My brain has been constrained through years of negative conditioning, ignited by harsh experiences. My mind needs a prison break.

Scottie once told me, "Sometimes you gotta be your own best friend." Sure, doctors and therapists tried to help me, but I held the inner compass. The voice I lost touch with was my own, my higher self. The voice that said to go right when fear was tugging me left. I needed to believe in myself, like I did when I was a child, before anyone taught me otherwise.

Until then, I found myself disrobing behind an impassive nurse holding up a faded gown. It was mostly uneventful and routine, much like the disorder in my life had become. Akin to a prized puppy in a mill, I submitted to the humiliation, hoping something better was on the way.

"We'll keep your purse and all its contents," a staff person spoke. "We'll go over your medication with you and keep it stashed behind the desk." They kept my cigarettes. Damn it. Now I understood why Grandma was so cranky at the nursing home. Oh well, I needed to detox from those anyways. Next, I passed through a locked double metal door. To the left was the nurse's station. To the right was a laundry room, then a sitting room with round tables and a TV.

"Follow me," the staffer instructed as she led me to the end of the hallway. "This will be your room. You'll share it with Marie."

The room was like a middle grade hotel suite, complete with bathroom, shower, and a lovely display of single serving toiletries. As I sat to use the toilet, I studied the towel hooks. Ah, this is so patients don't intentionally injure themselves. My reflection was visible through a faded mirror-like product that created a slight wave. A nuance that gave it a hint of One Flew Over the Cuckoos Nest.

Luckily we didn't have to line up at a pass through window for medication, and the staff were much more cordial than Nurse Ratchet. "Katie Sexton," a nurse gently called, and motioned me to her station to wash a Dixie cup of pills down with a miniature plastic cup.

Pill one and pill two were waltzing me through the front door of a new correctional facility. The synthetic brick walls being constructed in my brain were preventing me from spitting out words or sentences. Normally I could blab about anything. Now I had to concentrate to get the thought out, and good luck stringing thoughts together. Like a person who had sustained a head injury, I attempted to relearn motor functions and language.

They had given me Lamictal and Abilify. Experiencing side effects? Yes. Decreasing my depression? Negatory. Prior to the hospital visit, the medication caused me to develop a head twitch and slurred speech. "We'll keep the meds the same. The doctor will change them if he sees anything concerning," they assured me. Uh, okaaaay. I'm reading the fine print. Yeah no, the side effects are *worse* than the original condition. *Hey dummy, have you told them it feels like your brain isn't working right? I'm sure that will help.* Son of a bitch, the voice bypassed check in.

Focus on not slurring, like when you are feeling tipsy at the bar. Questioning medication while in the hospital is a no-no. The insert says, "your doctor has prescribed this medication because he or she has judged the benefit to you is greater than the risk of side effects." This is where trusting my inner compass came into play. How many doctors have taken these medications? I could describe to a man the act of giving birth, but if he hasn't experienced it, there's no fucking way he gets it. That's how I feel about psychiatric drugs and their side effects. Who's to say what's normal? On a scale of "normal," where does peddling synthetic, mind-altering drugs fall?

"Well, little missy, you're the one who went looking for help from a doctor who prescribes medication. This is what you get, medication," I imagine them saying to me.

I waived my judgment when I filled out their forms based on the current societal "norm." It's a tough one. My gut says, *now* you look like a crazy person. *Now*, your brain is short circuiting. You can't even talk right. This is the feeling of being doped. Here's a fun game: *Find out how to get out of the psych ward, while you're drugged!* What's worse than psych meds mixed with alcohol that causes them not to function properly? Just straight up psych meds.

When I finished in the bathroom, Marie had arrived in our room. She looked to be in her late forties. She was tucking her short brown hair behind her ears as she sat on her bed folding shirts. "My husband is pressuring me to get out of here. We are running out of money and my two kids have more expenses now that they are in high school." She's been here a month and this is not her first rodeo. "We are almost 90 thousand in the hole with medical bills at this point," she stated. If she wasn't depressed enough before, now she can feel hopeless about that too. "I like your sweater, especially those tortoise shell buttons. They are very pretty," she expressed.

"Thanks! My mom sewed them on for me. She likes to feel needed, so I asked her to hem a pair of pants and replace these buttons," I told the lady, sharing my tale of compassion and good-will towards my mother. I've been coached to find ways to help my mother feel needed.

With a dismal frown she scowled, "How thoughtful of you to throw your mother a bone. Is that all she's good for, a few buttons?"

There was a deep loathing in her tone, a sharp bitterness and scorn I rarely heard coming from the mouth of a mother. My mom was usually butterflies and la-la land, but possibly this is how she felt deep down, under all her denial. Maybe she felt as jaded as this lady.

I stuttered, "W-well, I was just trying to be nice to her."

"Oh yeah, of course," she replied with a half sunken smile. Dang! This woman was depressing me even more! I left my room to catch some air.

I sat down at one of the round tables in the common area, trying to get a bearing on my surroundings. The TV was on, but I wasn't interested. It droned with some garbage comedy I didn't find funny. The voices were exaggerated shrieks blaring with phony laughter, poking fun at my life. My stomach growled and I wondered if I had done the right thing by coming here. I put my elbows on the table, and studied the opaque speckle of the mass-produced hospital tabletop, until my eyes crossed.

As I blinked to refocus, I questioned, "What is the normal amount of time to look down at the table? Where else should I look?" *Quit obsessing, Katie!* For all they know, I was thinking about something really import-ant, not just counting the seconds in my head. I tightened up in my chair, crossed my ankles, and tried my hardest to be unseen. But my stomach was eating itself, pickled from the night before. I walked up to the nurse's bar height counter. I felt stupid asking and I hated not knowing what the response would be.

"Is there food here? I'm hungry," I told the lady.

She looked at me with kind concern, "Oh, you haven't eaten yet? You must have missed dinner while they were getting you checked in. I will have someone bring you a plate from the cafeteria."

I guess I was afraid the answer would be no. I was always expecting people to respond to me with an attitude of disdain. Like, how stupid of you to ask for food. Food? Not for you, dumbass. A few minutes later, a young man appeared in the room carrying a tray. Hot mashed potatoes and turkey with gravy. Milk. Water. Bread. A side of warm corn. I was grateful.

As I swallowed a few mouthfuls, warming my fearful belly, a woman cried out in pain. A shrilling wail reverberated through the room, and a shuffling took place. I caught a glimpse of her anguish, through the two-foot crack in the door, as they pulled her into an adjacent room. She looked like a bride, wearing a cream colored al-amira hijab, and layers of flowing white. The door closed as she continued to weep. This wing was clean and tidy, with a few fake plants to punctuate the neutrality. It could have been the waiting room to a dentist's office, but even the subdued decor couldn't hide the grave human challenges people faced.

A folder was placed in my room with a schedule of activities: meals, various group therapies, free time, and lights out for bed. I felt a draft blow into my room as I curled up under the stiff sheets and thin blanket. A yellow hue was gleaming through the crack in the doorway, like a sullen streetlamp on an overcast night. I wasn't used to falling asleep without the help of some substance, whether it be over-the-liquor-counter or prescribed. There were soft feet every now and again as a staff member walked the hall. Marie slept motionless. I bet she has Ambien on her script list. "At least I made it to the night," I thought, "I'm safe and alive." This consoling thought helped me drift to sleep.

I woke up feeling like I had been on a two-day road trip. Time for a shower. No razors meant stubbly legs and armpits, but I was glad I packed that extra shirt. Some people wore pajamas all day, like a giant psycho sleepover. After I freshened up, I joined the camp for a breakfast of champions. We lined up at the door. *Are we in grade school?*

You know who to call when you're getting dragged out to sea. I should call my older brother and let someone know where I was. I asked permission to use the semi-private booth. It had a gigantic white phone with cartoon-sized grey buttons. Dial 9 to get an outside line. I still felt strung out, despite being sober. Well, minus the psych meds. My fingers fidgeted as I forced them to focus on punching numbers.

My brother's calm dryness traveled through the satellite waves as he answered the call. Always the businessman, this time calculating circumstances, rather than numbers and dollars. Months prior, Jason pleaded with me not to do anything like Chad, the spitball friend of his I once beat in an arm wrestling contest. He said his arm slipped. However, as a sixteen year old, I gloated in triumph. He was cute, and much like myself, easy to get a rise out of.

Jason spent hours playing late-night card games in the basement of my parent's house, with Chad, among a few others. I would sit on the steps, in awe of the boys as they rumbled in fierce competition. Their sessions always ended with someone stomping out in a fury. Life had gloated in Chad's face one too many times, and he checked himself out early. Permanently. I felt guilty for toying with the idea of self execution, especially while calling Jason.

In my nervousness, I joked with Jason about the phones being tapped here. My bro, straight as an arrow, cautioned me, "You probably shouldn't joke about that." The poor guy probably thought our phone call would be cut short as someone excused me to provide a straight-jacket. "I'll come for a visit tomorrow morning," he said. His wife was sending some toiletries and a change of clothes. I wasn't planning on staying long, but some fresh clothes and a visit would be nice.

They don't tell patients the checklist of things to do to get approved for release. It's like playing Chess, without having the rules explained to you. Step One: Realize this is a game. Step Two: Uncover the rules. Step Three: This is basically Fight Club and you can't talk about the rules or they'll gaslight you by calling you "crazy." I detected hints of this tiny secret during one of my sessions with a counselor. She commented, "I'm pleased to see you reached out to a family member and showered," with a pause in her voice and glimmer in her eye. *Was that a wink?* I had made it through the Swamps of Sadness.

I bided my time with group therapy the remainder of the day. The greatest frustration of the majority of the group were their meds. Adjusting medication, changing medication, or sticking it out with the medication. The resounding retort from the therapist was to "trust the doctor" and "the symptoms of your disease are worse than the side effects of the medication." Cringe.

Maybe a few people appeared a little off, and maybe the medication was helping them. Who's to say? One woman felt laughed out of her job for sleeping with a coworker. A man told a tale of disappearing on a spontaneous European vacation, to the financial detriment of his family. Perhaps that lady really needed to get laid. And maybe that man needed to take a damn vacation, and that was the only way to break free. It's subjective.

An African-American girl in her twenties was called on… "The medication made me gain forty pounds." Her face was blank with despair. "I feel even more sluggish with the extra weight, and I can't wear my favorite clothes anymore." She looked defeated.

To add insult to injury, the counselor dismissed her comments with a generic response. "We understand. The sacrifice can be challenging when we need to take medication." Holy shit, it's the fucking *Twilight Zone*. Why can't we just go to the gym or sit in a botanical sanctuary? Because that isn't covered by insurance. Wellness is for the wealthy.

I carefully shared my reason for being there in a calculated manner. "I've been feeling like a loser and drinking too much."

"Do you feel suicidal?" probed the group therapist. Is this a new fetish or something? My inner voice started to wake up. *How long are we gonna do this dance?*

During free time that afternoon, I watched the girl next to me shade in a coloring book. A new girl loudly skidded into the seat next to me stating, "my boyfriend said if he came to pick me up and I was coloring he would leave me in here." She looked across the table in horror, as if the girl was sticking a round ball into the square hole of a plastic baby shape sorter. Others put together a jigsaw puzzle, looked at magazines, or mindlessly switched channels on the TV.

As she anxiously clocked every corner of the room, she detailed her journey to the hospital's doorstep. "I took a taxi ride in the ambulance last night," she said, "I was up all night in the ER and finally got transferred this morning. I'm a nurse here, but not this wing." Her secret was out. "Those assholes were whispering over my head they knew it was just a matter of time. Oh yeah, like they're so perfect," she added. People say they don't want to meddle in another's business, but they do. It's easy to make judgmental assumptions. People get a sense of power and stability by picking apart another's mistakes. They rationalize, if I'm smart and insightful enough to see your character flaws, then I must be less flawed. Wrong. Like attracts like. I can only see what also exists in me. It's a universal law.

Andi and her boyfriend had gotten into a fight while drinking. I'm sure alcohol helped her unwind from the night shift. They pumped her stomach and now she was wired with whatever was left over. "They think I'm with him for his money, or because I have daddy issues, but it's not true," she insisted. "He's the only person who understands me and makes me feel at home." Other than last night. Last night she felt like she wanted to die and took a bottle of pills during their alcohol-induced argument. She was pissed because now she would be put on one of those "lists" at work.

"He's getting me out of here ASAP," Andi bragged. "See, there he is. I bet he brought me some pills. The medication they have me on is bullshit. Plus, it's so easy to sneak stuff in here." *Holy fuck! Don't drag me into your shit!* I sat with my lips pursed and eyes stuck wide open.

"I hear ya, girl," I managed to squeeze out and excused myself to the bathroom. Then I hid in my room until dinner, and made a couple lists: Things to be grateful for and things I want to change in my life. After dinner I laid down for a nap that lasted until morning.

I woke up feeling energized, stoked my brother was coming to visit. After showering, I went to the nurse's station to borrow a comb, mirror, and blow dryer. It wasn't easy picking though a tangly cascade of hair with a black barber's comb, but I had time. I sat criss-crossed in front of an actual mirror and groomed myself. Hygiene—self-care—necessary. *Ding! Ding! Ding!* Previously, combing my hair felt like lifting a concrete block. But not today. I felt light.

"Can I have my make-up bag?" I asked the nurse. She handed it over and loosely monitored my application. Like a school teacher, she stood in close physical proximity, without staring. After a light coat, I was a cleaned-up version of plain old me. I dared bend a smile at my reflection. I'm going to be good to myself today. I glanced to my left, down the hallway to see if anyone had caught a glimpse of my Stuart Smalley moment. No one was paying attention. I breathed out. The nurse at the counter gave me a proud but modest grin, like the ones I would later give to my middle school students, when I accidentally caught them double checking their reflection in a pocket mirror as class dismissed.

Back in my room, I relaxed on my stomach, with knees bent and feet up in the air. I kicked them back and forth with a carefree joy I hadn't felt in a while. Maybe it was the window without drinking, the medication, or a reflection of my shift in perspective. Perhaps it was the refuge of the hospital, or my brother coming, but I felt optimistic today.

"How's it going, girl?! Look at you, all chillin' on the bed with your feet in the air. You look like a college student. You look happy, so whatchu doin' here?" a nurse asked, as he strutted in the door. He was a tall with a jovial smile.

I sat up with my folder of papers and pen. "I'm here for depression or mood swings or whatever. No one seems to know exactly," I told him. He looked at me with perplexity.

Lifting his chin to see out the door, he said, "Look girl, you work on you. You seem a-okay to me, not like some of the others that pass through here. Do what they want you to do, and then go home."

I smiled at him, "Thanks." His kindness filled me with warmth. If someone showed me an ounce of tenderness, it's as if they plugged themselves into a pre-existing hole in my heart and I felt a current finally complete its circuit. My head felt fluffy with the intoxicating surge of chemical reactions. But as soon as the person needed their cord back, *yank*, I morphed back into the draining void of a dead outlet.

As I walked down the hallway, I noticed a staff member seated on a wooden chair, in the doorway of one of the rooms. A middle-aged patient was inside watching TV. Why does that dude have TV privileges in his room, I wondered. So I asked the nurse.

"Oh, he doesn't like to leave his room," he reported, without glancing up from his book. Twenty-four hour surveillance. He was a suicide risk. God, I hoped he didn't hang himself with his bedsheets while I was here. I didn't want to see *that*. Shouldn't he be in the maximum security wing? What the hell does this say about me? Fuck. I wasn't *that* bad, was I? I wondered if he was hostile to others as well as himself. I guess the nurse was right. Even if you're just a little off, you don't want to be lumped in with people that are bat-shit crazy. This is at the root of stigma. A hint of fear makes us strive to stay behind the wall of perfection. A wall of perception.

I've heard that depression or alcoholism cannot be willed away. But there is something to be said about the power of mind over matter, and mind *creating* matter. It's a slippery slope to give up on your own mind. I hadn't given up on mine yet. I wanted to be more kind to it. Quit pickling it. Quit calling it names. I would start taking a few less pills, but I wouldn't ask the doc about that until I got discharged. He didn't recommend going cold turkey, but I did anyways.

"Your visitor is here," a nurse chimed. I lit up like a schoolgirl on show-and-tell day. Me? Someone is here to see *me*? It's Jason, I'm on in five. My feet floated down the hallway and I let the backstage chanting fill my body with a buzz. *Kay-tee! Kay-tee! Kay-tee...*

As children, Jason dove into a pile of shard glass for me. We were playing in the garage, surrounded by salvaged boards with rusty nails sticking out, a variety of saw blades, half empty cans of flammable substances, and a bucket of old Coca Cola bottles.

"Look how fast I can spin Jason! Look at me! I can balance on this board like a balance beam! How many jumping jacks can you do?" I called out at him, as he searched for a pocket knife among our father's highest shelf.

"Just a second, Katie. Ah, there it is," he said under his breath as he found my father's maroon Swiss army knife. His eyes studied it in the palm of his hand for just a few moments before sliding it back onto the top shelf.

"Let me show you how to make music with one of these bottles," I cheered with excitement.

"No, Katie, we are not supposed to play with the glass. Mom said," Jason said in his good deed voice.

"But that's how you do it. I'll be really careful." I grabbed a glass bottle and sat on the ground with it. I nestled into position as my shorts dirtied with sawdust. Holding the thick bottle carefully, I lightly blew over the opening in the top." A low vibration made a flutelike sound rise from the bottle like a genie. "See! I did it! You can make all kinds of different sounds!"

"That's really neat, but you should set it down before Mom comes out," Jason worried.

Quieted by my brother's purity of morals, I set the bottle down on the workbench, where I discovered an anvil. I grabbed a scrap piece of wood and started cranking it tight. With each rotation, the glass bottle crept closer and closer to the edge until *smash!*

"Katie! No!" my brother yelled.

I scrambled to catch it, but I was too late. Instead I tripped over my homemade balance beam and was headed straight for the pile of broken glass. My brother intercepted by pushing me out of the way. In doing so, he fell to his knees and planted his palm in the jumble of crystalline glass. With his teeth clenched together, he sucked in a breath, as droplets of rosy red blood began to stream down his hand and paint a cardinal path over his wrist. He frantically wiped it on his cut-off jeans and noticed it was dripping from his knees too.

"Are you okay?!" I was stunned at his heroic act.

"I'm okay," he said, still in a state of shock.

Earlier that year, I heard some boys remark while we stood at the bus stop how Jason was a wimp. Small as he might have been, I knew he was no coward. He wasn't as savage as other little boys. He reserved himself for when it truly mattered. My brother was stoic in his neutrality, but when push came to shove, he would put his hand in glass for those he loved.

A few moments later, my mother opened the screen door, "Oh my God! Get inside! You know you're not supposed to play with glass!" She swooped my brother up and tended to his wound, cleaning the mess before my father could find out what happened in his garage. The glass bottle incident, during a summer afternoon, would always be a marker of who my older brother was at his core.

"Hello there!" my brother bumbled, with reserved nerves. The nurse walked us to a room to talk with some privacy.

"I'll be back in 30 to check on you," she said. My brother is a peace-maker. Even if he has an opinion, he can appear nonchalant. In this case, if he was uncomfortable in this setting, or had any strong emotions, he wasn't letting them show. His unease was only slightly detectable with the subtle variances of his voice inflection. Presenting his best poker face, he politely asked how things were going.

I lifted my brows and said with a smile, "Well, I'm here."

He shrugged his shoulders and clenched his jaw, "Well, yeeaah…you know, aside from that." Detecting his own judgment, he quickly said, "No, it's good that you're here. I understand some things aren't going as planned. Does this seem to be helping?"

I chuckled on the inside. I've come to terms with tip-toeing around my life's situations. "Did you tell Mom or Dad I was here? Or Grandma?" I asked, knowing what I wanted the answer to be.

"Nah, I haven't talked to anyone the past few days. I've been bogged down with work," he assured. But I suspect he called our parents on day one. He was the proverbial "good son." I was of a more noticeable shade. But the most my mother could acknowledge of my uniqueness was, *Katie? Oh yes, she's very creative.* With a forced smile, swallowing a lump in her throat, she would attest, *she's my little artist.*

After a short meeting of small talk and receiving some fresh comfy clothes, it was time to part. "I'll give you a ring when I'm discharged," I told him. Like an eight year old girl who was old enough to be at a sleepover, but not enough to go alone. Did I miss something in "Adulting 101" class? That curriculum is missing a few crucial chapters.

Jason offered a stiff hug. It was characteristic of the awkward hugs exchanged by men in my family. It wasn't the kind of embrace people give, if they might never see each other again. His discomfort with emotions stood like a piece of petrified wood.

I was the kid who always wanted to squeeze tighter, and longer, until our heartbeats could synchronize. Over the years my hugs became weaker, consumed with a fear of being rejected. I wanted to avoid public displays of embarrassment, if my arms were peeled from the receiver. I felt foolish when the love I beamed out was not reciprocated, and fell flat into a soupy puddle. This time I hugged him back as close as I could and ignored the embrace-analysis whispering in the back of my mind. He showed up, and that was an embrace in itself.

After dinner, I sat with the unconscious mob, melting into the buzzing

TV. I needed a meeting of the minds, but I could see it wasn't going to happen in this circle of misfits. I was anxious because my "need to fix" list was running through my mind like a conveyor belt. I was ready to sort things out, so I could go home.

My romantic interest on the outside world wasn't fulfilling me anymore. The object of my affection was basically homeless, an alcoholic, and quite possibly a sex addict. I'm sure on some level I wanted to fix him, but I also felt an equality in our delinquency. He was attractive and charismatic when he was lucid. The only one who poured attention into me, not always *when* I needed it, but most certainly *how* I needed it. Sometimes my calls would go unanswered for days or weeks. Then in a unsuspecting rush of intensity, he would call and profess his need to see me—-now. That did it for me. Kai *had* to have me.

I would meet Kai in a bar, our silver screen, and he would announce to everyone, "this little filly is with me." He held me, petted me, and hushed into my ear, like a horse whisperer. He was the infatuated over-display of affection I craved. I enjoyed the super sexualized leading roles we served for one another. Sometimes I picked him up on the corner of the street, just before the light blinked red, and swooped him into my Jeep.

"Let's get lost tonight," I told Kai. The sparks in our eyes met briefly in the dim light of my car. There was no time for gazing into each others eyes. I only got a blink of his deep blue wonder.

"Can I kiss you?" he asked as if we had just met, with a smirky grin on his face. Desire washed over us as we grabbed each other's faces, quenching our thirst with our lips. Our chests heaved as we gasped for air between kisses. His tongue couldn't get deep enough into my mouth, petting the tool of my voice. God he tasted good. I was instantly wet. We frantically ripped off our shirts and wiggled down our pants while cramped in the back. I contorted my body against cool leather seats, which quickly warmed and grew sticky with friction. I told him how I wanted it, and he complied with the pressing of his tongue in between my legs. We were high on each other.

I lived for this sexual speedball. Nothing compared to the pulsing adrenaline rush of semi-public sex swirled with the blissful flooding of endorphins and release of oxytocin with orgasm. It was perfection. How was I ever going to let that go? Besides, this was a wave of passion my heart was familiar with. My energy would sync up with it right away.

Our connection was a build-up and a release. The deeper the breath, the more satisfying the exhale. I felt a strong, but short lived relief after our encounters, but it quickly turned detached and cold. He was using me, and I was using him too. My weakness for him was coming to an end.

The nurse at the front desk sent a counselor about my age. I told her I wanted to improve my life by cutting off ties with Kai. *Why would you do that? You know you need his kind of voltage. You're too weak and too slutty to turn him down.* "I'm not a slut. I just like sex," I defended to the imaginary church counsel in my head.

Kai was a growing source of anxiety and I was beginning to feel low about our relationship. I should be making guys take me out to dinner and meet my parents. But parents were a turn off, and the men treating me to dinner sucked at sex. They made me feel like I was studying the plastic butterfly cover over a static light at the gynecologist's office. I felt guilty for enjoying Kai's exploitation, but I also derived pleasure from being someone's lifeline. Even if it was for one orgasmic moment in my car. As long as he needed the fix I gave him with my panties round my ankles and his fist tangled in my hair, I was in control. It seemed.

My guard dropped as the counselor spoke to me as her equal. I shared intimate details of my romantic dilemma. She introduced me to the concept of being addicted to toxic people. She used her ability to relate by telling me she once had a boyfriend who was hard to shake off, despite all the negative consequences she was experiencing. I'd heard of co-dependency before, but never understood being addicted to an unhealthy person with poisonous interactions, until she shared her real life description.

The word toxic flicked on like a lightbulb for me. I couldn't set limits, couldn't resist the temptation, and romanticized relationships in my mind. Every sip of that noxious drug felt good at first, but always ended with regret. It drained me of self-respect. Surely I could do better for myself.

The counselor gave me a piece of paper and had me write down all the things I would do or say if he called. My list of options grew: 1) do not answer the phone 2) I'm sick with a cold 3) grandma is sick with a cold 4) grandma's dog is sick with a cold 5) grandma needs me to take her to the doctor 6) I have to clean the bathroom 7) I'm starting a new job 8) grandma's poodle is having a seizure 9) grandma might be having a seizure 10) the door to the house is frozen shut 11) my car won't start 12) grandma's poodle is dying 13) grandma might be dying and I have to take her to the emergency room 14) I want more than just sex out of a relationship *Oh come on, we all know that last one's not true.*

She had me write down the pros and cons of continuing to see him. I was to look at this list when I was feeling weak to his advances, lonely, sad, or in need of love. Finally, she had me write down other ways to fill my cup, to find that flutter of personal electricity in another way than letting him plug into my power source. It was a relief, like the sudden emergence of a putrid sliver in your foot. You're sure your whole stinking foot is infected with gangrene and a giant wedge of wood is about to come out, and finally you scrape out a flakey piece of broken saw dust from the ball of your foot. Instant relief. No more pressure. That was it?! That little poof was cramping my entire left foot?! I should have picked it out a long time ago, instead of letting it throb away at my resilience.

It felt good to be free from judgment. I no longer felt ashamed. I felt empowered. Having tools to pivot my situation was a game-changer. Maybe I was strong enough to give the real world another shot. I skated through the day, then popped into the TV room to kill some time. Three or four patients sat staring at the TV like a group of flies around a light trap. *Zzzzp. Zzzzp.* The counselor said the doctor wasn't in until tomorrow. I guess they don't discharge patients on the Sabbath.

Wait a sec, I've seen this movie before. It was *Dodgeball,* that corny comedy flick. It was the scene where they are taking a tour of 'Globo-Gym.' Okay, that's a funny name, I thought to myself. A poke at corporate gyms—I get it. *Ah man, I miss my gym.* I continued to watch as the testosterone-crazed, ridiculous main character pranced through the gym during his ad, informing potential clients if they're fat and ugly, it's their own fault if they don't hate themselves enough to do something about it. My funny bone tickled as I almost spit out my water.

I looked to the nurses' desk. Are they hearing this? They sure as heck don't talk like that in group therapy, but imagine if they did. I looked around at the other patients…not a flinch. I was in a room full of expressionless dummies, sitting like a flock of tactical decoys. No offense to them, they were still in a sleepy cloud of depression and pharmaceuticals.

I continued to snicker under my breath, fully entranced in this hilarious movie. The urge to laugh was unbearable, as my eyes welled up with joy. I don't know if the movie was actually that funny, but it triggered a one-woman laughing fit. The staff briefly glanced towards the commotion I was causing. One nurse gave me a satisfied wink that said, "welcome back, I see you've come out of your fog."

An imaginary loudspeaker belted out, "This one's ready to go home!

Start prepping the sheets for the next one! She's responding to our cheesy movies. Depression cured. She's been successfully re-assimilated. Send her back out to try again."

The switchboard caught fire. It lit up with calls to my therapist confirming follow-up appointments and so on. A discharge plan was typed out, printed, stamped, copied, filed in a cabinet and stuffed in my bag. It was like graduation day.

I packed my bag and waited in the patient lounge. It was nearing visitation time and Andi sat next to me. "Don't do anything *crazy*," she said. I gleefully gave her the finger, as I stuck out my tongue.

As her edgy and defensive looking boyfriend arrived, I pulled out a coloring book and started to work on my crayon shading. Andi snorted under her breath. He gulped in horror and shuffled her off to another table to talk. I smiled. Crazy is relative.

A nurse handed me my purse and other belongings. "Are you happy to be going home?" she asked.

"Yes! I'm looking forward to having a smoke on the drive home," I blurted out.

"Oh, I don't know how you did it. Being without cigarettes would be the hardest part for me," she replied. The parking lot was covered in a foot of white from the weekend snow storm. It was obvious who the patients were. Abandoned cars randomly spaced throughout, untouched by footprints, still sparkling with inches of pristine potential.

I hopped into my Jeep and put in a CD, Alicia Keys: As I Am. Her elegant piano intro played as I lit my cigarette and pulled out of my parking spot. A staff member headed in for the afternoon shift. We caught eyes. He gave me an open-mouthed grin, a big wave of congratulations, and a thumbs up as if to say "you made it!" Alicia's words echoed through my car and my heart. *People keep talking they can say what they like, but all I know is everything's going to be alright.* Yes, this song belongs on my soundtrack. Today the sun is reflecting off the snow. Same road, a different shade of brightness. I'm starting to remember my way home.

Energy Surge

Here it comes. I feel the surge crackle and wake inside of me. I become emblazoned with a passion and lust for life, unable to stay grounded through the excitement, swelling in my stomach like a growing bee colony. I was taught to dim my light, but no matter how hard the malicious ones try to trip my wire, my default was still set to shine.

When I feel the spark of life, my eyes beam with light. I'm not on the planet right now. I'm connected to the above. I've lifted off and exploded into stardust. I'm flying through the sky, through the clouds, into the rays of the sun, up to the stars, looking down below at the blue marble. It's beautiful, that place with all the noise and diversity. Earth. In my altered state of consciousness, I can appreciate it. This is one of my stations. I forget it's there sometimes. The radio gets staticky down there.

This state of mind is induced by life. It often comes after I've been feeling dull and bored with life, like everything is muffled and I have a vague memory that it wasn't always this way. I need time to zone out. Then little sparks of magic begin kindling, first in my gut, then a sizzling in my ears and eyes, until my head starts ringing with delight! I might hear a new song that makes me feel like I'm going to burst with joy. I put it on repeat to acclimate to this new vibration. What a gift it is to be in this body and experience these sensations! Music, doing new things, going new places, and meeting new people activate this elation. Gratitude energizes me until I can't relax. I don't want to miss one second of life. Until I learned to establish some routines, this inspiration could lead to insomnia.

One fall semester night, I lay in a cabin, chaperoning 7th grade girls in the middle of the Redwoods, and I was exhausted. The trip got off to an exhilarating start, and my blood was pumping through my veins like drumbeat. *Bah-bump. Boom. Ba-bump. Boom.* There's a song thumping inside of me and it won't let me sleep. I had to blare music into my earbuds to blend out the drums, and diffuse the ringing in my ears. The iPod probably added to the electrified current of racing thoughts. It traveled from my brain, down and up my arms, through my chest and belly, zipping down my legs, and tickling my toes.

They want me to contain it, but I want to embrace this stellar feeling. It wakes me up so I can blow my mind ball on some of the universe's majesty. It's the burst of energy that helps get me out of bed to walk outside at 3AM and absorb the wonder of a star-studded sky in a forest free from any light pollution. It's the tingling reminder of the web of protons and electrons doing a dance inside me, making this life possible. It's the 300 joule shock I need to revive me from the quivering limbo of fibrillation. *Charging five hundred...clear!* Get me back in the flow. Okay, not *that* much flow. I need to learn how to channel and balance this energy, before it becomes over-stimulating. Maybe one day I will no longer have to feel my skin crawl with discomfort, from the overwhelming flooding of sensations.

My merriment felt out of control at times, because I was told how to feel joy.

"You're at a ten Katie, and we need you at a five. Tone it down," Dad would say.

Happy could end in embarrassment, whereas quiet and subdued was safe and expected. This lack of balance created an atmosphere where pockets of bliss broke through in surprising ways. They came across as impulsivity. But when I was in this free state, I felt open.

In the work world, people are not receptive. They want a robotic base-line. But in the outside world, no one even notices. They are too deep in their own head box. Some may have shied away, thinking, whoa, she's a handful. Many people are attracted to it. Perhaps they wish *they* could be a little wild and free. Wouldn't it be nice to let loose, take chances, and reap the rewards of the unknown?

For me, it's not a choice. It's an effort *not* to be untamed, and making the effort to fit in leaves me feeling like a caged feral animal. I will gnaw, scratch, and plot my way out of the crate. Beware, when I make it out, I will run unbridled circles around every obstacle I face. I'll pounce on strangers and lick them in the face, with my puppy-sized paradise, overjoyed to be alive and free.

Part of me was ashamed of this energy, until I learned Reiki. My first energy transfer was emotional as I was not used to letting the energy of love flow through me. It was powerful in its tender nature. I had no idea my voltage was connected to the vibration of love, a frequency I had fallen out of familiarity with. I had worn off my wire gauge and it was time to recalibrate. This energy surge, this high vibration. What is it and why am I suspicious of it? I have been too afraid to be happy. Too afraid to be myself. I consider that I'm not being outlandish. Maybe this foreign feeling is actually the truth of me. Perhaps this state of euphoria is a state of being honest with my soul. My heart knows the answer to this question.

Starship Love

I was conditioned to think consuming alcohol to cope or celebrate was normal. It wasn't just the Midwest. It was on the television, in movies, and at every family gathering. Poisoning yourself with booze was not only socially acceptable, it was encouraged. I dulled down my being, in an attempt to sustain the toxic acceptance I was both addicted to and afraid of. But the watered-down approval was lackluster. I grew tired of trying to blend in and was discontent with the mundane life that came from mediocrity and self-denial.

In stepped my future husband. It's like he rolled straight out of a Tarantino film and kicked my computer screen with his John Wayne spurs. I was living in my grandmother's attic when my best friend Samantha had a brilliant idea. We were both working non-stop and done with the bar scene. I, for one, wanted much more. I took a break from binge drinking with the white knuckling help of AA. The gym was my daily oasis and I was harvesting confidence in regards to my potential in life. I was seeing a therapist and learning about setting boundaries.

"Let's try online dating!" Samantha suggested with enthusiasm. This was a new phenomenon and I wasn't sold yet. The only person I knew who had tried it was my aunt, who met an emotionally unstable man who broke her heart. There were a number of dating companies starting that boasted state-of-the-art security features. The infamous Craigslist killer was another reason not to put my delicate electrical system on the virtual circuit. The dangers lurking in this idea were many. On second thought, I could handle it.

I set up one of many future profiles. When I couldn't find a local guy willing to meet me for a date at any place other than a bar, I opened up my search to the entire fifty states. Surely there was someone interesting, attractive, and looking for a relationship with depth out there somewhere.

My next option is to go overseas, but hopefully my land-locked search will reel in a big fish.

When a clean cut Texan with a quirky Elvis sideburn, and a profile stating he only listened to techno music winked at me, I thought, "Yessss! Now I'm intrigued." Who is this man, Kane, who defies my stereotype of country bumpkin cowboys with Confederate flags waving from a junked up pick-up truck bearing a gun rack? I clicked past many other "likes," but this one I opened. Tell me, guy in tan jacket with collar popped, how have you been surviving rural Texas? What spaceship brought you here to meet me?

It didn't take more than a few email exchanges for me to feel comfortable enough to swap cell phone numbers with my admirer. Despite my recent self-improvement crusade, or maybe because of it, I confessed to him I had a strong history of being a little unhinged, out to lunch, and stark raving mad. Although I was interested, I put up all the stops to push him away. He called anyways. Codependent tendencies confirmed. Lack of getting laid lately, also confirmed. As I paced the hallway in my silk panties, daydreaming about Texas heat, my phone rang.

When I flipped open my cell, a gas light flickered in the attic. I didn't notice. I was distracted by the high-pitched twangy drawl that gushed through the speaker of my phone. Never had I heard a man's voice sound like this. Who was this creature? He was definitely from another corner of the universe than mine, and I liked it. My soon-to-be lover poured out a deluge of personal details. There is something I adore about a person who opens for too much intimacy. Why should you hold back? It's going to come out anyway. Sharing up front seems less contrived. I admire a heart that cannot resist sending out its full signal in order to summon the counterpart to its beat. My heart pulsed back in unison with his. With our pulmonary chambers finally in sync, we could take our first oxygenated breath as one. Circuit complete.

After a few months of love-struck delirium, I needed to meet him. Sure, the calls in-between the swing shift were titillating. I relished in having an enthusiast for my erratic happenings. He let me chat away about pouring a cup of Draino crystals down a clogged sink in grandma's 1940s kitchen. I told him about the corroded pipes flooding the room in a matter of seconds, at 5:30AM, right as I needed to leave for work. Not everyone would find this flaky fable as enthralling as he did.

He listened and laughed with a twangy cackle as I retold blips from my day. The morning my grey cat launched off my face and left me with a bleeding upper lip, he listened intently and requested a picture. So I sent him a photo of a gash landing a hairline away from needing a stitch, as well as one with me sitting by the pool, with my band-aid mustache sweating off my face in the humidity. He replied, "Looking good, Scarface." Gah! He was one step away from licking the blood off my kissers. Be still my heart.

I flew from Chicago to the middle of no-where Texas to meet the person I had fallen in love with over the internet. First, I arrived in Dallas, and was picked up by my over-the-phone lover, in-person stranger, then driven 2.5 hours into the sticks, after dark. Why would I do this? He seemed like the real deal over the phone, so I said, "fuck it" and went with my gut, hoping it was right. A few months prior, I was at the psych unit, how much worse could this turn out?

Before I set out on this weekend of amorous adventuring, I let Samantha know what I was doing. I instructed her not to tell anyone, but to be available via text for me to check in every hour or so. "If I go silent, you can assume the date has turned into a Texas Chainsaw Massacre situation. At that point, you have permission to call my parents and inform them of my possible coordinates." There were no hotels or motels in my soon-to-be husband's town. In truth, the nearest one was thirty minutes away. Okay, so I'm half committed to slutting it up already. This trip is genius in its planning. Five-star rating.

I had two pictures to go on, and no...not one of them was a dick pic. That didn't come until later, upon request. I had a respectable side profile pic and a grainy selfie of a shirtless slender man, full ashtray in the background, sleazy grin, wearing jeans and a black belt barely hanging off his pelvic bone. Quite frankly, he looked like trouble, and I wanted every single bit of it.

I was pleasantly surprised when a cobalt blue Mustang picked me up right on time in Dallas. My cellular suitor looked like his pictures, his voice matched up, and his demeanor was even more subtle than I anticipated. Dinner, drinks, and wandering through the dusk looking for fireworks made for an excellent first date with the Hardesty homesteader. This could work. I dug the thrill of taking the red eye to see a man I barely knew. There's nothing like a breeze of risk to get the libido stirring. A plane was a penny more expensive than the back seat of my Jeep, but the extra jolt it zapped me with was doing the trick. He pulled into a farm property where a revival of buzzing cicadas swarmed, and dogs howled outside the kitchen window. I felt the southern heat building up between us.

I was relieved my date wasn't a big drinker. Kane dabbled with recreational drugs in his early twenties, but had no need for them in his daily life anymore. I guess after thirty plus hits of acid, you've opened your mind enough. He was oblivious to his idiosyncrasies, which I found captivating. He offered me the couch, but I chose the bed in his Egyptian purple room.

I revel in my fantasy world. The only thing that makes it better is bringing it to life with multiple choose-your-own-ending scenarios. Tonight I'll turn to page 36, where he rips the black leather belt off and snaps it together between us with a *crack!* My heart quickened as I feared for a moment he might use it on me. But he tossed it aside just as my blood dumped a gallon of throbbing pleasure into my flesh. I lost myself in his smooth washboard abs glistening in the sweltering heat. He was perfumed with the aroma of a half-smoked Marlboro red. If this was a taste of the "dirty south"…don't mind if I do.

In the morning, I tiptoed into the bathroom to go pee. It was missing a door, but I pretended not to notice. The Texan waltzed in with his famous coconut creamed coffee and tucked his six foot boney body onto the tiled stoop next to me and said, "I hope you don't mind me being in here. I just want to be near you. We have to get used to each other's most intimate moments if we are going to be together."

I thought, "Oh no, is he one of those perverts that wants to watch me pee? God I hope not. There better not be a camera inside this toilet." Good thing I'm seduced by a high bar on the weird-o-meter. This strange new love was steadily declaring his affection for me, as I made a tinkle in his toilet. Some people may have thought that was too eccentric. I found it mesmerizing.

After a morning of coffee, we made way to the closest lake. Who knew there were lakes in Texas? Even a bath water temped lake sounds good in 104 degree weather. We parked on a mound of red ants that bit my ankles and left me with puss-filled welts to go home with. Texas welcomes its guests like that, and then placates them with a "bless your heart."

Certain parts of Texas are less formal than what you would expect from an area steeped in the history of grandiose plantations. Not everyone sits overly poised and repressive in nature at the dinner table. Some of its constituents foster the lawless undercurrents of a subculture sweating in the throes of nature's primal heat. Southern culture beholds a raw and ghostly juxtaposition of humanity.

On our way to the water, we brushed shoulders with a mini camp of motley lake inhabitants. "Don't eat any of the meatloaf the midget is cooking on the grill," my date advised me.

"Okaaay, any reason why?" I asked, taking a double take. There was in fact a shirtless small person cooking up some grub.

"It's squirrel meatloaf," Kane said. "That's Brannon, his brother was hung from a tree here a couple years ago."

Just like that, I learned how my future husband would pepper conversations with shocking oddities, like he was sprinkling bacon bits on a perfectly average salad. He moved on in the conversation, while I had to hurry to let each peculiar fact from his life sink in, with new questions after each one of his bizarre sentences—none of which were acknowledged. Did I just pass through the set of Jackass? The lake will wash away my concerns. Large bodies of water always do. A portal in a lake in East Texas. I allowed myself to be engulfed by this surreal symposium.

The sun glistened on the water and reflected on my lover's toothy smile. He noticed we had the same gap in our canine teeth. *My geeky twin flame, how can I resist you? I won't. Two months later I will drop everything and move here. A few months after that I'll marry you.* Lust leads, passion follows. If I had met anyone more mainstream, they would have never held my attention this long. I don't fall in love with ordinary. I fall in love with the one who personifies something more like the potential horror flick protagonist. A Sci-Fi hero who walks the line into a starry bliss. The stunt driver in Death Proof, so long as he's not actually going to murder me. The one with a Nashville wink and a heart of gold. Finally, our parallel universes have collided and fused.

Legend of Earth

A child embodies the knowledge that they were meant for something bigger. They zip through the grocery store with a parent, on a scorching afternoon in July, decked out head to toe in superhero attire. They are disguised as being immersed in play, but they know someone finally bought them an appropriate suit. Adults behold powers too, but with the trade of the costume, most accidentally traded in their access to the *Triforce* as well. Perhaps they suppress this omnipotent strength because false humility and the effort to fit in don't allow for altruistic aspirations.

I'm talking about finding the map to the overworld, attempting to connect to infinite levels within reality. I seek the magic compass that points to more than this uninspired existence I'm tolerating. Something tells me my strong flaming arms were meant to do more than fold laundry. I'm here to collect crystals and burst open heart containers. I can almost see the big key dropping down in a ball of golden light.

It would be easier to *fit in*, to find a niche and make a living at it. Happy. Simple. Take the medication. Teaching at a public school is purposeful, but it's becoming the death of my soul. I feel like I'm viewing a microcosm of the world's chaos, and it's about to implode. My guts keep tugging at my heart, which churn up my trachea, and whisper to my inner ear canal. My intuition rumbles, *there's more*. I'm hit with the trendy wanderlust everyone is Pinteresting about. But deep down I know I thirst for more than what a trip to Baja could quench.

Shut up, little voice! Sometimes you don't want to hear a calling. It can be an inconvenience. As a teenager, I was told my quest for more depth in life was nothing more than idealism, as if that was something bad. My pursuits of noble principles, purposes, and goals were poisoned with cynicism. Doesn't everyone want to know the meaning of life? Surely it's not just to make money and spend money. It can't be to blow up innocent *others* overseas. I also doubt it's to let some man up in the sky deal with it after we die.

Maybe wisdom, of both a masculine and feminine nature, has been lost over time. Theology is compartmentalized to one day per week. People who practice or seek out things of a spiritual nature on a weekday, are considered outsiders who are one step away from joining a cult. Who decided that anyways? The dude with a zillion Bible quotes and stickers on his station wagon in Kentucky—he ruined it for us.

In my effort to seek, I kept moving. Sometimes it felt like I was running away from things, but other times it felt like I was running to them. Sometimes I didn't know which it was, until I got going. I may not know what I'm looking for, but I'm sure as hell not going to find it while sulking in the recliner seat.

One freedom I've acknowledged in my life is the ability to change. If I don't like my situation, I can change it. That truth has kept me from giving up at times. It's halted suicidal thoughts. Change may not be easy. In fact, it won't be. Not at first. I focus on acceptance and work to move past the initial discomfort of change. I won't let the status quo suck the life out of me. It's easy to fall into a couch of complacency. "What if I make a change and wind up not even having a couch to lay on or pot to piss in?" That's the hard part—the unknown. The perceived risk or loss.

Years ago, my spouse hung onto a job that made him miserable. We both rationalized that quitting and starting our own business was too rocky. Stay with the company. Keep the steady paycheck, the 401K, and health insurance. We thought it wasn't worth the risk, but reassessed after the company liquidated the same month he had an interview for a promotion. The security dissolved like the imposter it was. The risk was there all along. The loss of his job turned into an opportunity to pursue his dreams. We chose to see it that way, and our lives were better for it..for awhile.

Fear can be paralyzing, but I know I can break free. Once I get the momentum going, I will monopolize on it. "When you've got nothing, you've got nothing to lose." People talk this way, but it's quite another venture to act on it. As you get older, there seems to be more at stake. But seriously, the only things of real value are my sanity, happiness, and my life.

At times, music acts as a soundtrack to the much larger life existing in my mind. My internal world is more magnificent than what I assume others are experiencing. Wait, is anyone else feeling this too? That used to be our test when my friends and I were tripping. If both people see it, then it's not a hallucination. We tested things like moving matter in between our fingers. We referred to it as the metaphysical plasma. If we both saw the cosmic silly putty being stretched and then condensed back down, then it was real.

She's a replicant! Sometimes I feel as though I'm surrounded by human robots. They didn't advertise that Vickie from *Small Wonder* circa 1985, was a true story. The impression of my co-inhabitants being AI's, sounds like a description from DSM-5, the manual put out by the American Psychiatric Association. However, this sensation can be one of the stages of awakening. If DNA is a like a computer program, then I've been dealing with some Apple II operating systems for quite awhile now. They are at the grocery store, my past jobs, and in the local mom groups. Just fucking upgrade. It'll be worth it, I promise.

I've had out-of-body experiences where I feel like my emotions have a color and pour out of me like paint on a canvas. I'm surrounded by light. My experiences are decorated with more than meets the eye. I wish everyone could see what I see, and maybe they do. But waking up is a singular journey. I know the electric sheep will wake up from their dreams. It is truly majestic to get through the layers of darkness.

As a young girl, I had vivid dreams that woke me to extraordinary visions. I saw fuzzies of light particles in the night. I wasn't exactly scared, but I asked my mom about it and I could tell she was disgruntled at my alien need to understand what "darkness" looks like. She sputtered something about the streetlamp outside coming in through the pastel blinds, then quickly changed the subject.

The fuzzies were something I came to accept as what midnight looked like, but when I woke up to a giant clown standing in my room, I was inflamed with terror! I froze beneath my quilt, not even a blink, until my eyes rolled back in my head and sleep came to rescue me. On another night I opened my eyes to a nefarious spider web entangling my room in the wee hours. My heart squeaked through a sheet of icicles. I saw something resting in the center of the web. I feared it had spun a cocoon around my favorite stuffed unicorn, so I crawled onto the floor and stayed low to the ground until I was in my parent's room. My mother woke from her deep slumber, with a fearful gasp. I threw up my hands and insisted they not go into my room, in fear they would be greeted by the Giant Spider Invasion that had set up camp. My loving parents turned on all the lights to prove to me nothing was there. No spider web. But I was awake when I saw it, and they knew because I entered their room like I was completing the low crawl pit at basic military training.

These incidents were chalked up to imagination, and possibly my asthma medication, which had a stimulant in it. I still don't know what the monster was, but I've learned these happenings are common for children with extra sensitive settings. Especially those with tendencies towards clairvoyance. To be clear, many children have psychic experiences that are discredited by a parent who can't remember. But kids are fresh from the other side. It takes time to forget. To help me through, my blanket was often my best friend and savior.

I try to quiet my mind, but sometimes it feels like it is fast forwarding through data, in search of a message that is deeply imbedded within the system. What is the lost message? It's like I already know it, but I can't retrieve it. It feels like when you know you are dreaming and try to wake yourself up. There's a hazy layer between the two realities, and it's hard to be awake in both at the same time. Donnie Darko..are you there?

I indulge myself in deconstructing the matrix. I am increasingly engaged with my inner world, or extended world, whatever the heck it is. It can allow me to feel the space I need when out and about in my body bubble. It's my buffer and my connectivity device, all in one. If I'm focused on my inner balance, then I'm not analyzing what others might be thinking of me. This is my Zen. I wish I had known how to develop it sooner. Many of us had someone who tried to squash our creative side. Someone who thought a heavy dose of logic and practicality would serve our lives better. It can feel suffocating to have your light buried, but in my case, the vitality of my soul wouldn't die. It lay dormant for a while, but now it's coming back. It needed the right conditions to thrive. I'm just trying to let my soul breathe. I think that's what it came here to do.

Shot Glass

The oppressive heat of Texas was causing my brain to swell into a slow grinding halt. But this was nothing new. It was accompanied by the suffocating straightjacket of marriage. Kane forced me backstage once again as he bragged that he was the artist of the house—even though I was the one who went to art school. He left bills unsigned on the counter I had prepared to be sent out, just to let me know *he* was in charge of the money. It was one of many red flags, but I didn't see it. My whole life was in the red.

Marriage was supposed to fix it all. Moving away from my hometown was supposed to fix it all too. But as they say: wherever you go, there you are. Kane was adamantly opposed to change on any level, and besides divorce, my only option was pharmaceutical drugs. One year had passed and I was already going through the motions. People excitedly asked Kane how things were going with the newlyweds, leaning into their fairy tales of marital bliss. He replied with a stale eye roll, "happily ever after."

So, there I was, slipping into a pattern of coping. I was drinking as an attempt to get motivated for life, or maybe I was trying to get numb. I did not have many other options to get out of this trap. Being a housewife was my preference, but became a predicament when I found myself alone and isolated in a rural setting. Where was my village? As three o'clock rolled around, I prepared for Kane to get home. I ditched my pajamas, and applied some make-up. If I didn't look tipsy, maybe our life wouldn't be a mess either.

My choices were wine and Lexapro. I wanted to choose vacations and traveling adventures. Kane wanted to choose the couch. It was the dusk of a summer day. I prepped this incident with five days of heavy drinking. Day one: Tipsy. Day two: Drunk but sleeps it off. Day 3: A little saturated. Day 4: I don't give a fuck. Day 5: My death wish is a sweet lover I talk to all day.

Kane trudged through the door in his usual way, "leave me alone. I've barely walked in the door."

"Okay sorry. I didn't know you never wanted hug and kiss from your wife," I snarked.

I was starved for his attention. How could he not notice how much I missed him. How could he not notice…me. He never did. We never talked about feelings, intimacy, or our deepest needs and desires. He made fun of me for wanting to discuss them. The abuse compounded. At the time I took the blame. I thought I was at fault for asking too much, but I wanted to be treated as a living, breathing, feeling human. There was nothing wrong with that request. This is the dance of the empath and the narcissist. I learned it from my dad. I thought this was a relationship.

Overwhelmed with the direction my life had taken, I fantasized about what I would be wearing when someone found me dead. The pink dress was on my top ten list. That day it almost made number one. It had a geometric pattern resembling something out of the sixties, with a silvery metallic thread wrapped through the fabric that went around my neck. I imagine there were plenty of misguided damsels in distress that overdosed in something similar.

Feeling ignored was a major trigger. I once heard someone describe a co-dependent personality like this: *treat me average, and I feel ignored; treat me special, and I begin to feel normal.* This applies to anyone in need of validation. I needed to be showered with positive attention, in order to feel like I was being mildly acknowledged. I lavished others with affection, and I wanted the same in return. I was coming from a place of lack, therefore the universe kept dealing me cards reflecting a deficiency.

When I was in love, I couldn't resist pouring myself all over my companion. However, no one was pouring themselves over me. I was the only one doing the pouring. Drip, drop, drunk.

"You could at least glance at me," I complained.

"Why are you so needy, Katie? Find something to do. I really don't care," Kane replied. He retreated to the living room and proceeded to pack his hitter box.

"Yeah, I can tell," I said. "You never care. What's the point? Why am I even here?"

"Here we go again. Not doing this," he stated as he toked on his weed.

"Not doing what? You don't do anything. We don't do anything. So what you're saying is, it's going to be more of the same?" I asked.

"Quit bitching for once. I'll eat later," he replied.

"Oh, so I get eat alone again while you play video games? Wonderful. I love this. I guess the video games are more appealing than me? Again, why am I fucking here then?" I began to shout.

"Quit," he shouted back.

"Quit what? Quit being alive? Fuck you, Kane," I said, now in tears.

I stormed to the bathroom and sunk into the mirror. I was going into Kamikaze mode. Desperate for affection, with no hope of getting it, I tossed back a shot full of an attention-deficit remedy.

Kane walked into the hallway just as I was swallowing it right out of the prescription container. He saw it with the corner of his eye, as he passed by the bathroom.

"What the fuck did you just do?" he yelled.

White out. Black out. When the sirens came for me, I didn't hear them. There was some scuffling and yelling. My body was limp. I think the swig of pills was too much for my 125 lb. 5'3" body.

"Get your underwear on! They're coming!" Kane instructed. He was shouting, but I was in a deep dark dream and could barely hear him. I was slipping into the void. It was filled with endless black space and twinkling lights. Were those stars far away in the distance? I want to see. Just as I started to connect with this space-like abyss, I was sucked back into my body. A nudge or sensation, like hot or cold registered, and sent a spark to my brain, popping me back into the one-thousand pound meat suit.

"Get your panties on! Can't you move at all? Come on! Help me!" Kane shouted with desperation. It must be hard to dress a body with nearly dead weight. My dense bag of bones was shipwrecked onto a cold hexagon tiled floor. His voice started to fade into the distance again. There was too much noise and drama on this plane. And I wasn't ready to deal with that just yet.

My consciousness went back to a place where time was limitless and I was weightless. I had a sense of my body being "over there," where life was play- ing on fast forward. But I wasn't in the bathroom anymore. I was in another dimension, floating in a stream of peace. I was aware I was in a different fre- quency. A frequency of pure potential and infinite love. An in between place, that wrapped its arms around me with the warmth of a womb. A place with no worry or anxiety. A place where I felt safe and protected. A state I hadn't felt for many years, perhaps my whole life. I was in the pause. In this place of darkness, I was light, in every sense of the word. Slam a bottle of Ambien like it's a shot of tequila, and it becomes an instant portal.

The deep space that enveloped me was intelligent, and I was a part of it. Information was not communicated with words. Here, there is only feeling, and ESP. Nothing is linear. I float in and out of worlds. A knowing was transferred into my heart. A gift that would slowly open like a lotus flower over the next few years.

Back in the land of heaviness, the ambulance workers rushed me out on a stretcher, then drove thirty minutes to the nearest hospital. I have no recollection of the EMTs being in our home, or the ambulance ride. I was completely emerged in another plane. I was taking a nap from my life. Maybe they were chatting about how I was acting out a "cry for help." My grandmother once told me, the ones who always threaten to kill themselves, never do. It's the ones who don't say a thing, and then one day, you find them—dead. Those are the ones who really do it.

A few years back, I worked with Jim, a gentle, considerate man in his late 40s. He didn't show up for work the day before winter lay off. Co-workers went looking for him, and after a few hours, the search was complete. They found him on the site of one of his side jobs, hanging from the rafters. He was a bit wiry, but always smiling. With a calm and unassuming manner, he taught me how my health insurance worked. I remember wishing my father would talk to me like that. At the time, my dad and I weren't speaking. I felt gratitude this coworker took me under his wing.

The last day I saw Jim, he was working with a bossy woman, and he mocked her as he pranced in her shadow. In an effort to make me laugh, he acted like he was dangling from a noose behind her, with his tongue hanging out. When she turned around he put his hands down and smiled. I giggled at his dark humor. It was an eerie foreshadowing, as that is the way he chose to off himself, just days later. He had a gambling problem, and spent all his family's money. Unfortunately, when you eliminate yourself, your family gets nothing from your life insurance. Some of the men at work called him a coward, because he did it to himself, but I felt sorry for him. He made an honest mistake. Some people don't know how much they're worth, beyond the monetary numbers.

I suppose I didn't want to die, or else I would have swallowed the pills while I was alone. I, on the other hand, allowed my monologue to spew out in an outrageous demonstration of my sorrow. I needed him to see me. I was desperate to be acknowledged, and didn't know any other way.

I drifted in and out of lucidity in the ER as I became aware of Kane's presence. He had driven separately, and found me at the hospital. Someone had propped me up on a chair in one of the patient rooms, but that bowling ball of a head was weighing me down. There was an IV jabbed in my arm, and I had to prop it up like some kind of mannequin, while my head bobbed towards my shoulder. The florescent lights buzzed with an idle energy that kept waking me up. The doctors were implementing a verbal questionnaire. *Ma'am, what is your age, relationship status, and religion?*

My head popped up. "Non-affiliated," I slurred. Get the most important information down first. God forbid they start praying over me! Up north I wouldn't have cared, but if I heard some Baptist nurse trying to "save" me, I might be tempted to swallow another round of pills.

The doctors asked, "Now what did you take? How many did you say you took?" and most importantly, "Why did you take the pills?" I tried to answer their questions, but all I could focus on was how hard it was to keep my eyes open. I wonder if they are just seeing ghostly white eyeballs. Maybe it would be more normal if I shut my eyes altogether while I talked to them. But I'll fall back to sleep if I do that, and they seem to want me awake. One doctor would leave the room and they would send in another to ask me the same set of questions. During these brief moments when the doctor left, Kane grilled me on what to say.

"You need to tell them it was an accident," he urged me. He was on damage control mode. I was back in the world of fast forward, but not fully assimilated.

I ineptly complied. "I took two or three Ambien because I really wanted to take a nap. I don't know why I took more than one. I just wanted to go to sleep," I groggily assured the doctor. They weren't exactly buying it, but it wasn't obvious enough to be classified a suicide attempt.

"That Ambien makes people loopy. One man we treated had driven to work naked in the morning. He was still in some kind of sleep walking state of delirium. After I saw that, I stopped taking the stuff," one ER nurse confessed to Kane.

A cocktail of Ambien and liquor mixes in the body system like a cryptic potion. I must have fallen asleep again, because the feeling of being moved woke me up. I was laying down this time, as I gazed up at a ceiling of rectangles passing by. My eyes discharged a flood of sadness. I was in the stage where I openly wept. The cold echoes of the rolling metal wheels and my devastated wails bellowed down the dark barren hallway. I wasn't sure where I was any more, but the reality of what I'd done was beginning to set in. My pain was surfacing. I was crying because I almost died, and because I was still alive. As I was whisked away by strangers, shrilling sounds fought to escape my empty vessel. The dismal sounds of the hallway on that night whispered to me in moments of weakness. They warned me of the groove I had dredged. Sometimes they tempted me, and in moments of clarity, they reminded me to heal.

A warmth passed over me. My eyes opened, and I turned to the side. He was there. Kane slept on the decor couch in my room. This made me feel like he loved me. Tears rolled down my face and I lipped the words, "I'm sorry." His eyes were welled with sorrow and concern. I worded, "I love you," and he worded it back. It was a relieving message soon to be forgotten. External validation is always fleeting. I could have woken up alone, but I didn't, and for the time being, I was grateful.

The IV was pinching my skin, prohibiting my elbow to move. The melodramatic mixture I swallowed the night before had left me a tad dehydrated. Life has a strange feeling when waking from a cry-for-help act. A bright hazy glow streamed through the window and sounds circulated through my eardrum like it was the first time I'd heard them. My fingertips tickled as I rediscovered my hands. I'm sure it was the Ambien wearing off, but it felt like time had slowed down, just enough for me to notice the beauty of stillness.

I looked around my room and thought, none of this matters. Not in the way I thought it did, at least. All these things, they are just things. But this place, this body, this moment, is precious. I have to remember the way this feels.

I turned to the opposite side of the bed. A sweet girl, appearing to be in her early twenties, was sitting upright reading a book.

"Hi. What are you doing?" I asked.

She looked up at me, with wide eyes, from the seat of her metal folding chair. She paused a moment, gently replied, "I'm reading."

Well, I could see *that*. I wanted to know *what* she was reading, and why was she perched next to me. Did I know her? I decided in my head, she must be training for school. That would explain the textbook. Wait…is this chick on suicide watch duty? Oh no! I've crossed over into the realm of "might hang themselves with a sheet" status! How did this happen? I'll just smile at her, as if I'm normal.

"I just got here," I shared as if we had just been seated for a show. "When did you get here?" I asked.

She looked at me with a baffle in her eyes and replied, "a little bit ago."

I nodded with recognition. I guess we'll have to see what happens next. Over the next few hours the staff played phone tag with my doctor who prescribed the Ambien. They thought he should know I accidentally took a few extra pills, and wasn't closely adhering to the "do not take with alcohol" labeling. During this waiting period, Kane went home, bathed, and picked up some fresh clothes for me. I showered at the hospital and washed off the filth from the night before, at least on the surface.

Everyone seemed to be in a big hurry for me to get "back to normal." But I didn't want to go back to normal. I didn't want to forget what I learned. Heck, I was still trying to process it all, and I didn't have the words to explain what had happened. In my memory, it was just a blink of an image, but in that simplicity were embedded worlds of complexity. But the people around me had their version of the truth, because they were conscious here on Earth during the event. But I was conscious during it too, just not in the same dimension as them. How do I put that into words? The more they tell me what happened, the more isolated I feel in my understanding. I want to tell them about the beauty, but they keep talking about depression and fear. They keep talking about pills and prescriptions, and I want to talk about oneness. I want to talk about how special life is and how my heart is filled with joy. But they are focused on some kind of desperation story of hanging on by a thread. I feel similar to when I was a child. The world looks and feels magical again. I am in slow motion, and they are plugged into a system I do not understand. The importance of slowing down, in order to witness and enjoy all this creation. They just don't get it.

I had a few more questions flung my way about drinking. Many people think alcohol leaves your system once it metabolizes, but it can settle in the muscle and fat tissues of the body for up to a month. The pain it causes can stick to the membranes much longer, because trauma gets stuck in the body. I met an elderly man who had "wet brain" and he was like a walking corpse. He managed to go to AA meetings, and was now sober, but his saturated brain was still suffering the damage. He hadn't truly healed.

Once the doctors were convinced I would be supported with continuing care via my psychiatrist, they released me. I made the right choice to get out of there. I wasn't going to receive healing in there, and I sure didn't have another ten grand to blow. I was on my own this time. I better go home and pull it together.

After I slipped into new clothes, my caretaker, Kane walked me out of the sleepover. He thanked the crowd of nurses who hovered near my door. One woman stepped away from the circle, and gave me a bear hug, like a long lost cousin. Her eyes teared as she told me to take care of myself. In my spacey state, I managed to utter, "I will." It dawned on me, she was probably one of the nurses who rolled me down the hallway last night. I thought hospital staff were numbed to idiots like me who try to annihilate themselves. Statistically, they get a few per week.

The warm-hearted nurse hurt because of what I did. We were a young married couple, and yet a tragedy like this had happened already. Maybe she knew someone like me, or was simply an empath. She was a plus-sized lady dressed in a pair of freshly pressed scrubs. I was a complete stranger to her, and yet she cared about what happened to me. As we walked down a quiet, carpeted hallway, I felt their eyes on my back. I sensed them wondering what would happen to me after I walked through the swinging metal doors. I wondered too.

I never guessed the same blue Mustang that scooped me up from Illinois would be carrying me from this spectacle. I needed to stop this unhealthy habit of needing to be rescued. But it felt nice to be willing to lose everything. That's what I wanted to feel. Like I have nothing to lose, say good-bye to all the years that led up to this, so I can have permission to be myself. That's all I ever wanted. To stop caring what other people think, and start caring about what I think. I wanted to create a new story.

The day after almost dying, I went home and took the warmest, coziest, most grateful-to-be-alive nap I had ever had in my whole life. Kane and I lay side by side, gripping each other's tired hands tightly enough to feel the blood of one another's hearts pumping. It was a comforting pulse, filled with gratitude. But the backbeat was still thumping with a residual bump of desperation. Even after an awakening, it takes a lot to rewire the system. They say you must relive the new pattern 300 times for it to resonate anew. As I listened to the ice crackling in the water glass next to me, and felt my cat's warm body nestle between us, I drifted back to sleep.

DSM

There's been a continuous attempt to chart my behavior. Anyone who has been on a similar path, knows how fine the lines of sanity are. Passerby's are happy to help scrutinize. I've filled out a dozen mood charts. "I'm sorry ma'am, looks like you just missed the cut-off for a sound mind. No wait, you're sound. No wait, you're not. If you chose the column with one less day per month, per ten month period, lasting 2-3 hours instead of 4-6 hours in a 48 hour period, then you would just be a typical housewife. As it stands, you are now...*fill in the blank with whatever label is popular this year.* I'm so glad we finally got this diagnosis right for you. Now we can get you on the right meds." Check back in six months and none of this "science" will be valid. But right now, we are going to shame you into paying us. A lifetime of inflammation due to eating processed food, not being breastfed, infant trauma caused by the societal practices of child-rearing, drinking polluted water...and on and on? No, we aren't going to look at the seretonetic connections of your gut-brain connection or root trauma. It's way more profitable to blame you, the victim. And when you have accepted that blame, we will teach you and society how to perpetuate victimhood while we laugh ourselves all the way to the bank. That's us too by the way. We are the Nothing, and we will swallow you all up unless you remember your Light. But who can remember anything when they are in a cloud of forgetting. *Where is your Consciousness, Katie?* I uploaded it to the cloud before I finished reading the black label warning:

Common Side Effects for Common Psychiatric Drugs: Clumsiness, unsteadiness, continuous, uncontrolled, back-and-forth, or rolling eye movements, aggressive behavior or other behavior problems, anxiety, concentration problems, crying, depression, false sense of well-being, hyperactivity or increase in body movements, rapidly changing moods, reacting too quickly, too emotional, or overreacting, restlessness, suspiciousness or distrust, irritability, or other mood or mental changes, confusion, convulsions, blurred vision, dizziness, fainting, cold or flu-like symptoms, delusions, dementia, hoarseness, lack or loss of strength, lower back or side pain, swelling of the hands, feet, or lower legs, trembling or shaking, worsening of depression and/or the emergence of suicidal ideation and behavior (suicidality) or unusual changes in behavior, increased risk of suicide, homicidal ideation, insomnia, ejaculation disorder (primarily ejaculatory delay), nausea, sweating increased, fatigue, somnolence, sensitivity to light, fever, chills, headache, stiff neck, seizure that will not stop, trouble breathing, unusual tiredness or weakness, chest pain, discomfort, or tightness, mask-like face, muscle spasms, nosebleeds, lightheadedness, fast heartbeat, trouble with sleeping, memory loss, hallucination, euphoria, general body swelling, shuffling walk, slowed movement, slurred speech, indigestion, and pain.

Nature, meditation, and yoga? Grow up you fucking hippy. This is science.

Did you take "your meds"? Barf. Oh, you mean the legal pharmaceutical drugs that don't belong to anyone, especially not in my body? Yes, I took those under the guise of being a responsible citizen. I took those according to the program plugged in when I was 4 years old wanting approval for being a "good girl" who did her chores. But I don't have a shortage of Lexapro. I have a shortage of my soul. But I'll take *your* lab-created pill to block out that connection even more, so long as you groom me with your acceptance. You take the pill to block out Consciousness. This is why people feel blank or numb on them. They shut off the receptors, the receptors that bring the human experience to life. I haven't been taught the power of self acceptance-the energetic pill that washes away all need for outside approval, all anxiety, all depression, all feelings of being lost. No, I haven't been taught about the wonder drug covered by my self-assurance-insurance that lives inside me. The most powerful one of all, the free one with no label and no side effects. The one they don't make a commercial for. I need a dose of my Self, and it doesn't come in a child-proof container.

The first doctor I saw in Texas gave me Geodon. I took it one evening and woke up unable to move out of bed. My body was the consistency and weight of wet cement. I crawled through the quicksand of my floor, across the house, and over to the kitchen table. *What is this shit? I can't even move. Fuck this. I'm not taking this. It feels like I've just taken a horse tranquilizer.* Sure, I didn't feel depressed, but even if I was, I literally couldn't lift my arm to pick up a gun. Maybe that was their goal. I couldn't sit upright on the toilet, or open my eyes enough to grab the toilet paper. *This isn't practical. This is like being in a coma. A stay-at-home-coma. Thanks, pharmaceutical company. I see what you did there. Nice one.*

After the Geodon experience, I called nearly every psychiatrist in the state of Texas. There was a shortage in my area. Most were children's shrinks, probably cramming some Adderall down a juvenile's developing throat. On a scale of 1-10, if you are a 1, 2, 9, or 10 you might be on the spectrum, if you can't answer scripted, canned questions in group interviews..if you feel something human..you know what-everyone who isn't an exact five-you get a diagnosis. Private practices had waiting lists as long as the side effect disclaimers on the medication they prescribed. When I finally found Dr. Delair, a large, southern man with friendly wrinkles and silver sideburns, I felt utter relief. His wife was from Ohio, so I had hope he could understand how to best communicate with me and relate to a north plus south marriage.

My heels clacked against the dark mahogany flooring as I waited for my appointment to begin. To my delight the mantels were adorned with statues of the virgin Mary, Shiva, Buddha, and other spiritual icons. The multi-cultural religious acceptance was reassuring. If more than one perception was possible in this office, then maybe there was room for me, too.

Dr. Delair was always sweaty, as most people are in grueling southern heat. Little pearls of moisture would form on his brow when he told me we had yet to see if I would "take root" in Texas. I told him about the Geodon, and he responded, "Well, that's like taking a sledgehammer to a cockroach." I tilted my head and looked perplexed. What the heck does that even mean?

He said, "It's overkill. That drug is too strong for you. It's not working for your body chemistry. That medication is for people with severe Bipolar disorder. Maybe you don't fall under that category. Sometimes medication helps us narrow things down. Based on the history you described, I think you are experiencing some obvious PTSD symptoms."

"I feel like an unbalanced version of me right now, and I don't know how to get back to who I was, or who I'm supposed to be. I feel like *I* got hit with a sledgehammer, especially this past year."

"We need to treat the anxiety and panic. Remember, it's not the label that matters, it's the symptoms. You can address those in many ways, but we'll start with prescriptions, talk things out, and take it from there," Dr. Delair assured.

"I was told the anxiety, depression, and panic are the result of growing up in an alcoholic family dynamic. We were always walking on pins and needles. I was an obvious scapegoat. Then that incident last year, with the sexual assault…that put me over the edge," I shared, hoping he would understand.

"Yes, ma'am, that is what I think caused the PTSD. It has created anxiety around feeling safe at work, since it happened to you at work. If you can't move around the world and be alone in a room with a boss, how could you feel safe. It was an unfortunate experience. The legal system was likely an unfortunate experience for you as well. Most survivors of sexual assault feel shame, fear, and a challenge to reintegrate after such an event," he communicated.

"Yes, that's how I feel. I fought so hard, but no one wanted to get involved. I had just met Kane, so I moved to Texas. It seems like things got worse," I shared.

"Well, you never had time to heal. Let's slow things down for you. Get your nervous system calm. Baby steps," he suggested. He looked at me with the endearing eyes of a father, "We are going to get you back on track, little lady. You have your whole life ahead of you. I have a feeling this is just a hiccup. Time will tell."

His solution was a mixture of four different prescriptions. Gabapentin and Lexapro for the daily maintenance of anxiety and depression, Xanax as needed, and at first, Ambien to sleep. It was an arm sling for my brain, but I tried it. I'd take arm sling over gurney for the time being.

Panic is a nightmare, and nothing seems to help it when you're in the grips of an attack. It starts with jagged flutters in the heart, then the battery acid rises from the gut, burning the throat and settling in the temples, disturbing the activity of my brain. The wiring short circuits and then my eyes begin to dart around, desperately clocking every danger. No thought processes are involved at all. It's simply a clockwork of horror. Enter Xanax. *Get to the pill. Swallow. Wait fifteen minutes before you do or say anything. Just wait.* It washes away the red, each and every time. But it is a band-aid to a deluge of repressed emotions. Can I learn to eliminate the panic altogether? I want to teach myself how to not need the pill. That is my ultimate goal. To get to the root of the matter, and heal that. Return to a state where there is no panic, like when I was a child laying in the green grass.

Dr. Delair was a hoot. He was a deacon for the Catholic Church, but he never preached to me about religion. He thought spirituality was a positive outlet for a healthy life, but that's about all he said on the matter. He had eight children. While out with my husband, I saw them all together at the movie theatre. He had a warm, patient, and yet matter of fact demeanor, like a favorite uncle.

The routine appointments were routine. There was a comfort in knowing that, on schedule, Dr. Delair would be there to talk and realign me. He coached me how to taper off the pharmaceuticals when I was ready to start trying for a baby. He was very conservative in that respect. He said, "You are starting with one single cell, that divides and multiplies. The first thing to develop is the nervous system, the spinal cord. You don't want to mess with that."

I appreciated his respect for the creation of life. "Things have been calming down for you. When it's time, you will be okay. That's my assessment," he shared.

I had an appointment with him the week after I had my first miscarriage. It was a hot summer day in August, and I was on a mission. I felt the loss of my baby like an anvil had been tied to my leg and thrown off a skyscraper. Shitty things happen to me, I told myself in a state of numbness. I trucked on over to the local animal shelter and found the tiniest black kitten they had. She was adorable and coming home with me, but only after a quick stop at my appointment with Dr. Delair.

The secretary in his office was an animal lover. When the poofy-haired Miss Kandi, saw the tiny creature her eyes widened behind her thick glasses. My last appointment with my favorite uncle doctor was spent with all three of us juggling this adorable ebony kitten with golden eyes. The secretary watched her for the first half of the appointment and let her run and climb all over the front desk. About half-way through, she brought her into the appointment room. Dr. Delair gave a deep belly laugh as the kitten climbed over his powder blue thinking couch and up his dusty bookshelf. The doctor had lost weight; his formerly plump cheeks visibly hollowing out and dark circles deepening under his eyes, but he said his wife had put him on one of her famous diets.

With a voice gentle with compassion, he said a kitten was a nice remedy for the loss of a baby. "It's hard to be sad with a fluffy creature, tickling and cuddling up with you every step of the way," he soothed. "When you are ready, you can try again for a baby. Children are even more fulfilling than a kitten. More work, but deeply gratifying." I left reborn, full of hope to try again for a life bubbling with the innocence of a child's reality into my home.

I didn't get the chance to tell him I was pregnant again. I was about seven months along and off medication when I got the letter in the mail that Dr.

Delair had died of leukemia. Another loss. I buried my sadness. His wife sent a letter saying he had been diagnosed about a year earlier, but wanted to keep treating his patients because it brought him great joy, and a will to live. He did not want to hinder our progress with his personal challenges. So, he kept seeing patients until he couldn't, and he died shortly thereafter.

I don't know whether I grieved more for my miscarried baby or for Dr. Delair. Did I grieve at all, or did I shove it deep down inside me? Therapists are an important extension of your support system, and sometimes they can feel closer than family. He was a giving man who loved helping people even more. Who would guide me now that he was gone? I must accept he was a marker on the path, but not the path itself. I had to move on. His advice settled in my heart. His words took root, even if I didn't.

Channel Changer

It comes in like a wave. I feel the cool breeze and the smell of salt in the air. As I playfully jump in the ocean, sand between my toes, I feel ecstatic and am loving life. Then a little mist hits my skin. It feels good at first. Tingles. All the same, it's a hint of what's to come. The ocean is about to swallow me, but not before it smacks me around a bit. The situations fluctuate, and I don't know how to avoid the sway. This is just my life, I've told myself.

Something trivial like a wood chip could turn into an oak board that whacks me right in the face. I get blind sided, frequently. The nerves come back, zinging up and down my arms and legs. The blood beats against the walls of my arteries, and I become hyper aware of the heart pounding in my chest. What did I do wrong now? There must be a grizzly bear chasing me. I feel like I just got "Pulp Fictioned" with an adrenaline needle. I do not want to live in fight or flight anymore.

Someone changed the channel to the ten most annoying stations and turned the volume to max. To make matters worse, everyone around me is expecting me to "behave normal." I can't focus with this noise. Living in downtown Chicago was quieter than this. Even the countless ambulances, fire trucks, horns honking, L trains, people talking in the alley and pissing on dumpsters at 3AM, became background noise after a while. This? There's nothing background about this. This is all foreground chaos.

Kane's words confuse me. They flip and turn, twist and burn. The inconsistency is torture, like sleep deprivation tactics at Guantanamo Bay. The noise softens and stills, then *boom*, the volume gets cranked when I least expect it. The ringing in my ears could shatter glass. Arduous self-improvement procedures seem to lengthen the process, and I have to be at work. I want to smash all of the clocks. Skip the protocol. It's time to reprogram.

"I forget how hard it is until it happens again," a vet tech recently told me. She was referring to the death of a pet, but that is a good analogy. I forget how chaotic Kane and I's life can be, then one day, it blows over and life goes on, like nothing ever happened. Just a flick of a switch on the remote control.

Triptych II:

The Garden of Light and Dark

Tastebud

"I want to be a nun!" I cheered to Mom. I was eight and it was my first spiritual calling.

My mother, a devout Catholic, looked at me with horror as she warned, "But nuns can't get married or have children." That didn't register as a concern for me. What she was trying to say was, "You won't ever be able to have sex!"

I was consoled by my Higher Self, and patted on the head, as I accepted my mother's disapproval of my desire. My future Self knew I was a voyeuristic, exhibitionistic, sexual heathen, destined for sketchy parking lots. The path of a monk was never for me. Masturbation, yes. Monk, no.

I sat in the yellow pine pews, worn smooth by followers, staring at the electric blue carpet, juxtaposed with soft murals of angels floating around a beautiful hippy holding his sacred heart. I listened to the words of the priest, encouraging us to listen to the voice of Jesus.

He would say, "Jesus is all around you, and inside your heart." I pictured a miniature Jesus standing in the chambers of my heart, a dwarf sized clubhouse for Jesus to reside in throughout my school day. He was usually leaning against the wall, glancing up at me like a Bop magazine cover model. Tiny Jesus.

I had a different understanding of "God." The traditional religious teachings never jived with me. Only a few lessons resonated, like the teaching that God was everywhere, all the time, always has been and always will be. As a child, Eternity was fairly accessible to wrap my head around. I absorbed the notion that God loves without judgment, along with the seemingly simplistic mantra, "God is Love," which, to me, epitomizes hidden complexity in plain sight.

I knew the other lessons of punishment, guilt, and judgment were bullshit. The two concepts of God could not coexist. The negative was hypocritical, and translated as an afterthought. I sought out hubs of like-minded people in the spiritual realm. Why did this feel like an underground sub-culture, while the swindlers on stage hypnotized the mainstream with fear? I favored the grittier clubs. Give me the dive bar of Enlightenment. Invite me to the church with fire and nudity, sacred geometry and strangers, that meets in the jungle after dark.

Likewise, I didn't believe in Hell. Grandma agreed. A priest once told her, "Hell is on Earth." I was surprised a priest said this, but not shocked at the meaning under his words. I enjoy insight that is free from indoctrination. The human experience seems to be on a plane that mingles with darkness.

A boyfriend philosophized, "Hell is how far away you are from the Light." I liked that. It insinuated you have a choice in the matter. And the choice isn't reliant on you avoiding punishment. It is more akin to leaning into the light of home. Finding True North when you are cold and lost. Returning to the embers of your creation.

During a month-long punishment of being grounded in high school, I planned an adventure for myself. The only place I was allowed to go to was the library. In the back of one of the Outdoors magazines was an ad for Outward Bound. I recognized the name of this organization. A classmate went on a trip with them. As a sixteen-year-old, I wrote to the organization, received brochures, and began training for my two-week backcountry hiking journey. Sometimes goals are the best distractions. And it never hurts to be in good physical shape. It led to a pivotal experience that opened my eyes. It was my first guided meditation.

Towards the end of the trip we went on a solo hike. I got to be alone in nature, for a full 24 hours, somewhere in the Rocky Mountains near Durango. The afternoon prior to our solo excursion we sat in a circle and did a visualization to prepare us. Our guide took us through a process of contemplating our size, relative to our immediate surroundings. "Imagine yourself larger than the blades of grass, grains of soil, and petals of a Columbine flower. Then realize you are smaller than the Evergreen trees, the mountain side, and the Rocky Mountain range," he suggested. Then he expanded the comparison to the body of land that made up our country, and the Earth. Leaving our bodies on the mountainside, we were to allow our mind to continue moving upward, to a bird's eye view, from outer space, and gaze back down upon ourselves. Now, as a part of the solar system, we were but a small dot in the universe, smaller than the initial grain of soil.

It was the first time I'd heard an adult describe his own insignificance. Our guide, Auden, shared, "I have to make it to the back country at least twice a year to remind myself of the impermanence of it all. You have to periodically distance yourself from the materialism. Nature helps you regain perspective."

I didn't know grown-ups thought this way, let alone encouraged it. One day I'll come back to this place, I thought. The mountains. I love them.

I admire those who can deny themselves material possessions. Those who can unplug their brain from the overwhelming flood of culture insisting we put utmost importance on *things*. It's a trap. I want to harness a feeling. Materials provide instant gratification, but they are fleeting in their fulfillment. Even identities and labels are manifest things that eventually dissolve.

My adolescent draw to nunnery stemmed from a desire to make people feel happy. Giving smiles, hugs, and love would be a wonderful way to spend a life. At eight, I felt the difference between the spike in joy one experienced from a new Barbie, and the resounding peace that warmed me when I shared a heartfelt embrace and exchanged a message of love with my eyes. My list to Santa may not have reflected this, but I didn't need to ask him for something I already had.

In the past I have burned through a stack of cash like many others. It's not hard to do just to have a roof over your head. But *they* call it a symptom. I thought it was an Ikea commercial. Christmas season? Being festive? Fitting in. Giving in. Get that loot before it's gone. And when it's gone, it's gone. And so are you.

In middle school, I learned about the sixties and hippies living in communes. My affinity for the non-traditional received hope. My solar plexus exploded with recognition, *yes, I like that. Sounds like a good plan. Enough with small town suburbia.* I came across a book about Timothy Leary, the Harvard psychologist who led studies using LSD and Psilocybin for psychiatric therapy. My twelve year old self was already requesting peer-reviewed studies and valued his credentials. I eventually found the tribe I was seeking, though they were spread out across decades and chapters of my life. My tribe…they are a nomadic people. Some die, some live. They've all breathed fire.

A high school friend landed in Taos, New Mexico, building Earthships. I flew out for a visit at age 19. Andrew had a rusty, tan colored 1980s era Subaru, complete with a faux wool steering wheel cover. It was his girlfriend's mother's car. Come on, hippies don't have their own cars. We all know that. *Blister In The Sun* by the Violent Femmes played on the radio. As we drove up a winding, dusty dirt road the golden sun spiraled behind the foothills, casting a blazing blanket over the little cottage we were aiming for. We arrived at his girlfriend's parents' house on the mountainside.

We smoked a hay bale of the most pungent herb, delighting ourselves into a cannabis coma. I was hypnotized by the glowing cherry crackling its way towards my upper lip, sizzling through the herb's spirit like a mower through a lawn of dandelions. We hung out in the den of an artist, a father figure, and a painter, until I couldn't see straight.

I managed to sneak past Andrew's girlfriend's parents and carefully climb up a ladder and fall asleep in a cozy loft. I woke to the sounds of Flamenco dancing below me. Castanets clicking the tune of a new day. I had cast a request for the colorful ribbons of life, and the Universe delivered. The following nights I slept in the "The Castle", which was a giant Earthship built to resemble a castle, with aluminum cans left exposed, like apocalyptic bricks. Average doesn't flow through habitats like this. Free spirits, vaga-bonds, drifters, dreamers, outcasts, and idealists leave their watermarks along the walls.

To truly sink myself into the off-grid bliss of limitless possibilities, I must expand. Dan was my go-to person for this option.

"I can't believe you hang out with Dan outside of the party realm. Are you like, friends with him?" my college friends probed with raised eye-brows. He was a war veteran from the 90s, and they were convinced he was a few screws loose.

"Of course! He's super interesting," I offered them. I could connect and vibe with Dan in a way others seemed to struggle to access. Dan and I took hikes and dropped acid. But we never drank alcohol together. He said alcohol was too low of a frequency for him, and on some level I understood that.

Dan and I were bosom buddies. We took a road trip to the wilderness of the Pacific Northwest late summer and he gave me my first shooting lesson.

What better teacher than an Iraqi War Veteran? First, he showed me how to hold his semi-automatic rifle. I was concerned about a stray bullet shooting a hiker or someone off in the 400-yard distance range. Dan showed me how to use the scope and encouraged me to pull the trigger and go for it.

"You're a natural!" he exclaimed. I hit the tree we lined out to be my target. I guess the visual acuity that made me a skilled softball player served my marksmanship skills as well. Although I had ear protection, the sound it gave off was louder and higher than I imagined. It rippled through my body like a vibrating wave. I can see how people get fixed on this feeling. With a surge of adrenaline still pumping through me I said, "Wow, that was powerful! I feel like this could do some damage."

My friend looked at me with austerity and said, "That's the point."

Next he showed me how to shoot his handgun at close range. I hit pretty darn close to the target, which was a dead tree stump. The handgun was a little clunky, and heavier than I expected, but I could see how people would like these as well. I imagine that's why I chose to stay away from them from that point on.

Dan said, "It's not the guns that make veterans come back with PTSD. It's seeing the way things really work that's hard to integrate. Impossible to integrate, because it's just plain wrong."

Tripping with Dan felt like staring into my own soul for the first time. I could be one hundred percent weird and awkward around him, and somehow it felt safe and welcome.

"Hey Katie! What kind of tea would you like?" He would ask, in his gentle voice, as he opened a cabinet filled with non-caffeinated options. He leaned in for a hug that locked in a long healing pause. This warmed my heart and soul. Dan, in a room full of tapestries that breathed, allowed me to nervously play with my hair, fidget through sitting positions on his couch, and giggle at socially inappropriate times.

"Come on over! Okay, heads up, I'm in the bathtub, so just come in," Dan said over the phone. He had a hit of LSD waiting for me on his kitchen counter. I let myself in and chilled on his couch until it kicked in. Then I laid in his hallway, and contemplated the meaning of his wallpaper, which transformed into Egyptian hieroglyphics.

"How long have you been in the tub," I asked him.

"A few hours. I like to soak with these Epsom salts to raise my vibration. Then I can connect with the intergalactic entities. They want to dance in the limbo with me," he feathered out. These were summer Saturdays with Dan. He was too much for some, but just right as my best friend.

We laughed in amusement at the oddities of being human. I felt like I had tapped into a state of mind, or consciousness that was familiar, yet unspoken in other circles. We had a cosmic kinship, and joked of the secret messages our star-struck selves tried to send down to spark a memory of who we really are and where we really came from.

As we sat on his front porch steps, one psychedelic Saturday, a delivery truck with the logo advertising "Milky Way" chocolate bars drove by, and we burst into awe. There's a sign! It's literally a sign. But it's also a *sign*. Clutching each other, we bent over in fits of laughter, tears streaming, and voices breaking in high-pitched hilarity. It's comical. It's celestial. Does it feel a little psychotic? There's a fine line, when pushing the boundaries. I try to hover in an oasis of Stephen Hawking, rather than dive into a black hole with John Nash.

Dan was the first one to talk with me about the concept of everything and everyone being connected. The familiarity was a blanket of comfort long before I'd had the courage to discuss these internal concepts and beliefs with anyone else. If I had ever whispered an inkling of this knowing in my old circles of friends it would have been met with a blank bewildered stare. Suffice to say, these are not new and outlandish concepts anymore.

Dan compared, "collective consciousness is like being a part of a much larger body." He said, "We are like a tiny, little taste bud on the infinite body of consciousness. We are all performing and existing as one, however, like a tiny hair on the top of your big toe, you are performing within your niche, completely unaware of your place in relation to the greater body."

I heard him, but I never really "got it," until later.

I still get swept away with memories of Dan on warm summer evenings. I reminisce about staying up all night, watching fireflies calling to their mates in the Midwest country fields. Like itsy bitsy glowing spaceships of love, they land to meet their lovers atop blades of grass. I watch it play in my mind. I feel the thick humidity swell my face and cool grass tickle my bare legs, beneath my cut-off jeans. I know the feeling of my flip flops dangling off my suntanned toes. I watch the oak trees sway in the soft midnight breeze, leaves turning into peacock feathers that become hundreds of pupils gazing back at me. The whole Earth breathes. It is alive.

My ability to sync up with people on the same wave-length is just as miraculous, magical, and seemingly implausible as an insect who puts out an iridescent signal to locate its match. My code of light pulses until my equals detect the signal. We silently seek each other with our neon flickering Morse code. In the course of time, we find each other. Illuminated.

Sunny Side Up

I'm looking for the light at the end of the tunnel. Right now I'm stuck, and it's dark, with frightful noises echoing at every curve. I'm afraid I'll never make it to the other side. But the tunnel is a vortex of growth. Bravery pushes when my resolve is weak, but trust is the magic carpet effortlessly carrying me farther. Every time I've arrived at the opening on the other side, the light is brighter than before I went in. It's the illumination of a new reality. A layer of color I never knew existed.

My heart never stopped, but I was reborn a few times. It wasn't a religious "Born Again Christian" scenario. It took more than mumbling some promises to God to birth a new version of myself. *A palm forcefully smacks me on the forehead*, "Healed!!!" I didn't plan a spiritual awakening. Something happened, without me expecting it. I woke up, just like I woke up from the previous world I came from when I was a baby. And when this happened, I was someone different, and yet the truest Self I always was. I wish it happened as quickly as a smack on the forehead. In reality, it's more like a cyclical process. The "healing spiral"…it's the number one ride at the amusement park.

I couldn't un-see my revelations when I was sixteen, but I could only go so far at that age. They were a peek. I met Lisa in high school art class. My new best friend warned me, once I dosed, I could never go back. She said my mind would stretch and I couldn't return to thinking the way I did before. I had a slight concern about my brain being turned into mush, but a tiny drop of apprehension has never been known to stop me.

My short, curly red-haired friend was wise beyond her years, at least when it came to LSD. Her body suffered the crippling soreness of an elderly person, due to Rheumatoid Arthritis, but you would never know. She rarely complained, and only explained her condition to me once. Smoking cannabis helped soothe the aching, but that was before medical marijuana was legal. In the 1990s, you were simply labeled a stoner. I felt like a six-year-old when I was with her, like the world was a huge playground to run around, laugh, and be happy in. Or maybe that was the acid. In any case, the sun was always brighter after we hung out.

I lost touch with Lisa for a few years when she got married and had a couple of kids. Then, right as she came back onto my radar I found myself reading her obituary. It stated complications from a lifelong battle with chronic arthritis. I'm not sure what kind of healing she sought out, but I hope her expanded awareness gave her a fuller life than most people experience in eighty years.

The expansion unbolted a gate for me. I looked through it, but was afraid to step across the opening. The voices were still telling me, *none of that bliss is real. Do what you're told, and don't you dare dream about the other side.*

Dilated pupils, dilated dreams. Psychedelics can wake a person up and loosen the programs that confine our understanding of existence. This is not the only way, but it's one of them. I won't take so many of them that I wind up staring at the bread rack for four hours at the local grocery store on a Saturday afternoon. Especially if it's twenty years after I've stopped dosing. Legend says, the high school quarterback of my uncle's era took one too many hits and became the bread contemplator. He was a cautionary tale, much like the health class video that warned us about becoming the guy who stared at a brass doorknob for eight hours because he thought it was an orange. That doesn't sound very enlightening. Set and setting were not with him on that day.

I haven't reached enlightenment. Peeks of dillusionment, sure, enlightenment—let's not get ahead of ourselves. I'm also of the belief that preparation is key. It determines what can be unlocked. In high school there was little prep work, other than, "get ready to see some cool shit while we're tripping balls." That kind of mindset lacks the honor and dignity necessary to precede any attempt to expand your mind, allow consciousness to speak to you, or heal your soul.

In my mid-thirties, I went through a more organic tunnel. The sun blinded me as I passed through the opening. When confined to a room in a hospital, it seems like years pass before crossing the threshold to the outside world again. Muffled sounds coddled me in my room while the random beeping of machines became the ticking of a timeless clock. Time has no meaning inside a hospital room. The world floats by, as time submits to an automatic loop in my room. The outside world ceased to matter. I watched the trees blowing outside my window, but nothing in my sterile room was alive. Except me, and a new human. In our cocoon, about to blossom.

I had been reading all about giving birth, each stage of development in utero-fascinating things I had never been taught. I remember seeing the stages of a fetus' growth in jars filled with formaldehyde in the Museum of Science and Industry. As a child I asked my mother, how they got the babies in there. She said they had to get special permission. They were babies that died during pregnancy. They were translucent, all spine with grey eyes forming under the skin. Having one inside of me growing felt like there was an unknown being latching on, and then it shifted. I felt overwhelming love, then anger, then exhaustion, then warmth, headaches, then all-consuming "nesting" urges. Hormones are amazing. They guided me through the process. They unified us. Within those first few months, my baby and I became one, and that is a process I don't think a man will ever understand. How could they? After twenty years of having a monthly bleed, I didn't even understand it, until I went through it. And that is why I honor it so much. I honor mothers and their bond with their children. No one taught my body how to unify with my baby-it just did it. THAT is Divine wisdom.

As a science teacher, I hear them trying to explain it away like a series of chemical releases and functions in the brain, like they do when people have near-death experiences. But there was something else, in both occurrences. There was a spiritual aspect. A soul aspect. A Divine love that goes beyond any dissection of anatomy. This is the part Western medicine doesn't address, and that is why I knew we weren't completely safe in their hands. I spoke with my cousin who had had a natural home birth. She was enrolling her son in a Waldorf preschool in Colorado. She sent me raspberry leaf tea and some other tips, which I appreciated. I didn't know her well, but she seemed to be the only one who knew what I was researching. Apparently other women just didn't look. Or they only looked at mainstream information I guess. But when I mentioned my curiosity about home birth to my husband and the grandparents, they were opposed. They took agency over my pregnancy.

"That's our grandbaby too! You could lose the baby trying to take risks like that!" they would say. And then they wove in the paths of the past. "Haven't you taken enough risks, Katie? Why would you do that? Be smart for the sake of your baby," I was guilted. But I was smart. I had dove deeper into the information than them, and I lived through some of the research as a personal guinea pig. So why couldn't I trust myself and ignore them? In the past I wouldn't have had to ignore anyone. I would have been surrounded by mothers, elders, doulas, midwives, and townspeople as they guided me through this rite of passage.

I was always health conscious. My process with asthma had led me to various philosophies and nutritional practices. I was into healing root causes, and therefore aware that birth is a root beginning, and I took this very seriously for the life I was bringing into the world. My choices and the way I did things, would imprint her immediately. As an educator, I knew about this through the lens of child development, and I was forming opinions about public school as well. The programming didn't appeal to me. I had questions about if the system was natural or healthy. Working as a teacher while pregnant didn't feel healthy. All I wanted to do was rest and take care of the life inside of me. I wanted to be present.

At this stage I was convinced a return to the natural science of organic food from the earth was the healthiest, most scientifically perfect nutrition available. I was engulfed in gentle and attachment parenting. Due to the my background with anxiety, I wanted to take every measure to prevent my daughter from developing those tendencies. I had gone down the environmentalist rabbit holes, and now I dove down the pregnancy one. I watched *The Business of Being Born* and I had a flashback of all the trauma Western medicine had caused me with asthma and depression. It seems the medical field had its grip on the process of pregnancy too. They medicalized a natural process. My father would say, "thank god they have hospitals now, back in the dark ages women and children would die during childbirth." And although that was true to some degree, it wasn't the full picture. Many women die due to interventions during labor. This documentary was showing the full picture. Capitalism and for-profit medical procedures got its greedy hands into the process of giving birth. And profitable it is. Humans are always being born, and since they got rid of the midwives, they now had an entire population of women without wisdom being passed down. And no woman wants to go against the system and be told she's a negligent mother. That's the biggest threat of all, and it's been effective on separating us from our own process of birthing children.

I discovered Ina May Gaskin. I wanted to know more. I searched for midwives near me. It turns out, the Christian community I was so opposed to, were the only ones having home births with midwives. They weren't vaccinating their babies either. They believed in the divine intelligence of god to protect them. I wasn't sure if I had THAT kind of trust, but I did understand pharmaceuticals could do more harm than good in many cases, and the medical field had often pressured me into doing things that were unsafe for my body. Birth control was a disaster for me, and likely contributed to much of my mood dysregulation over the years. So I was curious. I called around, but due to the rural location I was in, and how far along I was, I couldn't hire a midwife or doula to assist my birth near the due date. I was devastated, and horrified after watching that documentary. The best I could do was stay calm and come up with a birth plan. Surely, they would honor my written birth plan.

"Kane, I don't want to do all the things they are going to suggest," I shared with my husband.

"That's the hormones talkin'. Everything is going to be fine," he said as he played his video game. Kane was handling his stress over impending fatherhood by playing hours on end of video games. He would come to bed at 3AM on weeknights. I knew because I hardly slept for nine months. First it was the headaches, then the nausea, then the sheer discomfort of having my skin stretched and organs crammed into my ribs. The last three months I had constant heartburn. I tasted stomach acid around the clock. It burned my throat, and all people could say was, "that means the baby has lots of hair."

People weren't nearly as kind as I thought they would be to a pregnant woman. I felt I had to wear my wedding band all the time, despite how snug it was on my swollen fingers. I didn't want anyone to think I was pregnant out of wedlock. They would be even less polite if that were the case. I flew home for a baby shower Mom was throwing for me. I planed alone. Just me and baby. Hardly anyone opened a door for me. It was more like they were annoyed with a pregnant lady being near them. I felt it. But why did they act this way? Like I was a nuisance? When did this shift take place in society? On that particular flight, take off was delayed for an hour on the runway. We were supposed to stay seated so it could take off immediately when cleared. But like any pregnant lady, I had to pee. The baby was squishing my bladder, and so it could barely hold much urine at this stage. That was the other thing about being pregnant I didn't expect. The 24/7 sensation of having to urinate. It was highly distracting and uncomfortable. Try to work with that feeling or sleep. All I could think was, "men and women aren't equal. They aren't equally experiencing this at work, and yet I'm still getting paid less."

"I have to use the restroom," I told the flight attendant.

"I'm sorry ma'am, we could take off any moment. You'll have to wait," he replied.

"We've been sitting here for 30 minutes. I can't wait. Like physically, it's about to be not possible," I said with irritation.

"I'm sorry but it's not allowed. You'll have to wait until the pilot takes off the stay seated light," the flight attendant said sternly.

"Are you serious? I'm might pee on this seat," I mumbled as he walked away.

Then I got up and waddled in between the tightly packed seats. People were sweaty and growing impatient, and oh great now here comes the pregnant lady. I could feel them praying to themselves, "I hope she doesn't go into labor during our flight."

In comparison to how people responded when I told them I was pregnant, they weren't nearly as excited in my daily life. There was no honoring the woman bringing life into the world. I picked up on that. I remember my neighbor's comment when I was a kid, stating how women who had more than three were "baby factories." I guess human life is only special within certain constructs, according to our culture. I was still getting the message that babies, children, and pregnant mothers were meant to be seen and not heard, or hidden altogether. I felt shame in public as a pregnant woman, and that wasn't what I expected. I was pressured to start having children after marriage, and after having one miscarriage, then trying for year without birth control, this was not the response I had anticipated.

However, I liked feeling the baby kick. That was amazing. I could see it happen. Her little foot or elbow would move across my stomach.

"Kane! She's moving! Come quick!" I would shout to him. A few times he made it down the hallway. This part amazed him.

"It's like *Alien vs Predator*. That thing is in there!" He exclaimed.

"Stop! She's not an alien!" I would say.

"I know, I know. Does it hurt? She must be getting big," he commented. He looked as though he couldn't fully comprehend what was happening. And I think that's how parenthood starts, and it never really ends.

I would play our baby classical music at night time…anything to support her development. I sang little songs to her so she would know my voice. My voice outside the classroom, barking at middle school students. If babies experience all we do while pregnant, then despite my soft music playing at night, this little being had been taken through a daily whirlwind rounding up kids in my 7th grade science classes. In the early stages when I had morning sickness, which really lasts all day for three months, we were dissecting baby sharks and cow eyeballs. I would close my door and lay on the floor on my break periods. The odor of formaldehyde overwhelming me with its smell of death. The opposite of what I wanted to experience. It was absolute torture. In the later months, I would sit on my spinning chair and let the kids do the reading and passing out of papers. I was short of breath and I think they all felt lucky I hardly graded a thing that semester. Honestly, my brain was in such a pregnancy fog it's a wonder I accomplished anything. I floated through my day in a haze. That's what the hormones do. They create a bubble for you and baby. Nothing else matters. That becomes your existence. Bonding. Every cell. Every moment. Day and night, for nine months straight. There is no 50/50 split. There is no equal division. This is between me and baby. We are one in this experience of becoming, growing, and birthing.

"I'm serious Kane. I need you to stand by me, because they are gonna try to make us do things, but we can say no," I pleaded for his focus.

"Alright Katie, what do you want to do?" He asked.

"I want to be able to move positions. They say its easiest to give birth in a squatting position. So I want to do that for as long as possible. I don't want an epidural. They are bad. They lead to all kinds of interventions that could lead to a c-section, and I do not want that. It's important for the baby to come out the birth canal. I read about it. It helps their lungs and helps build their immune system with the flora exposure," I informed him. "This is my responsibility and I want to make sure these doctors don't fuck it up."

"Um, okay? I thought the epidural took the pain away. Why is it bad again?" Kane wondered as he was distracted by his game pinging for him to keep playing.

"It's in the spine and I don't want to be paralyzed. It's the path of the Divine fluid. There's lots of reasons. I'm writing it in the birth plan. No epidural. And no vaccines for the baby. I haven't had one while pregnant. We already talked about that part. Did you read the articles I gave you? Do you have any other thoughts?" I asked.

"Yeah okay, write it down. And of course, I'm not letting them stick the baby full of stuff. Fuck the government. I haven't done any of those shots for decades. We got less than half of what they are doing now it looks like. If anything we could wait. It seems strange they do it to a newborn. Sheesh, let the kid see the sunlight first," Kane commented. "I don't even go to the doctor anymore after I slipped that disc in my back. They wanted to do back surgery. I watched that screw up every man I've ever worked with.

Backs messed up forever after that disc surgery. I fixed it myself with a few chiropractor appointments and my own stretches at home. I can't imagine if I had followed my original doctor's advice. Fuckin' nut jobs with knives."

He had similar views, but they didn't come from exactly the same place as mine. Due to being the woman carrying the baby and my history with autoimmune issues like asthma and allergies, I had strong convictions why I didn't want interferences that would cause over-activations of her immune responses. I understood inflammation, and wanted to avoid it from the get-go. Kane was on board. That side of his "Texas Secede" programming made sense for us. He didn't even want them to have a social security number. He posed to opt out. We actually looked into it. We got them, but the process of looking into the actual laws was certainly interesting. We didn't leave one page unturned when thinking of this baby's future.

"Are we gonna school her is the bushes of the forest too, sweetheart?" Kane asked with a smile.

"Preferably. You know how I feel about public schools after working as a teacher. Just read 'Dumbing us Down.' You'll never be the same," I replied.

"I'll let you do the reading. All she needs is a dirt bike and a dream," Kane laughed, "I'm going to show her all of my favorite jet ski spots when she turns two."

He was warming up to the idea of his little girl, and just in time. "Montessori, Waldorf or homeschool. I think that's the only way to bypass all the nonsense. But we'll see. We got to get her here first. Find out what she thinks," I smiled as I held my tummy. "I want her to be able to play outside for hours if she wants."

It started at midnight. They say babies come in the middle of the night, and here she was coming. I felt the cramping start. It was a tidal wave that washed over me. The pain started as a soft roar, and then increased with intensity. The sensation was completely foreign, and the unfamiliarity added to the heightened sensations. But a calm washed over me too, like getting a tattoo. First the pain, then the body releases endorphins to assist. When I had a contraction, the world stopped. I couldn't even access what the pain or sensation was. It was like I was being set aside, and a wave of energy from somewhere else was passing over me. Through me. During the cramping I was powerless. I remembered they said to breathe, so I did, slowly. Then I moaned into a surrender of sorts. And when the cramping stopped, I felt fine. I actually put on make up. To have the baby. Something familiar. It calmed me. Then I got my bag ready.

"Kane, it's happening," I nudged him as he slept. He had come to sleep early that night and was in the bed konked out. But I was wide awake.

"What? Are you in labor? Do we need to leave now? He asked with a yawn.

"Yes, I'm in labor. But the contractions are still ten minutes apart. I've been up for an hour with them," I said.

"Okay, lay down. Let's wait a little longer," he consoled.

I tried to lay next to him, but I was so antsy. It was happening. My body was doing this amazing thing and I was filled with emotions. Fear, excitement, love, anticipation, and aloneness. I looked down at my belly and rubbed my hand over her. "It's time little girl. We are gonna do this together," I said to my baby. And that was the truth. Kane was here, but it was the baby and I who would go through the physical experience together. This was a tunnel for two.

"Oh god Kane, it's getting bad. This one hurts," I cried in fear.

"What? Okay, I'm up. I'm gonna start the car. It's okay," Kane said with more alertness. The tone of my voice had cued him into awareness.

While he was in the garage the pain paused and I went into the bathroom. And that's when it happened. The gush. I was in my nightgown with no underwear and it just poured out of me onto the tile with a splash. It was a feeling of relief. My water had broken, and the pressure it had been creating in my body was temporarily relieved. Then quickly followed by a more acute, tender, visceral pain with the next contraction.

"Kaaane, help me!" I yelled to him.

"What happened? Did your water break? Are you okay?" He scrambled through concerns as I stood in shock staring at the pool of water.

"Yes that's the water. That's okay. But the contractions. Kane it's so bad. It hurts so much," I tried to tell him. But talking itself hurt. The pain was the type of pain that made you feel like you would pass out. Things went white for a few seconds, and my body felt like it wasn't shaped right. I was being twisted in half. I felt it. It was happening on the inside.

Kane got me into the car. We had a thirty minute drive to the next town where the hospital was. There was no way I was putting on that seat belt. My belly was burning. I felt like I could rip a door right off the car with my bare hands. There must be adrenaline or something at work. This is supernatural.

"You're doing good honey. It's going just like you said. Right on time," Kane offered as he drove. He was right, my body was doing exactly what it was supposed to. The contractions progressed in the time frame every book reported, and my water broke on its own. My body was doing what it knew how to do. All I was doing was taking the cues and giving into the process. I felt sure the baby would be ready to come out when we got to the hospital around 3am.

Kane brought us in through the emergency doors. "My wife is in labor," he stated.

I moaned as I tried to cradle my belly.

"Let's get her a wheelchair," the nurse bellowed to her deskmate.

As soon as they wheeled one up, I felt relieved. He got us here. Now I could get some assistance. They put me in a room with a bed. I showed the nurse my birth plan. "This is my birth plan. It states my intentions," I told her.

"Okay, thank you. Let's set that right here," the nurse replied as she set it on the table sideways. Why wasn't she reading it? She was more concerned with handing ME paperwork. "You're gonna have to sign this stuff for us to treat you today," she informed me, "I'll be back in one minute."

Treat me? What strange wording. I wasn't sick. I started skimming the paperwork. It wanted me to comply with whatever the medical team saw fit to serve me best.

"Kane, it wants me to sign my rights away, and I have the birth plan. I don't know what to do. I don't want to sign this," I panicked.

"Let me see it," he said as he grabbed the paper. "This is only for extreme situations. They aren't going to do anything. What are they gonna do, make you have the baby outside if you refuse something?" Kane said with annoyance.

"I don't know. Why are they using that wording? I don't like it. Maybe I should have my baby outside," I said to him as I felt another contraction coming on.

"Katie, I think you should sign it. They will help you have the baby. Everything will be okay. I'm gonna stay right here," Kane assured me, but he had a lost look in his eye.

"Okay," I said with tears coming. It's not like I was gonna argue with anyone in this state. I felt vulnerable. It wasn't the time to be signing stuff. I can't believe this was the procedure. Something in my gut, that wasn't a contraction, was giving me a yucky feeling. Like in a movie when the character goes outside because they hear a noise. And everyone in the room says, "I didn't hear anything." But the main character goes anyways, despite the sinking feeling in her gut. That was me. I went against my intuition because

I didn't know another way, and I was already in the brink of the next wave.

"I have to use the bathroom," I said to Kane.

"Okay, do you need help?" He asked.

"No, I'm okay," I said as I took a step. And then I went to my knees. I crawled to the toilet. It felt good to be on all fours. I attempted to urinate in the toilet, but it just felt like I had to take a shit. The pressure was insane. This body was not mine right now. I was becoming the portal. I felt it. I got back on the bathroom floor on all fours. Yes, this is the position. The pain is less here. Like an animal. I am an animal. This is as primal as it gets. I stayed there moaning loudly, soothing the pain with the sound of my moans. It was starting to put me in a trance. This is the way. I didn't even have to think. I just followed what felt right, and it was right.

"Ma'am, you need to get on the bed now," the nurse scolded at me like she was the warden at a foster camp. The hospital was a stale environment. The floor, as close to earth as I could get.

"Not yet," I said. "This position feels best. I'm gonna stay like this for a minute," I told her.

"Ma'am, that's not allowed. I have to hook you up to the monitor to hear the baby's heartbeat," she said.

"Well I'm sure it's beating. I can feel it moving. I don't need the monitor," I said.

"We need to make sure the baby is alive, and the cord doesn't stretch over there. This is procedure. Don't worry, we will take care of everything. All you need to do is lay on this bed," the nurse informed. I could hear her irritation, but this seemed like a line she had said before, so there was also a hint of apathy. No, this wasn't how I wanted it. I wanted to stay right here on all fours. I'll birth my baby right here.

"Ma'am, do you need me to help you?" She asked. But it sounded more like a threat.

"No, don't touch me. I'll get up. Kane..come here," I said. I was getting mad. I don't like people threatening to overpower my body. Kane got up and helped me off the ground. He didn't say much. I don't think he knew how to compute what was occurring. I started to cry.

I wished we had stayed at home now. Why did I have to be on the bed. It made no sense to me. I understand if the baby was crowning, but literally nothing was happening except contractions. The further I laid back on the bed, the worse the pain got. Then she strapped the monitor over the exact place where the pain of the contractions was the worst.

"Oh no, not there. That's right where the pain is worst. It's unbearable. Take it off," I told the nurse.

"Well I have to keep it on. I can move it to the side. There, that better?" She asked, not wanting a reply.

"Not really," I said. Arguing with a passive aggressive nurse? This isn't how I wanted my birth. I was getting pissed. But as soon as the anger would rise, a contraction would hit and I would be sent into a state of helplessness.

"Try laying on your side," Kane suggested as the nurse stepped into the hall. He looked helpless too. As cocky as he was at home, he didn't like to make waves. We were like two kids in trouble trying to come up with a plan. Only he kept making me do all the talking. Why couldn't he tell these nurses to fuck off and leave me alone? Because he didn't actually do the research with me. He didn't actually know what was happening. But I knew. It was just like that documentary. We were in the belly of the beast right now. The center of the system.

"Kane, don't leave me," I stared at him with bulging eyes.

"I won't. I'm right here," he said with brows bent. He wanted to help, but he couldn't.

"Kane it's getting worse, I can't stand it. This bed. This monitor. It hurts so bad. I want to move. I can't lay here being tortured. I don't know how much more I can handle," I pleaded with him.

"Babe, I know, you're doing good," he fed me the lines men are taught to say to a laboring woman. He couldn't hear me. I was in this alone.

An hour went by, but it felt like a week in that bed. They kept checking to see how dilated I was. I was progressing on schedule. But on schedule in this environment was intolerable. I wanted Kane to do something. But no one was going to do anything. Except offer an epidural. The lack of support during this belt-biting pain, had me backed into a corner. No-worse- a bed, in the most painful position there was, that actually slows labor because your aren't utilizing the force of gravity.

"Kane, if they won't let me get out of this bed and onto all fours, I don't think I can do it. I might do the epidural. I can't stand the pain any longer," I said to him, feeling like a failure.

"Only if you want to. Can you last a little longer?" he said, "I'll get the nurse if you really want it. I'll tell her."

He will tell her I need something they are peddling, but not stand up for me when I want to birth in a natural position. So this is how it is. I was afraid if I started getting argumentative they would ask me to leave and I would have to have my baby in the parking lot. And then what if there was a complication? If I was already kicked out, would they even help me in that circumstance? These were the thoughts running through my head as I contemplated my alternatives. They weren't what I thought I would be pondering while in labor. They aren't what anyone should be pondering while in labor. I wanted to feel safe. I thought I was supposed to be doing breathing exercises while Kane rubbed my back. But they wouldn't let me off my back. I looked down at my belly. "Baby, I don't know what to do. What should we do? I want to get you here safely, but I'm in so much pain," I talked to my baby. It seems everyone else forgot she was in the room. Her. The soul in human form, trying to get out peacefully.

"I need help little baby, so I can meet you and have this pain be over," I told her. I felt so much guilt. I said I would never do this. I knew it was wrong. But they wouldn't let me move. They had me pinned down. And that's how they win.

"She wants the epidural," Kane told the nurse.

"Okay, I'll notify the anesthesiologist. He shouldn't take long to get here," the nurse answered.

About ten minutes later, a man walked in with some equipment. He had an air of confidence about him. "Alright mama, let's sit you up," he said. Finally, I'm allowed to sit on the edge of the bed with my feet dangling. The feeling of freedom. The relief was confusing. I got to feel relief because I was giving in to one of the procedures they recommend. It's twisted. "Okay, I'm gonna thread this right into your spine," said the anesthesiologist. "You're gonna stay still and you won't feel a thing, but a little cold. And in a few minutes, all this pain is goin to be gone. Easy peasy," he recited.

I felt it hit my back. It was cold and it felt like a stiffness rising up the center of my spine. My mind went blank. I couldn't think about the potential risks. I was like a cat you put a collar on. I froze. This was unnatural. I felt it. I knew it. But what's done is done. I should have had a midwife from the second the pregnancy test was positive. But I didn't know better. No one told me. And I didn't arrive at the necessary information until it was too late. And even then, they fear-mongered and shamed me into this mess. So now I was here, with a hollow needle poked into the cord that is the literal life force pathway. It couldn't be more sadistic. This was the downward spiral.

I laid back in the bed, as they put on IV in my veins. Now I was tied to more wires and tubes. Kane looked like he was in shock.

"Katie, oh my god. You should have seen that needle he threaded into you. How do you feel?" Kane asked.

"I don't know. I'm scared. The pain is starting to go though," I told him.

Time had lost all meaning at this point. I was lost in the process. Not the process of birth, the process of procedure. Medical procedure. The contractions softened until I couldn't feel them any more. The only detection was the beeping on the machine. I was having them, but I couldn't feel them anymore. I felt detached. Where was my baby? I could no longer feel her.

"It's time to push," the nurse said, "we are on a schedule with what the machine is reporting. When the contractions happen we will ask you to bear down.

"But I can't feel anything. How can I push?" I asked.

"Just imagine it. Think hard. You can do it," the nurse instructed.

I tried. I tried so hard, but I felt nothing.

"Is is doing anything?" I asked.

"Push! Push! Push!" The nurse encouraged, "the baby isn't dropping further. We'll try again next round. I'll be back," she said.

"Kane, it isn't working. I can't feel a damn thing. What's happening?" I asked him.

"It's going to be okay," he said. That's all he could say. He looked confused and sad. This was a storm he wasn't expecting. And he didn't have any instruction as a man. He was the first of his generation to even be allowed in the birthing room with the mother.

"You're failing to contract. We are going add some Pitocin to your IV," the nurse informed me. Wait, Pitocin, that was the dangerous drug they talked about on the documentary. It was going to mess this all up. It was a synthetic form of oxytocin used to induce labor. So they shut off my body's natural release and added their synthetic form to counter the epidural. That's what epidurals do. They stop your body from performing labor. They stop your divine power. And all I wanted was to get on my knees and crouch to birth. But now...now I couldn't feel my knees.

"Kane, my legs are twisted! I know it! Check my feet! I need to see them!" I cried to him in a panic.

"What? Katie, you're okay..see, there they are. They are straight," he said as he lifted the sheet to show me.

"Oh god, I feel sick. Kane, I'm gonna puke. That stuff, it's making me nauseous," I told him.

Just then the nurse walked in. "How you feeling honey?" She asked. The sun was up now. I was on a rotation of pushing with no feeling every 20 minutes. But hours were passing. I was exhausted, yet felt nothing. Nothing but this nausea. They increased the Pitocin.

"I feel doped up. Does the Pitocin make you feel high? Is this normal?" I asked the nurse.

"No, you shouldn't feel high. You're just tired. Here's a bucket in case you get sick," she said as she handed me a clear plastic bucket.

I felt the next dose of Pitocin kick in. I did feel high. I know what being drugged feels like, because I've been drugged before, and this was just like that. And then I vomited into the bucket. Kane just stood there ready to rinse the bucket. I tasted metallic pharmaceuticals in the vomit. I was saturated with them. And my baby was sharing everything that went into my body. What was this doing to her?

The nurse came in again to check the heartbeat. She called another nurse and I heard talking. They were talking over me like I wasn't there. I hated that. It reminded me of being a child. It was dehumanizing.

"The baby's heart rate has dropped. We need to keep an eye on that," the nurse told me.

"Why? What's wrong?" I asked her.

"Well, we don't know. But this can happen. That's why we have the monitors," she talked at me. She was like a machine. Repeating a program. But I knew the heart rate was dropping because of all the medications. My body was fine before all this. There was nothing wrong with my baby. There was everything wrong with this cascade of interventions.

"I'm gonna have you push one more time. Right now you are failing to progress in labor and the baby can't go long with the decreased heart rate," the nurse said.

"Kane, I'm not failing. Why is she saying that? They said the epidural woundn't inhibit labor, but it is. I know that's what's wrong," I said to him. But I was too sick to keep talking. It couldn't be reversed. This dam had already been broken and it only led to one outcome.

"Push! Bear down now! Push!" The nurse said. But who could "bear down" in this position? They said to imagine I was making a bowel movement. But who take a shit laying on their back? She had to prop my legs up because I had lost all ability to move them on my own. I pushed as I held the bucket and vomited Pitocin. This was their version of giving birth. They had bastardized the whole process. They had taken my power. My divine power. And lined the birth canal with drugs.

"You did good sweetie, but we are going to have to take next steps. Your body isn't laboring in time," the nurse said. In time for what? I had heard stories about women laboring for days. Even my mother, she had labored for a couple days in the hospital. But it was getting close to late afternoon, and someone's shift was ending for a Saturday. Births had to take place by 4pm. The nurse stepped into the hallway and spoke with Kane.

"Kane, no, what are they saying?" I pleaded with him. I didn't want the answer. I knew the answer.

"They are saying they have to do an emergency c-section," Kane told me with reluctance in his voice. "I'm worried about the baby. What if she isn't getting enough blood to her brain without her heart beating enough. I don't know. I think we have to do what they say," he shared his concerns. I started weeping. This is the nightmare I didn't want.

"I want more time. She will come out on her own, I know it. Let the medicine wear off," I told the nurse.

"Well mama, I know that's what you think, but we just don't know what's causing this. We have to keep the baby safe," the nurse said to me. Were these people even human? It's like they were reading a script. And they were. The medical script. I wanted to rip that epidural out myself. But would I get paralyzed for life if I did that? Do I even have the energy? I can't feel anything from my ribcage down. They made me disabled and detached, during a time I was supposed to be the most present in my entire life.

"Kane no, I don't want to be cut open," I cried to him.

"I'm sorry, Katie. I don't know what else to do. They said they will let me be in the operating room with you," Kane replied as he held my hand.

Then the nurses came in. They transferred my body, limp on the lower half to the bed they would wheel to the operating room. Birth wasn't supposed to be an operation, and my body wasn't supposed resemble a corpse. I cried. Bawling at this point. I cried shrieks of emotional pain and grief, knowing this is not how I wanted to bring my baby into the world. I wanted her to be surrounded by beauty, presence, and love. Instead she was met with scalpels, resistance, metal, and strangers.

"No. I don't want this. This isn't what I want," I said as they wheeled me. But they kept wheeling. Ignoring me, talking over me.

"Hey there mama, how ya doing?" Another man asked as he scooted his chair up by my head. "Is your husband coming in here?

"Yes," I said.

"Oh yeah, what's he do?" The new anesthesiologist asked.

"He's a welder," I replied.

"Oh yeah? Does he weld these little things?" He asked as he pulled up the metal cart the IV was hooked to. Him and the doctor started laughing. They were making fun of Kane, because welding is lower class. It was their inside joke and I caught it. You couldn't drug me enough to miss classist jokes. How dare they demean me and my husband as I lay there paralyzed on their table.

"I don't want this," I said as I started crying again. I was so overwhelmed with all of it.

"Here we go. Get her some morphine," the doctor said.

"What? Can't that hurt the baby?" I asked.

"This is gonna make you feel all better. We need you nice and calm. The baby is going to be out before this even gets to her," he said as he tapped the IV.

More drugs. I was barely conscious. Kane stepped in as they put up a sheet so I couldn't see the process. He was right, I couldn't feel a thing as they slaughtered me through six layers of abdominal wall and sliced open my uterus. Then they handed her to me. She still had the white vernix coating all over her skin. She started crying. Good, that meant she was alive. I felt her skin on my face. My baby, I could finally feel her again.

"Do you want a picture with her?" Kane asked as he grabbed his cell phone.

"Okay," I said, "Yes." I was so doped up, everything sounded like it was in the distance. I cracked a smile through my morphine haze. Is this what I got sober for? No. It wasn't.

"We need to weigh the baby now, mama," the nurse said as she took the baby from my hands. "You still have work to do. That placenta needs to come out."

"Okay mom, you might feel a tug here, just lay still," the doctor reported from the other side of the blue sheet. "There it is," he said as he put something on the cart next to me.

"Whoah, look at that Katie, it's huge," Kane said as he observed the placenta. It was the size of a liver, I imagined. Bloody. I can't believe that gigantic thing was in me with the baby. No wonder my stomach felt so heavy.

"One last step mama," the doctor instructed. "We have to massage everything back into place so we can stitch you up. You are going to feel some pressure and movement, but it shouldn't be painful. The epidural should still be working along with the morphine. If not, we can tap it for little more."

I felt the tugging. I felt the pressure. But I was like a helpless animal in a crate at this point. The same as one of those animals taken to slaughter. There was no use in crying, or talking, or resisting. I was defeated, and it was happening regardless of how I felt about it. In the background I could hear Kane talking to the nurses, and I could hear my baby screaming louder and louder. What were they doing to her? Kane had the birth plan. Was he telling them? All I could see was the metal table they had her on. I heard water running. They had washed all the vernix off of her. To "clean" her. But I read that it was a protective layer and they should massage it into her skin without washing it. But they were washing it. Kane came over to me. I was dozing in and out at this point after they stitched me up.

"Katie, they said we have to do the Hep-B shot," Kane whispered in my ear.

I woke up. "Kane, no, we talked about this. Don't change anything. I just want to breastfeed her. I'm supposed to feed her. I need the baby on me. Bring her to me," I told him.

"Katie, I can't. They told me I can't hold her yet. They are saying it's really easy to get Hep-B in the hospital and it could kill the baby. I don't know, but I don't think we can leave without doing it," Kane said.

I was so sleepy. I couldn't operate enough to verbalize logic. I wrote the logic down. Questioning me while I was paralyzed, drugged with morphine, and still laid out on an operating table was not the time to be propositioning mothers or parents.

"Kane, I can't. I have to have you do this. Keep the baby safe," I told him.

"They want to do all three, but I told them just one," Kane said. "They seem to be okay with just one." A fear started to wash over me. What did he mean we couldn't leave without doing the shots? Were they trying to keep my baby? Could they do that? Was that in that paperwork I signed? I couldn't remember yesterday. It was less than 24 hours ago, but it was dimensions away. But I knew one thing, they could do a lot of things you didn't think you agreed to. They hospital was its own entity.

"Do what you need to do. We need to keep our baby with us," I said to Kane.

He walked back to the nurses and our baby laying on the metal table with one blanket wrapped around her. Through my blurry vision I was trying to see what they were doing. Then I heard an ear-puncturing shriek from my baby. That was it. They stuck her with the needle. Then they brought her over to me.

"They just did one. She's okay. Hold her for a minute before they move us back to the room," Kane said. I'm surprised they even let me do that, as I nodded in and out of coherence, waiting for the ability to locate my legs to return.

I gazed at my baby. Only a few more moments until they are out of our hair and we can be together again. I felt intoxicated by her smell and skin on mine. No one else in the room was real. She was real. And then they took her again.

"Okay mama, I gave you one more little pump of morphine to hold you over," said the anesthesiologist. "They are gonna transfer you back to your room so you can rest. Baby will be in there soon with papa."

I dozed again to the sound of wheels. I woke as the nurses shifted my limp legs once more to the new bed. "You still have the catheter in, so the urine will gather on its own. Just rest and dad will be here. I know it didn't go as planned, but at least your baby is here and alive," the nurse attempted to console me. I wasn't consoled. Just be grateful the baby is alive, even though that train wreck just occurred? I would hear it numerous times during the first year of my baby's life. No one wanted to hear mother complain. How dare she complain? How ungrateful. More shaming. That was motherhood to them.

Kane walked in with the nurses pushing the baby in a cart with a plastic bassinet of sorts. "I promise, I'm not gonna let them take her anywhere without me," he assured me once they left the room. "I had no idea how pushy this place could be."

"No more shots, Kane. We don't need them. You have to say no. She's been through too much already," I said to him.

"I agree. We all need to rest. They said you could hold the baby. Do you want to hold her? She so cute. She's a little scrunchie!" Kane said, adoring his new daughter.

"Yes, I want to hold her. Maybe she will nurse. I want to try," I said as he gently placed her in my arms. Her presence on my chest calmed my whole nervous system, like a piece that was missing. We had been joined for nine months. It didn't feel right to have her separate from me. That's why they call it the fourth trimester. You're really supposed to be co-regulating outside the body, but still touching for the next three months. Maternity leave ended before that. Unpaid. I didn't want to think about it. Not now. Right now my only concern was holding her.

"What if I fall asleep? I don't want to drop her," I told Kane.

"I'll put the side bar up. She'll be fine," he said as he assisted then left to shower at home and bring a change of clothes.

I spent the rest of the day trying to nurse her. The nurse told me she had a different temperament than most babies. "Don't all babies cry?" I asked her, thinking she was in the maternity ward and heard crying all day.

"Yes, but this one doesn't give you much of a warning. Some babies gently wimper for 10-15 minutes. Your baby goes straight to a full cry in 1-2 minutes. I think it's her temperament. Some babies are just impatient. Keep trying to get her to latch. Here, let me show you how to position your nipple so she can get a good latch," the nurse said.

It seemed this shift was nicer. Or maybe they liked babies on the outside of bodies more than the inside. The whole thing was confusing to me. Their behavior didn't make any sense to my natural instincts. My baby wasn't latching easily. By the end of the day my nipples felt raw like a chaffed blister. They gave me a special cream with instructions for others. They said I might want to look into seeing if she had a tongue tie. If that was the case they would do a procedure to remove the skin that was prohibiting her from getting milk. This was more complicated than I thought. It occurred to me, I was grossly unprepared for any of this. As much as I read during pregnancy, none of the support systems I actually needed were in my field of reach. Yet another enormous betrayal. It seems they were always adding on more information I was not aware of. And then someone had the audacity to ask me when I would be returning to work. Work? What the fuck was that? THIS was work. This was my new job. There was no question about that.

For the next 12 hours my baby and I drifted in and out of sleep on an endless rotations of sleep, diaper, nurse. We made it through our first night. Then it was time to go home. I wiggled my toes. They were finally back. I called for help to the bathroom. The nurse encouraged me to shower. I smelled like blood, vaginal fluid, and armpit odor. I could definitely feel again. A sharp stinging pain registered on my lower abdomen.

"Can your husband help wipe you down? It might be hard for you to reach things on your own right now. And we don't want you falling in the shower. Keep the gauze on that scar honey," the nurse said, "Those stitches need to stay in for awhile. It's going to sting for a few days."

Sting? I've had a bee sting. This wasn't a sting. This was slasher horror torture. The tenderness was beyond what I could have fathomed. I think this experience has shown me types of pain I didn't know existed. And I don't think it had to be this bad, but it was.

"Don't lift anything over 10 pounds while you're healing that c-section," said the nurse.

"What about the baby?" I asked.

"She's only 7.7 pounds. She's fine. You have to hold her. She's the exception no matter what," she answered. And then she looked at me with serious eyes. "Mom, we have to go over this. It's part of a safety protocol. Listen to me. There will be times, after you go home and all the visitors go back to their routines, and you are up for days on end with this crying baby. And you will be more tired than you ever imagined. You will get exhausted and emotional as your hormones adjust. But DO NOT shake the baby. Ever. It causes brain damage, swelling, and they can die. People are at risk of doing this when they are tired, and it seems they are rocking the baby but they are being too forceful and it turns into a shaking. The baby then quiets and it seems the baby has been rocked to sleep. But this isn't what's happening. It's shaken baby syndrome and it's very serious. So I'm going to say it again, DO NOT shake the baby. Ever. When you feel like you can't take any more crying and the baby is unconsolable, set her down someplace safe, like in her crib, and you walk away and take some deep breaths. The baby will be fine. And this will keep her safe. Do you understand mama?" She stared into my eyes.

"Yes, I understand," I answered her. I understood and I was terrified. Why was this so common? Why was she so serious? Mom told me babies slept. But this nurse is telling me otherwise. And for my baby, she was extra concerned because I had a baby with a temperament towards crying quickly. It was going to be extra hard and she knew it. So she was doing her due diligence. But again, why is this the first time I'm coming across this information? How is it possible I know so little about raising a human, when I am human? The segregation of people with children and people without children would begin to unfold for me over the next few years, and it would make more sense how we got this way.

"How's mama and baby doing?" Kane peeked inside the door. "Are you ready to go home?" He asked.

"Yes, please. I want my surroundings. I'm done with this place," I replied.

"I'm going to pull the car up and the nurse is going to roll you out front with scrunchie. Okay?" He asked.

"Okay, let's do it," I smiled at him. I don't know what we just went through exactly, but we made it out alive. And there had been moments I wasn't sure that was going to be possible.

The nurse came in and positioned me with the car seat and baby on my lap. She rolled me out an endless series of double doors. This was the first time I'd left a hospital with an additional entity dropped down from another world. The nurses and assistants talked around and over me. This was part of their routine: roll the object out the front door, make sure the object can belt the other object into the car, have them sign these papers, then go eat your lunch.

They seemed oblivious a miracle had just occurred. I didn't know how to embrace this supernatural marvel myself. A new being just landed on this earth ship. Mother's instinct began to settle in my breast, and a fierce mama bear growled from my core. She has awakened from her slumber. I must consider, if my baby has been born so perfect, just as she is, then so was I. I will relearn my path of acceptance, as I nurture her and protect her at all costs. Another precious layer of Creation has been revealed to me.

Like a knight in shining armor, Kane pulled up in my silver Subaru Forester. My broken body fumbled into the car, and after numerous safety checks, we pulled away. There was that noise again, this time from the stereo. The radio hosts were blabbing a bunch of nonsense. Nothing significant happened in their lives this weekend. They were churning out the same old drama. In mine? I birthed a baby. Love poured into my heart like a golden fountain. Nothing was the same, and it never would be. Exponential change was thrust into motion.

The week and months ahead were a blur. Kane accompanied me to two of the first appointments where we continued to argue with doctors about declining vaccinations.

"Jesus Christ, I was almost thinking we should do one or two after they scared me at the hospital, but now their pushiness has me feeling like they don't even care. They are pushing an agenda. I can't even try and reason with them. They don't want to hear our reasons. They just argue even more. Just say no. I have to go back to work. You can do this on your own now. I know it, Katie. You'll be fine," Kane encouraged me. "And don't tell my mom we aren't vaccinating. She'll freak out. They are filled with fear."

"I know. Mine either. They keep talking about polio and the measles. What about asthma and allergies. Do they not know how much my body has been through? It's risk vs. benefit, and for DNA like mine, there's way more risk. And don't they wonder why so many kids have a peanut allergy since the 90s? Not to mention the whole vaccine injury thing. I don't even want to get into the discussion over blood-brain barriers and neurotoxins,"

I said.

"Agreed. We got this," Kane said. I knew he didn't get into the nitty gritty nutrition and science stuff. He followed his gut, and that was enough. Our next battle was telling the grandparents we weren't going to let the baby cry-it-out, and that they couldn't set her two inches from the tv screen playing Fox News in a baby carrier when they babysat her. They would crack jokes about putting Mt. Dew in her baby bottle, and question why I was still pumping breast milk. Even after I had the tongue tied procedure done, she wouldn't latch. She screamed at the nipple. I wondered if her temperament had anything to do with that traumatic birth. She was now calibrated to the speed at which the milk flowed out of the bottle. If only I knew how important it was to get a lactation specialist working with me sooner. But my mother didn't breastfeed me and she had zero interest in these conversations. She only wanted to buy the baby outfits and take pictures to post on Facebook. It was like she was playing with a doll. But I was nurturing a human. I never lost sight of that. I pumped in my car, in school janitor closets, I did everything I could to get my baby human milk. I wanted to pass my immune system along to her. I listened to videos of her cooing to get my breastmilk to let down. In reality, the baby is supposed to be with mother for much longer...like a year, two years...kinda until they are 18. This crazy idea of women being pumped like cow in a factory, is inhumane. And now that I officially know how the cows feel, with mastitis and separation trauma..I'm not consuming dairy anymore either. The sadism was everywhere.

Despite the unveiling of those darknesses, I was revealed new layers of light. I was a part of the portal, it's impossible not to see the light when you are that. I didn't know how to embrace this kind of brightness. I felt unworthy and vulnerable to the role I was just granted. Family members acted like it was a spectacle to be displayed like a commercial. That bothered me. They were missing the whole essence of the baby and motherhood. I drew inward. A kaleidoscope of dreams was just created. Where there was nothing, now there is something. My amazing daughter, a beautiful gem of Light from the stars.

Tornado

Righteous spirits weren't meant to go with the grain, they were put here to carve new paths. "There is no way I'm raising my daughter in rural East Texas. Either we go to Austin, or we leave this state. We don't have to go to Chicago, but we sure as hell are not staying here," I delivered with assurance to Kane. He was sick of my ultimatums. Our marriage began on one. I was threatening to leave before we were even engaged. It took me ten years to follow through.

"I saw an opening for a position at my company's branch in Colorado. If there is anywhere I would move, the mountains would be it. I'm fixin' to go," he relayed to me. I was shocked. Perhaps he was ready for a change too. We had lived in his dead grandparent's house, three blocks away from his dead dad's house, and one block away from where his father was murdered, for long enough. It was time to let those ghosts rest.

Three months later, Kane secured a job in the foothills. It was the night shift, but nothing short of a miracle to get us out of this energy pit. We were apart for three months. He left for Colorado to begin work and I stayed in Texas until the house sold. I longed for him while he was gone. I was alone with our four month old baby, pumping breastmilk, teaching middle school, and praying for the block in our lives to be removed. When it finally started to flow, I packed a baby, a large Labrador-Pit mix, a breast pump, and three cats into a Subaru. The Motel 6 became our home until the house in Colorado closed. The market was booming, and we barely made the cut. Our honeymoon lasted a few months, like most honeymoons do.

I lie in bed staring at the stark white ceiling. The dimmed light from the bathroom crept in. I saw a gray tornado whirling over my head. It was filled with stories, letters, cards, notes, suspended in a spiraling mess. The tornado circled a path over my forehead, down to my heart, and back again. The tears and frantic cries of my life followed me. I thought I got rid of them, but they are still here. Unseeable to the eye, they remain a detectable ping on the radar.

I dug through a bin of old cards I'd lugged around for two decades. "I might want to read these when I'm old and bored," I thought. How presumptuous of me to assume I might live that long or predict I wouldn't have something better to do. The box contained loads of graduation cards with generic signatures. They're just taking up space.

I pried open Pandora's box, and lost myself that afternoon. I let my daughter toss cards all over the family room. As she enjoyed the pictures of silly cats and rainbows, I read through a lost history. I found recognition of things that had infuriated me over the years, as well as perspective on the destitute relationship with my family.

Only days before, I reacted to my mother, "Screw you!" With bubbling resentment. I was filled with rage that she'd come over with a terrible cold, claiming it was allergies. Engulfed with blame, I decided she got us all sick and I was steamed. I couldn't stand being stuck at home, let alone being sick. Kane had move us into a rural location again, despite my request for us to be near a town. How would I raise kids way out here? How would we make friends?

I was not the typical, "I wish I was feeling better and out with my friends" kind of sick. I took it to another level. I became Colonel Kurtz in *Apocalypse Now*, suffering from a malaria of discontentment, introverting like a savage amongst severed heads. "I have no friends. My life is a huge mistake. None of this has any point. I'm trapped in a shitty shit hole that I will never get out of." A discontentment that surfaced with the common cold.

Mom lacked awareness. She was recklessly concerned about satisfying her own needs first. She fed the monster that said she must gain love from other people. *Wait, I can't possibly relate to that.* Her entity was a bottomless pit called "need." Her quest for love was a black hole. She had become a vampire for attention. I felt drained and empty. I now recognize this mindset was not my mother, it was a negative thought pattern adapted by my mother.

When I tried to advocate a boundary, my parents defended their actions as well-meaning because they loved me. I was spoon fed another dumpster-worthy thought pattern: we hurt the ones we love. Bullshit. No, we don't. Furthermore, if they spent any time or money on me, I would be reminded of it. That lunch cost more than five dollars. It was years of obligation. The energy blobs of guilt, blame, regret, shame, and sorrow swarmed their heads like a hornet's nest. I wished I could help them, but only oneself can exterminate such personalized vermin. My efforts were futile.

Mom assured me Dad's heart was in there somewhere, "He loves you very much. Your father is a very sensitive person. People just don't understand him." She taught me it was my job to make excuses for men who refused to communicate or take accountability after having an adult tantrum. I only saw a glimpse of this fantasy character when I witnessed his eyes glassy with woe. It happened rarely, but I perceived a depth of pain that went beyond his interactions with me. But my sympathy for men who do not self-reflect would prove to be a vicious virus. It became an infection that affected my neurological pathways.

The failed relationship with my parents made my heart shatter at its core. I tried to ignore it, but I felt bitter with a toxic resentment blistering me on the inside. I was asphyxiated on a rope of whys. In every letter, Mom obsessively wrote how much she loved me. Her handwriting was as familiar as a voice whispering in my ear with a crinkled smile. In letter after letter she promises, someday things will be better. Most of the time she appears to be writing to convince herself. Then she rambles on about shopping. It fills her cavity. I watch her deteriorate in an endless tomb of temporary relief.

I suppose it made her feel like she was taking care of me when she bought me things, but things are not what I needed. They were a "get well soon" card to a person on the kidney transplant waiting list. She did her best within her universe of reality. I found forgiveness for a woman overlooking the need to heal herself. I will not repeat the pattern. I will choose a path through the unpruned forest, in lieu of the Mall of America.

Dad wrote notes of encouragement on life goals, but his heart followed corporate regulations. I froze in the company of a paternal figure who was unable to show love. His handwriting drew a response of anxiety in my body. It looped with the intention to prove he was doing his job, rather than sharing a heartfelt gesture. His dense shadow puffed its chest and influenced my self-image. It was as if it duplicated itself and attached to me.

I could hear his disapproving tone, "The only job you have is to keep your mother happy, and you've failed. If you were my employee, I'd fire you." I was a nuisance to him, but he couldn't trim me like an undesirable branch in his manicured lawn. Instead, he tried to mold me into the extension of himself he needed to construct. "Come talk to me when you have actually accomplished something," he'd say. Rejection became etched in my story. My challenge became learning how to like myself, when the most significant model in my life did not. To let go of needing an apology. I dissected the internal programs that kept me cycling through dysfunctional relationships. The most heavily imprinted one was: *It's normal to try and convince men to love you.*

Mother's instinct drives a woman to protect her children at all costs. But mine chose denial. She didn't stand up for me. I stopped being surprised when I acknowledged, she could hardly stand up for herself. She was wooed by my father's gifts and vacations, which fed her self worth. She bragged to me about how much Dad loved her. She wrote, "He surprised me with a limo! He said I look beautiful and deserve to be pampered!" Jealousy became a malignant sore on my heart. Eventually I learned they were intertwined in a codependent tapestry. An overpriced rug at the flea market, to sweep all their wounds under.

The tornado rose and fell. Sometimes it slowed down enough to drop the debris in random places. Like a Kansas summer aftermath, I spent hours and weeks picking things up, trying to re-categorize them. It never packed the same. At this point, my parents didn't even return my texts, unless it was about seeing the grandchildren. I hoped the funnel cloud would remove my problems without my focus. I didn't want to consciously pick apart the whats and whys. That sounded tedious and uncomfortable. I would rather whisk it up into a fire.

It worked in Texas. I ignited a blazing bonfire in my kitchen by dumping a stack of litigation papers into a bucket. They were from that nightmare of a sexual assault case I filed before I met Kane. I wanted to erase that horrible memory. "You're nuts dude," Kane said as he passed by me to play more video games. I begrudgingly chunked the pile of papers into a five gallon Lowes bucket. It was a ceremonial instinct to purge and transmute energy.

"This is happening," I replied, as I squirted lighter fluid onto the mound of crumpled white papers. I wanted the flames to reach the ceiling and burn in a bombastic display. Energy into ashes. Dust to dust.

I decided to throw out a brown sack, overflowing with cards. The resistance was akin to not wanting to lose someone or a part of myself. I had a strong desire to understand my life, and the letters were like puzzle pieces. I was afraid if I threw them away, I would never solve the mystery. Or worse yet, I would never understand it. This notion kept me clinging to the old stories. It was time to let go.

When you become an architect, a question arises, "Will this help build the bridge or will it weigh it down?" I became attuned to what helped me, and what hindered me. Letting go itself didn't get easier, but the need to do so became easier to identify.

Putting on the Brakes

My peeping eyes were level to Grandma's kitchen table of wood. Grade school fingers rounded the corners, waxy from hundreds of hands being laid on them during deep discussions. Her petite, Leave It To Beaver kitchen fostered life lessons beyond my immediate family. I overheard varying opinions, stories of far-away places, and chronicles of people long gone. Ghosts of the Depression era taught me street smarts, like how to swear in Polish, and rejoice "*Nostrovia!*" Being permitted to eavesdrop in her kitchen was a rite of passage.

I sat at her table as a young adult, asking for advice, support, and the ears of someone older and wiser than me. I keep hopping tables, looking for the same comfort I found in that magic crystal ball made of oak, but Grandma's kitchen has lifted into the stars. Its wisdom is somewhat elusive these days.

"The man was so bloody mad he was seeing red! They better not mess with him anymore!" exclaimed the plump woman in Grandma's kitchen. I imagined one of those color wheel toys I had as a toddler, where I could turn the transparent plastic wheel and see through a lens; either blue, yellow, or red.

One of the adults was seeing through the red lens. I asked what it meant. The elders chuckled with amusement. They glared at me with a look of pity that said, "You've got a lot to learn, kid."

As an adult, I understand it's a red curtain draped over my eyes, causing me to see nothing but blurred crimson images and the nebulous shadows of life. My limbs flail as I swat at the invisible sheet of red. It's like a magic trick, where the scarves keep coming, and coming, and coming from seemingly nowhere. I want to rip the red curtain off the hooks. I try, but the maroon blanket keeps falling, until I'm tangled in my own suffering.

Securing a home in the Rocky Mountains was a milestone. Yet I dashed out of it disgruntled most mornings, feeling like we had gone from pillar to post. Life was shifting quickly. Much like the cell phone service backing up to a national forest, my life was losing reception.

I pushed through. *Just get out the door and start your car. Go to work. Don't fuck this up, Katie.* This is the mantra going through my head. It's my daily pep talk to avoid throwing in the towel. It's hard just to get out the door. I don't know how other people do it with less than a three hour window. I fantasize about not going in, ever again. No call, no show. I'll dissipate into thin air. They won't know what happened. It'll be like a dream, a bit hazy, then administration will call the next person on the list and someone new will show up to work. I feel foggy. I better hide my tendency to disengage, or I won't have a choice in the matter.

I calm myself with the reminder that I am the condensed matter of stardust. I've thrown on some silly "work" clothes and I currently reside on a spinning rock, floating around an endless outer space of shining stars that are so bright and so far away, they don't even exist anymore. None of this matters. I am an intelligent vibration inside a human vessel. I'm on Earth. Planet Earth. Time is a new concept for me, and the average human life span isn't long enough to acclimate. That's why I suck at being on time. This is the game I'm not so good at. The game of being human. *Okay, now that we've got that covered, let's head to work.*

When I'm running late, I play a game in my head that says I can slow down time with my mind. So no matter when I leave the house, or what speed I drive the car, I will get there on time. Ironically, on the days I indulge in this game, I skate in on the dot, if even by one minute. I'm not sure how long this method is going to work, but I'll take it for now.

An abrasive woman is stressing me out at work. She doesn't know she's bothering me, but it's making my nervous system go bizerk. I can't focus when I'm there. People try to talk to me, but all I hear is a buzzing noise. Can I construct a sentence? English. I speak English. How do you say, "I had a nice weekend. How was yours?" This is awful. I'm in some kind of anger-induced stupor. I'm annoyed with small talk and it's rendering me illiterate.

Days like this I am looking out the window to see if someone has called the paddy wagon on me. I feel like an absolute alien in a world that makes no sense to me. *Are those sirens? Hmm, must be an emergency close by. Where's the back door to this place...*

I distinctly remember Dad cracking up during Sunday morning cartoons. His laugh bellowed. I rarely saw him this amused. He explained a paddy wagon was for people who have lost their minds, gone crazy. It takes them away to the loony bin and locks them up. This was delightful to him. He demonstrated how being taken to the nut house was way more shameful, and clearly more humorous, than being put in jail.

As I grew older, I observed many stigmas attached to how the human brain functions. Societal paradigms have confined our minds to specific behaviors. Thought patterns outside of the current norms are punished or worse, "disordered." I began to consider that the humans forgot how to be human.

My brother Jason used to call Mom "Mental," as if it were her name. He was taught to taunt a woman who was facing her own abuse and trying her best to be nurturing. I laughed with him. If I only knew, I was getting the same programs as her. I would soon have to face my own reconstruction. And when I did, they would shun me. I need to exist on mountain time. Show up when the wildlife gets through crossing the road, or whenever my spiritual moment in nature allows me to continue. There's no need to hurry. That deer is staring into my soul, and mountain people know, I can't just look away. If an elusive black stocking fox crosses my path, then I might as well take a vacation day to decode the mystery. After all, maybe it's whispering the answer to a question I had a long time ago. Spirit works that way, speaking through animals, plants, and dreams. That's what we practiced when we were more connected.

As I sped down the road my brake light turned on. Damn it. I'm being blocked from getting to work on time. The sign was in red caps, "BRAKE." Unmistakeable, located above the speed I was going. Seriously? Is the parking brake on? I pulled over and jiggled both brakes, then shut off the engine completely. I'll let the program reset itself, then turn it back on. Nope, there it was. Bright stinking red, front and center, BRAKE. Holy crap, the Universe is talking to me, and it's being quite literal. I put on the brakes. I listened. Not to the chatter in my head, but I slowed down and listened to the motivational speaker on the radio.

He spoke about letting go of adversity. Just when one of his comments clicked in my brain, I looked down and the brake light shut off. It stayed off. Funny things like that happen to me. I'm sure they happen to a lot of people. Except no one wants to sound like a schizophrenic, so they don't share their stories very often. Or they preface it by saying it was woo woo or a coincidence. They make sure their audience knows they are telling the story for entertainment purposes. We're amused by these happenings. But perhaps deep down, we want to hear the whispers of the Universe without someone laughing at us.

This isn't the first time the Universe has sent me a message. One time it was delivered by a piece of fruit in my throat. I was driving my manual-steering, stick shift truck, while eating a fruit salad with a fork. Reckless multi-tasking. I started choking mid-shift change, on my way to a massage therapy appointment. I was too busy, all the time. A nice lady named Mary sat with me for an hour until it dislodged from my vocal cord. She was a nurse, a massage therapist, and unafraid to tell me it was the Universe, or God, or however I thought of it. She told me everything is connected and that sometimes the Universe wants you to slow down, and it can use a tiny piece of fruit to deliver that message. After being raised Catholic, I'm certain any time a stranger named "Mary" crosses my path to save my life, it's not a coincidence.

The Omen

There it was, a dead bird on my doorstep. I considered brushing it off as a delivery from one of the local stray cats, but it was too creepy. It spoke volumes. Things were changing. Sometimes when a change is coming, bad things have to happen. People say that during any massive life shift. It's going to get worse before it gets better.

I was trimming mental baggage and eliminating negative people from my life. While I tried to manage an unmanageable group of family members, that bird flew right into our window at top speed. It was bye-bye birdy. It was the death of everything I formerly knew.

Things don't go well when I force them into being. Motherhood was finally teaching me that.

"You gotta work. I don't want to pay all the bills," Kane griped at me as I entertained a toddler while cooking a home made dinner. Which "work" was more important? The office work, or growing a human baby work.

"Do you know how much day care is? And with the drive from way out here in the mountains? It doesn't make sense. She's happy. Why would you want to change that? I don't like you pressuring me. Isn't everything I do here good enough for you?" I pleaded.

"Come on, can't you do Porn Hub or something? I bet those rich guys up the hill would love to be spanked by you. You might as well be fucking someone if you're not fucking me. Bringing us home some money while you're at it," he charged. I was speechless. I'd rather he be jealous than this. My heart sunk. This man didn't love me at all.

Kane didn't let up, so the following month I took a job with a chaperone assignment right out of the gate. I started marching to the tune of the bell again. They tried to groom me by calling me professional. Insinuating *this* is what being an adult is. To me it felt a repressed, bottled, and scared version of myself. Then I miscarried, the day before the trip. I had no time for self-pity. I wasn't going to get any more empathy than I got for my monthly periods. I packed my bags, got on a plane, and was dropped off in the middle of Times Square, responsible for numerous tweens. Life lessons 101; dealing with any hurtful loss later, usually equates to dealing with it now, later, and a little extra after that. Good night, sweet baby. I'm sorry you weren't meant to be. I consoled myself as we flew over the sea to shining sea.

A local clairvoyant assured me, "the ones who seem to be out to break us down, are actually set in place to cause us to reflect upon what needs to be healed inside of us." Kane didn't feel like a gentle lesson from the Universe. He felt like pain, and his micromanaging made me feel rebellious. All the stress from trying to be everything at once, was too much for me. Does he want me to be the man, or the woman, because I can't be both. Especially not when the children are young.

I've had a fiery edge since forever, and I say things, that I guess you aren't supposed to say. I remember when they first installed cameras on school buses. I was in middle school. My primal instincts kicked in as I stepped up the oversized, grimy stairs on a sweaty Midwestern bus. I paused and glared straight into the camera. My whole body said "no." So I flipped it off. Whoever "it" was. Being a child of eighties freedom, surveillance introduced in the 90s was foreign. I didn't trust it, and I let them know I didn't like it.

"We got to watch a lovely little video of you at the PTA meeting tonight," Mom reported with a sigh. The principal, my aunt, who was a school bus driver, and a slew of acquaintances of my parents, were able to view my political debut. It resulted in two visits to the principal and a week of after-school detention. I would have evaded the detention, had the secretaries not snitched on me for rolling my eyes as I walked out of the first visit to the principal's office. The whole thing was absurd. "Just wait until they put cameras on their every move, and see how *they* feel," I thought.

I got into teaching to help shift things, but that was like joining the military to change the military. Nevertheless, I had a soft spot for the underdog, the non-conformist, the tenacious spirits who question authority. The ones who can't help but refuse the box. I love those types. I delivered pink slips to those kinds of students with a stern look followed by a side smile. *You do you, kid, and the world will be a better place for it.* I was disheartened with public schools because I realized I was required to spend more time churning out an agenda to tread water, than to actually bettering students' lives. But much like joining the military, you don't know what you don't know. And once you do, you're already there..in the system.

I arrived home from the chaperone assignment, welcomed by a card from my daughter, and an air of resentment from Kane. He wanted me to "go get a real job" to help with money, but this would require me to be away from home. This inconvenienced him, and he didn't like it. But there was no reasoning with him. He was like a child throwing a tantrum, not mature enough to engage in the dialogue of division of labor or scaffolding a plan. The schedule drained me so much, I began returning home a withered resemblance of my former self. I put in 97 hours a week as a Mom, but no-one was counting that, certainly not Kane.

I wanted more. I *want* more for everyone. I'm not talking about a poster saying, "The Mountains are Calling!" I'm not trendy. I want to know how far do I need to go? Because I'm already gone.

Tunnel of Light

I'm playing Hopscotch with timelines, taking periodic jumps through tunnels of light. The birth of my second daughter brought me through a recent one.

"This baby is going to be early," I told the nurse at my third trimester check up.

"Oh sweetie, it's normal to feel 'more full' with a second baby!" she blabbed at me.

But I knew otherwise. My abdomen was tight and crampy—a gut feeling kicked in, urging me to put myself on partial bedrest. If I moved too quickly, this baby was gonna drop out. I knew it. I sat on a sofa chair for days trying to ward off the onset of early labor.

On a Tuesday morning, five weeks before my due date, the cramping became severe. It was a typical morning playing with my toddler and attempting to fold some clothes amongst the attention-starved dogs. I got up to ue the bathroom and somewhere between the couch and the center of the hallway, I doubled over. Straight to the floor.

Dear Lord, what is happening? It's too early. This can't be it.

I crawled to the bathroom and crouched on the floor, like a deer who had been hit by a semi truck. It came on fast. Kane had been working in the garage, but ran up the way to the hardware store. Sometimes his errands took hours. I think he liked to wander around in the mountains, or maybe he was just talking to the desk clerk at Ace. He was like that.

I wailed in agony. My two-year-old daughter fed her stuffed animals at her miniature table at the edge of the kitchen. We were at our home in the mountains, one hour from any hospital. *Just stay calm, Katie. Call someone. Get your phone.*

"Mommy, why are you peeing blood?" my little one asked.

"Mommy is okay. I think the baby is coming," I told her, leaving out that a pool of blood was not a good sign. I crawled to the edge of the couch and grabbed my phone. I began making frantic phone calls to my midwife and doula. I had a gynecology office too. The midwives were connected to it. I was going for a VBAC. I had read everything about it, and this was not one of the things I expected. What was this. I sat on the toilet because I felt like I had to defecate. This can't be a sensation due to labor progression. Not this soon. Only minutes had passed.

I listened into the trusted female voice on the other end of the phone.

"Trust that your body knows what needs to be done at this precise time. If you are going into labor, then there is a reason and your body is making the right choice. Trust it," my doula encouraged me.

My daughter climbed onto the kitchen table and proclaimed herself the circus ring-leader, as she tossed hot dogs into the air. One by one, they landed in the mouths of our eager dogs. Our Lab-Pit mix and Blue Heeler were thrilled to keep her anxious mind distracted. My moans were being drowned out by her brigade of loyal canines.

My phone rang with another caller. It was my midwife calling me back.

"Hello? Wait. I can't tal…." I tried to get out between another set of severe cramping. I leaned on my daughter's stepping stool. I hugged it as I looked up at my sweet girl running laps around the island in the kitchen.

"Mommy! Mommy! Look at Baxter! Look at me! We are playing chase!" She cried out. She had dressed herself in her favorite flower printed pants, layered with a tutu, a long sleeved shirt, a striped tank top over it, and a sequin hat. She had fashioned herself with every bracelet she could find. I could hear them clinging as she dropped a few while she ran, leading the dogs in their favorite game.

"Okay honey! That's so silly. Are you okay?" I tried to check in with her.

"Why are you crying, Mommy? Are you hurt?" She asked with concerned eyes, afraid to look. She slowed down to take a peek.

"The baby is coming. Isn't that special? I'm okay. Mommy is calling for someone to help. You play. Okay? Okay," I managed to get out.

I turned my attention back to the phone.

"Katie, are you in an accelerated stage of labor? You know your body, you've done this before. You know the timing, is this what you're experiencing?" The midwife asked.

"Yes, I think that is what's happening," I confirmed. Within the thirty minutes of phone calls, I could barely speak.

"Where is your husband?" She inquired.

"He's on an errand. He's not responding to text. What should I do?" I asked with confusion. This wasn't part of the plan.

"Katie, if you are in labor, you need to call an ambulance for assistance. That is what I recommend," She said with the most serious tone. "Can you do that?"

"Yes," I replied.

"Then I'm going to get off the phone with you so you can make that call right now. They will stay on the line with you until the EMT arrives at the door. If it's unlocked, give them permission to enter," she instructed. "You can do this."

In-between breaths, I dialed the numbers. 9-1-1.

"911, state your emergency," the voice said.

"I'm in labor. I'm 5 weeks early and I'm bleeding a lot," I said with fear in my throat and tears in my eyes.

"Where are you miss?" They asked.

"I'm at home, in the mountains. My two year old daughter is with me," I explained.

"Give me an exact address and I'll send an ambulance out immediately. Stay on the line with me until they get there," they said.

I was in the tunnel now. Going deep. It's loud here, and quiet at the same time. Sirens once more.

I was getting a call on the other line. Kane was texting me back, just as I heard him burst in the basement door.

"Katie, are you okay? Where's scrunchie? I left the door open for the EMT. Wait..I hear them. Stay calm honey," Kane said. He was getting frazzled. Blood startles people, barking dogs, crying women, and screaming children. This is it. This is our journey. It's as wild as the howling coyotes outside.

The local mountain EMTs maneuvered up our winding staircase like a team of lumberjacks. "Miss, we need you to get on this stretcher. It's a seat that will convert once we get you downstairs," they informed me, with the boasting assuredness of every man I've ever met.

"I'm not going anywhere," I growled at them from all fours on the bathroom floor, centered on what used to be my favorite bathroom rug. Now it was soaked in marroon. "I'm going to have this baby right here," I contended.

"We know that's how you feel, but your baby is very early. We need to find out why. If we get you down to the ambulance, we will have access to all our equipment if you and the baby need help," the woodworkers appealed to my logical side.

"No! You're not listening. I can't move. It hurts," I told them, trying to convey the contractions had me locked into a ball. I couldn't reverse into a standing position. My body would no longer straighten.

"We will help you up, if you let us. We can help you do this," they said, moving quickly now that they had my partial compliance.

As I spat out pain-induced profanities, they hoisted me into an upright position and strapped me onto the stretcher and rolled me into the ambulance. I screeched in sharp pain with every thump of the turning steps. They got me inside the van, and started hooking up all the gizmos.

"What ya think, mama. You wanna make a go for it down the hill? If you have the baby on the way, we can do that, but if we make it to the hospital, it might be better," the one closest to me confided. "It's up to you. Should we give her a whirl. You say the word. What hospital we shootin' for?" He asked.

"Fairview Adventist," I told him, remembering I was just there last week, filling out paperwork exceedingly early. I liked being prepared, so I could feel calm. What a plan this was.

"Okie dokie. Can we go?" He asked as he gave a glance to the other EMT and the driver.

"Yes, let's go," I said.

"Hear that?! Let's go! Hit those sirens!" He bellowed. "He's an excellent driver in the mountains. We are in good hands with him. Now let's keep an eye on you. We are gonna get this IV started miss. I'm gonna be as gentle as I can. I know you're in pain. Breathe."

Deep down, I knew they were angels with beards ready to jump into the tunnel with me, and as feisty as I was feeling earlier, I was grateful they were here.

The furriest EMT consoled, "I don't know exactly what you're feeling, Miss, but I understand pain. I broke my femur once. That's about a nine on the pain scale. I'll help you get through this."

"It feels like my body is being cut in half with a chain saw, while I'm alive and watching it," I shared with him, as he jabbed a giant IV into my arm with the van bouncing over an un-graded dirt road.

"Okay then, I think that's right around a ten on that scale," he said with a matter-of-fact look on his chin.

I stared out the back window of the ambulance as it wound round and round, spiraling down the mountainside. As we made our way through the canyon, I gave into the pain of being unmedicated and almost fully dilated. I thought, *my life is a series of disappearing and reappearing horizon lines.*

As I gazed at the swaying mountain, the other EMT documented my status. "Have the contractions stopped for you, Miss? Your vitals suggest you might be having one, but you seemed to have calmed down," he spoke with confusion.

"I'm having one right now. I'm just trying to give in to the pain," I worded through the trance Mother Earth guided me into. This is what it feels like to surrender. You go into the trance.

His eyes froze. "Okay Miss."

As the ambulance whipped to a stop, the back doors opened. A moment of silence started to wake with movement. When the ER doors swung open, my trance was broken by the blaring noise flooding back into my field. Multiple voices shouted stats and orders at one another. Traffic beeped and blared from the sidelines. Nurses argued over a sea of tangled cords, tugging at my arms. Intercom calls buzzed and machines beeped with insistence. An undertow of emergency ensued.

"You made it!" gleamed the only voice I cared to hear. It was my doula, Merrilyn, waiting beyond the doors with a smile that rejoiced in my arrival. Her glow made me forget the machines and placed me back where I belonged...in the present. The tunnel of birth paused with gratitude.

"Your baby is very early. Her heartbeat is slow. I'm getting confirmation from your midwife on next steps," a nurse spoke with blunt urgency over me, as four staff members lifted my body to another stretcher.

Moments later, "Okay, we've got confirmation. Miss, we are going to take you into surgery now. The anesthesiologist is going to put you fully under, and when you wake up this will all be over," the nurse relayed as she hovered over me.

I looked at Merrilyn, "It's going to be okay, Katie. I'll be right here with you," she spoke warmly as she held my hand. Her eyes flashed a million different outcomes at me, but settled in one of peace. She was a magician in that way.

"What does this mean?" I thought to myself. I'm going to the center of the tunnel again. Three. Two. One. Lights out.

The transcendence of birth and death are two experiences you undoubtedly face in singular. Within minutes of arriving, I was put under anesthesia and my baby was birthed through the uterine rupture that was tearing my womb in half.

A series of muffled sounds, finger squeezes, and hazy faces were attempting to reach me. As the density cleared, one began to register.

"Your baby is safe. When you wake up, you can meet her," a soft voice spoke as my hand was squeezed.

Where am I? My baby is safe. I heard that. Where is she? I need to hold her.

"You were asleep for awhile. They must have really knocked you out. It takes some people longer to wake up. Do you feel okay?" The nurse asked me.

"Okay. How long have I been out? Where's my baby? Who's holding her?" I questioned.

"Your doula has been holding her. She's beautiful and healthy. Are you ready to see her?" She shared.

"Yes. Please let me see her," I said. I was happy my doula was with her. If there was anyone other than me or Kane, it was Merry. She knew me and all I prepared for to bring this baby in with love and support. She was an angel too, who flew in right at the right moment.

Kane hadn't made it to the hospital yet. He was tied up in a series of phone calls, trying to uncover where they were rushing me. So Merrilyn held our sweet baby in a cocoon of motherly love until I awoke from my medical slumber. My preemie smiled in her sleep. Our little Buddha had arrived.

"I made it. Holy crap I didn't know which hospital they took you to. I called all of them!" Kane squacked as he snuck in the door. "Where's that little nugget? She okay? You okay? Holy crap, what a day," Kane rambled. He was overtaken. Wired. He said down and started talking a mile a minute. He was excited, and I was exhausted. After holding her awhile, I fell asleep again to the sound of Merry and Kane chatting it up, cooing over our baby girl.

A Colorado blizzard had been blowing in outside. Kane headed home to be with our other daughter. A neighbor had been watching her all night. In a couple weeks it would be Christmas. The following day, Kane brought our oldest daughter to see me and meet her new baby sister. The hospital echoed of strange uncertainty. I had been there by myself overnight and I hadn't seen scrunchie since the ambulance. What would she think? Was she okay? Was she ready for this? The lights in the hall were dim, and I shuffled in discomfort towards my family. Our daughter clung to Daddy like a lifeboat. Her eyes bulged with fear.

"Mommy? Are you gonna come home?" she asked with a worried heart.

As I saw the tearful distrust in her eyes, I knew I would never leave her. She came here to find out what happened to me. I was hit with a realization. It felt like the ghost of my future beamed into my presence. He showed me a movie of my life from another angle. I was shown the pain, sadness, fear, and heartbreak that could flood my daughters, for quite possibly a lifetime. A blood bath of could-have-beens gushed through the vacant hall. In that moment, I chose to be here more than I ever had my whole life. For these brave, loving girls.

On this occasion, my daughter's fear was softened with the new life of her sister. Her dismay was disarmed with sparkly stickers and a stuffed animal. She reached out to me for an inseparable hug. Mommy was still here. She began to trust again.

"When will the baby be able to talk?" she asked. Soon, my chatty angel. Soon.

I stayed with my second daughter for a week in the NICU, attempting to nurse her on a schedule. After day two they noticed she was getting jaundice and had to be under the Bili lights for a few days. She was given extra oxygen to help her fully arrive. I wouldn't leave. They tell you you can, but I wouldn't leave her side. I sat up next to her for hours while she napped with her little eye mask on. I knew she needed her mother's skin-to-skin warmth and love to keep her thriving. I held her until they forced me to put her down, so we could sleep. They let me stay in my room as a "boarder." I set my alarm to promptly wake for each time I was allowed to hold her again. I wouldn't miss one minute. Not after all that. No way.

My girls need me to take care of myself. They need me to heal every ounce of my being. My only option is to keep evolving. To keep growing. For myself, and for them. We were going to be the strongest family. The closest family. Connected. Always.

Under Pressure

I stood in the kitchen, holding an infant on my hip and picking out the red puffs from the cereal my toddler likes. I've been trying to work off the 40 lbs I gained during my last labor. It's not easy while still nursing around the clock. But my preemie is big and strong now. No one could guess what a start we had. Transitions were hard for my oldest. Prior to the birth of her sister, she struggled to transition for more than one errand today. The books called her "spirited." Aren't we all. She took special attention to acclimate to our expanded family. I devoted everything I had to their wellness and development.

Kane trudged up the stairs from his shop in the garage. "Isn't it time you went back to work?" He greeted me with a grumble.

"That's funny. I'm pretty sure this is work," I answered.

"No seriously, Katie. Just put them in daycare. You need to split the bills," he continued. *Where is he getting this crap. The son of a single mom. Oh, so that's why he thinks I should be doing everything.*

"*Kane, what* are you talking about," I stuttered. "When we took your transfer to this state we agreed that wiped out my teaching career. And with two kids, commuting out here in the mountains, none of it would make sense financially or time wise. Plus who would do all this stuff at home? I'm not getting any rest as is." His words hit my nervous system with a jolt. He didn't labor fifty percent of those childbirths, nor the aftermath. My brain was hit with so many thoughts of frustration, I began to lock up.

"I'd love to just sit around all day. Looks like a piece of cake. I don't know why you're always whining about how tired you are," he served up.

An internal gas leak silently hissed through my cells. What will be the flint that sets me aflame? Pressure builds, my muscles stiffen as if rigor mortis is setting in. Who am I kidding? I've been holding things in for months now, a decade, my whole life.

I'm being triggered, and Kane's index finger is on the mechanism. I thought my buttons would diffuse in time, or his attempt to push them. But that isn't the way it worked. The whistle blew louder each time the lesson circled back. This pattern of being unseen. I can't unsee it much longer. My neurological pathways have created a groove that I need to disconnect and restructure with intention. Neuroplasticity: nature's rematch.

Kane walked to the sliding glass door to perch himself with his vape pen.

"Let's talk about this after I get the kids to sleep. I'm in the middle of dinner right now," I suggested. He stared out the back door. "Kane, does that sound okay?" I prompt.

No reply. His body is half facing me, but his eyes look coldly into the distance.

My mind condenses. "How can you keep ignoring me?" I ask a deafened room. Once again, I'm invisible. That story has been on repeat for decades. He only notices me when I'm panicking. He responds to the stuff that invokes the rescuer. To get his attention, I must always be the victim. I must always be in crisis. But when I confront him with intelligence, I get stonewalled.

A wave of rage rolls over me. As I lift my hands I see them tremble. I belt out, "Why can't you say something!" I begin to leave the room to get away from him.

I need to relieve this tension. I used to drink, but now I have kids and I'm never off-duty. I swore off hangovers years ago. I'm beyond sober. I have zero interest in poison of any kind. When the wound of being chronically unseen is ripped open, it's like a natural gas explosion. There's a "pop" and everything gets muffled with a deafening noise. My hands and arms shake. But I don't know about tapping or somatic therapy yet. I cannot endure this one more second. *Get it out of me.* I feel like I'm losing my mind. *Good. I was outgrowing it anyways.*

"Look at you. You're such a mess, Katie. I bet you couldn't even hold a job. You can barely sit around here and do nothing, without shaking like some freak," he chimed in as I went down the hallway. *So now he has something to say.*

I was feeling like a leper until I remembered guys from high school who would punch through walls or head bang someone during a fight. I watched a prominent tennis player repeatedly smash his racket over his head, during a match one time. It reminded me—I'm not the only one on this planet losing their shit. There are intelligent, talented, unsuspecting people just as frustrated.

The noise in my head is too loud. I feel like an animal in captivity. "Why is that lioness charging the wall with her head?" the zoo onlooker asks. *Because she hates it here, that's why.* The world is asking her to be something she is not. They've made her into a spectacle, and yet invisible at the same time. This is a place of hell for the lioness.

This is the last stop before I make a life-changing decision. Things are about to shift. I can feel it. The pressure to sustain composure has been cranked lately, and I'm not doing well with that. I lead a local crunchy parenting playdate group, and I feel like a hypocrite. I promote all things unity, support wholistic well-being for children, and yet this is what I endure at home. I am torn. I am the organized homemaker people see on the outside, and I am also the lady coming undone behind closed doors. Neither of them feel like me. They are symptoms of me. Where is the free spirit? I must find her again. The one who floats with joy, grateful to be in the body. The one who doesn't let others hold her back. The one who believes in herself. The one who believes in magic.

As I stumble along a path of spiritual awakening, Kali has been summoned and she is on a rampage. One Katie is dying, and maybe it's me who is killing her off. They say on a path of enlightenment one needs to let go. It sounds so peaceful, to surrender. I guess I'm the kind of monk that goes kicking and screaming, ripping her Ego's clothes off to leave it shamed and exposed on the street. *There, we're done with you.*

With divorce on my mind, I returned to therapy. As I opened up, my therapist began to ask me questions, in which I had no response.

"Katie, where did you go just now?" she asked in a soft voice, like she was addressing a shipwrecked survivor who has been lost at sea, assumed eaten by sharks, and unofficially pronounced dead months ago.

"What do you mean?" I responded, feeling disoriented, and not quite understanding her question. I was listening to the waves. They got louder for a moment.

"You had the look of being shell-shocked. I asked you how you could advocate for yourself within your home, and your eyes lost focus and you appeared to freeze up. I'm not sure you were with me, in the sense that you normally are," she said. "Can you describe to me what you were thinking a moment ago?"

"Well, I could hear you talking, but you seemed to get farther away. It was like a tunnel experience, the way you feel just before you faint," I answered, feeling like I was talking about myself, not *as* myself.

"I think you were dissociating, Katie. It's a coping mechanism our brains have when presented with something that is too difficult for the senses to fully absorb."

I'm terrified by this comment. This is what I've feared. Losing my mind. And now it's literally fading off during my therapy session. When people ask me confrontational questions, I began to feel a wash of confusion. Paralysis. It was similar to an out-of-body sensation.

"What is dissociating?" I asked.

"Dissociating is something clients with severe trauma experience. It's a survival tactic of the brain," she informed.

"Oh, you mean like split personalities? Doesn't that happened to people who were sexually abused as a child? That never happened to me. Is it going to get worse?" I pressed her as I started to worry about the implications.

"It's not a split personality or any disorder. Well, maybe PTSD. It's a trauma response, and a bit of brain fog. Dissociation can happen in response to complex trauma. That can be emotional, mental, or even financial abuse that's gone on for years," she suggested.

"How can you tell if you've been subject to those things?" I asked her.

"This. This is one of the indicators. But let's talk some more about your father. Katie, have you heard of the term narcissist? Do you know what it means?" She asked me.

"Like self-centered?" I answered.

"It's more than that. It can be very subtle or very loud," she continued. "I have a book for you to read. You decide if this confusion you're feeling has been accompanied by examples similar to those in the book. There's more than one type of abuse, Katie. But only you can speak to what's happening. Let's pick this up next time, after you've dipped into your reading."

I resisted this new idea. My parents were humanly flawed, but they weren't evil. They loved me, didn't they? Am I unloved? How is love displayed. I'm not sure I know. Yes, I do know. I love my children. That is one of the only things I'm sure of right now. But what about the emotional stuffing I was raised with? If that's abuse, then we'd have a whole generation of people recovering from trauma. I think back to every emotionally avoidant man I've ever dated, including the one I married. Perhaps it's not me who is sick, but my environment. What a trip that would be.

When I tried to self-advocate, Mom, Dad, and Kane called me selfish, or flat out ignored me. They didn't listen to each other either. They were always yapping over one another like a pack of dogs in a frenzy. So concerned about being heard, that they never heard anyone. Around and around it went. Until it landed on me. I will dismantle the programming. My redemption lies in my willingness to look inside, deep down to my inner child. Childhood is the complete consciousness of freedom, innocence, curiosity, creativity, wonder, the belief in what you cannot see, and absolute love without bounds. A point in existence, such as childhood, deserves to be free from judgment. It deserves presence. It deserves love. We all do.

Necessary Evil

My creativity blooms in the fresh mountain Spring, but as I carelessly breeze into my home, each wildflower wilts. The lack of light suffocates every petal until it crumbles into a forgotten dust. The squeeze of irritation and discontentment deplete the oxygen in the room. The fighting in this house is blowing my withered remnants of self, right out the door.

"Work sucks. I'm tired," Kane declares. The sobering tension drags out. He flies a kite of negativity that dives and pierces those within his perimeter.

"What's wrong? I thought you liked working for yourself and having your own schedule," I inquired.

"Everything is fine," he lies between his teeth.

I press him, "It's not fine. I can feel it. It's uncomfortable. What is it?"

"I'm happy," he slights. "I'm always happy. I'm whatever you want me to be."

I can't handle the condescendment.

"Obviously you are not happy, and I don't appreciate the way you're speaking to me," I reply. "Can you be honest and communicate with me? I'm not a mind reader. Is it me, or is it something else?"

He continues to unpack groceries and act like he doesn't hear me from where he stands two feet away. I'm fuming. I demand a reply. He hatchets me with sarcasm and here it comes, like a rolling flame.

"It's a yes or no question. Either you are upset with me, or you are upset about something else, that isn't related to me. Which is it?" I push for a response.

Nothing.

"Ignoring me is torture. You're abusive! I can't take this anymore!" I yell at him. The flammable gas is rising. The switchboard starts smoking, lights flashing. The panic button is throbbing.

No response. Button pushed. I rush to our bedroom that has been void of any real connection for years. I let out a primal scream. The kind you howl when you are out of options. A rally cry to my pack, so they will know where to look for me as I am going down.

Kane peers into the bedroom at me. I plead, spitting through desperate tears, "Why do you do this to me? I'm your wife! You're ignoring me and it hurts! I'm not invisible!"

He doesn't care. I think he wants to see me go crazy. I fall to the wooden floor, bumping my elbow and knee on the hard Hickory planks. My stomach is having piercing pains again. Every time Kane inflicts this psychological warfare on me, I get doubled over. I crouch on the floor and hold my stomach. I can't stand up the pain is so bad. I hang like a weeping willow. I beg for something…anything, "Please, why? Please!" He calms, flashes that once loving toothy smile, and looks down over me. His face swells with a smug grin as he begins laughing. "You're fucking crazy, Katie. No one is going to want you."

"And you're a loser, just like your dad," I slither under my breath.

I peel myself off the floor as I feel the blood pumping through the artery in my throat. He stared at me with blank opposition. There's a snake in my gut, curled up in fear over what he might do. Last time I stood up to him he broke my glasses. Smacked them clear off my face. It was only that one time, but I would never view him the same again. From this coil, grew an aggressive instinct that has been turned on from the act of being cornered. I. Will. Show. You. Crazy.

He backed away and disappeared into the sandstorm. Men have been in the habit of using those words to trigger women. That's how they avoid feeling and it's how they exert control. That's what I was learning. All of this was about control. Those two gaslighting words: "You're crazy."

The prize for staying married is class, status, and the ability to survive. It's like my uncle said, "you're basically a high-priced prostitute." I'm certainly not doing this for a gold-frosted cake in 50 years. As it turns out, the gold-star conditioning expired for me. I crunch the numbers. They don't add up, unless I want to live next door to a crack house and hookers on Colfax. Not exactly what I had in mind as a former teacher. Financially speaking, I can't afford to leave this loveless, sexless, dysfunctional marriage. According to our world's construct, I can't afford to be alive.

Even if I transfer my certification and land a full-time teaching gig, I'll barely be able to pay for myself, let alone my daughters. I've heard horror stories about men who are self-employed finding ways not to pay child support. So then what? Do I have to stick with a relationship that has become deathly toxic? I ask the Universe. If there is a better way to heal this, please show me. Because I've come to a fork in the road, and I fear that both paths lead to a lethal drop off.

Kane owns numerous guns. He doesn't hunt, but he wants to be prepared in case of the apocalypse. In times circa 2019, I thought, well *that* will never happen. He keeps them hidden and locked in different places. I think he's afraid of murder. The essence of the gun. In paradigms of oppression, guns are an unnecessary threat. The real damage is done on litigation paper.

I know what it's like to hear a mother say she wants to die. One rainy evening, when I was in high school Mom said, "I'm ready to drive my car into oncoming traffic, into a semi-truck." She had just gotten back from a drive to get some fresh air. A comment like that leaves a child feeling helpless and hopeless.

I was stunned, "Mom...what? But why?" She echoed with discontent while walking back to her bedroom for the night.

Other times I remember her kneeling and begging. Sobbing and pleading. Her voice shrieking, "Why?! Why am I not good enough for you! You don't love me!"

A child rarely gets a bird's eye view of an adult. It was perplexing to see my guardian, who normally knows everything, brought to her knees, begging for answers. I thought, "We must not love her enough." I felt sorry for her and disappointed in myself. I wanted to help her, but I didn't know how. What does an eight-year-old kid know about lifting mom up off the carpet. What does an eight-year-old kid know about convincing mom her life is worth living?

I didn't understand her tendencies, until now. But there are other ways to show yourself mercy, besides a mercy kill.

"If you're depressed, just reach out for help!" preaches the commercial on the TV. "Connect with a Domestic Violence representative now if you feel you are in danger." Our world boasts a lot of assistance, but once I realized the emergency I was in, I found out just how false those billboards were. They expect you to show up with a black eye and then *maybe* they can qualify you. The systems were as equip to handle a crisis as a person wearing crocks on a 14er. *Ya ain't gonna make it buddy. This hike is meant for mountain goats and $600 gear.*

Slow Cheetah

"Think positive!" everyone told me. It's bullshit, I thought. I hit a plateau with traditional therapy, so I started asking myself, "How else can I dig deep? What else is out there I haven't tried?" I set the intention to heal, and to my surprise, opportunities began to find me.

I needed healthy organic food. I'll have to manifest a greenhouse. Why live in a rural area if you aren't going to be self-sufficient. His agendas continued to perplex me. But I knew digging in the dirt was good for my body, mind, and soul.

"The cold dirt will cool me off," I thought. I can stick my hands in the soil, rub it on my face, sit on a pile of it, roll around and ground myself. They'll call me Dirt Lady. Second house on the left.

"We should build a greenhouse!" I shared my idea.

"That hilarious," Kane responded.

"Well I'm not really into remodeling the inside. All this stuff isn't very useful. You know that, right?" I said.

"I never liked your decoration propaganda, so ya ain't hurtin' me," he boomeranged back. We've tried hard to emulate what a healthy family looks like, but I feel empty and caged. Real health comes from habits, and I want those. I want a partner.

"You know, it's not a crime to be healthy. Some people would value a wife like me who is into nutrition," I defended.

"Why don't you take that anti-depressant the gynecologist prescribed you. All you ladies are so hormonal. Thank god they have those pills for you these days," he said.

I was concerned about waking up in a fortress of white cubicle walls one day, with a series of numbers patched onto it. *Type in your ID code. Wait time is..22 minutes. I'm sorry, that code is invalid. Please try again.* Some Twilight Zone shit. The next thing you know I'd be teaching middle school in some

Orwellian nightmare. Reading an email pressuring me to "norm" the kids at the beginning of each day.

"How about *you* take the pills?" I reacted as I threw the bottle. I know what those pills are. They're not a happy pill. It's a contentment pill. A complacent pill. A don't-overreact pill. They're a shrug-your-shoulders-and-sigh-when-your-insurance-rates-go-up pill. A don't-over-analyze-your-marriage pill. A going-through-the-motions pill. A numbing pill. A death-of-my-soul pill. They're a patriarchy pill, and I won't take them anymore.

"Real nice, Katie," said Kane. "Mommy is upset today," he called out as if the children needed to hear our qualms.

"Do not make it their fault," I instructed Kane. "It's not their job to fix us." I didn't want him cautioning our children, like my father did. It was too easy for Kane to point the finger at me, when he was every bit a part of this toxic dance.

I crouch in the corner between my ebony dresser and a white door to the adjoining bathroom. Kane has me triggered again. I don't feel safe anywhere in the house when he is home. I gasp for air repeatedly. Tears stream down my face. My toddler looks at me with bewildered eyes. I smile and use my baby voice, "Hi sweetie, it's okay." She smiles back.

She leaps with superhero flight next to the legs I have tucked together, rocking my trembling body in a hug. She squats down with her knobby knees pointed towards me. Looking at me with her wide eyes she thoughtfully recites, "Do you feel like a cheetah is chasing you?" It's a line from a book on body awareness and emotions we have been reading together. I didn't know she understood the lesson, and here she was, her little voice gently pulling it out at precisely the perfect time. My little Jedi. I should be her She-Ra, not the other way around. Like a wounded animal, with its heart pounding to the beat of survival, my instinct is to hide when I am feeling weak. I do not want the children to be exposed to this stress, to these family dynamics. I want to break the pattern. Perhaps my vulnerability and endless drive to get back up again will be a demonstration of the courage it takes to manage the switchboard. It's hard to watch someone walk through the fire, but once you do, you know it is possible.

I used to be able to hide it, but there is no compartment to shuffle my emotions into anymore. I am scarcely absent from watchful eyes. Motherhood. No breaks. No breathers. No village. My body betrays me with its overload of adrenaline. Every time Kane snubs me, it ignites a wave of anxiety over me.

I think to myself, "I want out of here."

"Mommy," my sweet angel whispers.

The rush hour train in my head comes to a screeching halt that ends with the chime of a pin dropping. In an instant I snap back into reality. The one my daughter is in. I can never leave them, especially not with him. He doesn't know anything about nurturing children.

"I'm right here baby. Mommy is just a little tired today," I assure her.

She drifts peacefully back to sleep. As her angelic body lay there, her tiny chest rising and falling and little eyes fluttering in a dream untainted by the filth of life, I choked on the thought that maybe she'd never know how hard I was trying to heal—for her.

A mother is designed to respond to her baby's cries. It's a survival response. It's natural. I had a strong mother's instinct, but my wires were wound tight. I couldn't predict how the high-pitched sounds of my own children would make me flinch. As I'm startled, my chest cramps and a shiver of discomfort vibrates through my body. It stabs my eardrum with a needle. I never noticed how sensitive I was to sound. I put my hands over my ears, or avoid letting her cry at all costs. I wasn't allowed to cry like that when I was a child. There were negative consequences to strong emotions. That is why I was having these strong reactions as an adult, and they were compounded by issues with Kane. To learn how to hold space for my children, I must first learn how to re-parent myself. It's time for my emotional quotient to surpass my parents.

Kane sits on the family room couch. The room is grey with the pale moonlight falling on his shoulders, his head in his hands. Silent. Helpless. Hopeless. We are worn. It's time put this sullen night to rest. Tomorrow will be better. It has to be. I do not want to keep reliving this day.

I want the "enjoy-the-moment" pill. That's what life is really about. A series of moments to be cherished. But that pill doesn't come in a container.

Moving Energy

The warmth of the July air folded me in her arms and whispered of my youth. I'm ready to venture out.

"Mom is going to join her cult. She's getting all spiritual and is going to leave us," Kane sarcastically joked to our daughters. "Don't drink the Kool-Aid, sweetheart!"

"Very funny, Kane," I remarked as I looked for my car keys and sunglasses. I keep things in methodical places. I developed this habit to help myself in college to create order for my life. I liked everything in a viewable display. I had every drawer in my life memorized. If I didn't memorize them, they would cease to exist. I discovered this on my own and created solutions to be more successful. I was constantly running through a mental list of what was in each pile of papers for school. I had to picture it all in my mind, or else I could forget something important. Mom called me a "visual learner." Which made sense to me, since I was an art student. But it seemed everyone else was operating with some kind of autonomic system to manage this, and I was having to concentrate on each heart beat to keep my blood pumping. I felt exhausted, but my parents and now my spouse, called me lazy and immature.

Car key and sunglasses placement were part of my crucial method. I had a key holder, and my keys, no matter where I lived, went on the far right hook on the series of three hooks. Always. My sunglasses were placed in front of my purse, so I could see them, in the exact same location on the kitchen counter every time. They were reliably available the second I needed to exit the house. The essentials were always in my field of vision so I could be reassured I had what I needed to exit the house. When I began prepping diaper bags, it helped that I had previously established this routine. I already had a similar system down.

"Kane, where are my sunglasses? Did you move them? I always set them right here, and you know how sensitive my eyes are. I need them to drive," I called out to him.

"Sunglasses? I don't know, what color are they?" He replied from the balcony. He was sitting with our toddler watching me through the wooden banister rails. "Did you look next to your keys?" He asked.

"Yellow. You know what color they are. I wear the same ones every day. And my keys were sitting on the counter, which is also why I'm asking if you moved them for some reason. I always put my keys on the hook. Did you use my car today?" I continued.

Kane waved his hand, prompting our little one to do the same. "Look at Mommy, she lost her keys again. She's so silly. Wave to to Mommy," he said. "No sweetie, you must have done that. It's easy to set something in a different place when you're in a hurry," he offered.

This sounds plausible, but my system is so engrained, I could be sleep walking and I would place my keys on the third hook, furthest to the right. I have trained it to be an autonomic system. It's interesting. I don't lose my keys when it's just me in the house with kids. This only seems to be an issue when Kane is home. I'm starting to piece this together.

"Kane, I'm serious, I don't want to be late," I called up to him.

"Katie, I don't know where they are. Try not to get so flustered. Did you take your meds today?" He asked.

"What? What meds? I don't take antidepressants anymore. You know that. Why are you even asking me that? Can you help me find my sunglasses?" I pleaded.

"Well maybe you should. You seem awfully upset," he answered in a pout voice. "Look at Mommy down there rummaging around. She gets so confused. Poor Mommy. Can you say, poor Mommy.." Kane spoke with our toddler as she attempted to mimic his words.

His tone is giving me that spiraling feeling. I need to be on time. I went over each surface area where my sunglasses would be, knowing most of our furniture is designed with ultimate baby-proofing. Adult objects are only accessible to things waist level and above. I broke from what seemed logical and peered into a red fabric basket of toys that was placed on a shelf slightly above my eye level. There I saw a shimmering gold frame. My sunglasses. A shiver washed down my spine and settled in my stomach with nausea. There is no way a child could have put them in this location. The days are routine as a stay-at-home-mom. My system runs perfectly when it's just me and the kids. Even the toddler meltdowns are routine with my system in place.

I have everything timed with a 30 minute buffer for children transitioning from carseats. My background in teaching and Montessori method trained me to group each toy by category and place them in labeled bins. I had them laminated with a colored graphic so the kids could learn to identify the items and discover a sense of order. Kane seemed to be the only one who didn't identify the system, and he thought I was easily fooled. And maybe I was up until now. I had been so trusting of him. That's what they told me to be in a marriage.

"I found them. Kane, did you put them in this basket?" I asked him.

"No honey, one of the little ones must have thought they were a toy," he replied.

"But they were in a bin that is stacked and put away. It's been that way. I rotate the toys and this bin has been up where they can't reach it," I said.

"Well it's obviously in a toy bin. I didn't put it there," he answered, then looked back at our daughter. "Mommy is upset again. I bet she's gonna be late again. She just can't seem to remember anything," he spoke to our toddler.

I do remember things though. I have a system. The chaos only seems to surface when Kane is home. My nervous system was getting lit up, but I carved a path to the door. His words fell like grenades. They were his last attempts to keep me trapped, but I slipped outside the burst radius.

"You're moving energy," a person suggested at the workshop.

"A shooting pain keeps pinging through my arms," I say, describing the sensation of panic.

"Everything is energy. You know this. Your nervous system is set on repeat. Instead of continuously reabsorbing the message of pain, release it," he coaches.

I began to re-program my nervous system. I've done Cognitive Behavioral Therapy before, but I was ready for more than talk therapy. I understood that neuroscience shows what neurons fire together, wire together. I was ready for a quantum transformation of all my dysfunctional pathways, while I searched for their point of origin.

"Visualize yourself as a magnetic portal. Halt the energy from being internalized. Acknowledge it and envision sending it up and away, past the atmosphere, and into the void," my mentor guided. "Mothers and their children are energetically corded with a genetic rope. You're managing more than just your own energy," he explains. "It connects them to their source of safety and survival. Right now that's you. Be gentle with yourself."

If it authentically helps negative energy roll off me, I welcome it. This is my new method when I feel the overwhelming sensation of pressure, anger, fear, or any kind of claustrophobia arises when I have toddlers hanging on me. My perspective has changed. I acknowledge I am absorbing their nervous excitement. It's like an energetic umbilical cord. They need me to ground them into our bodies. I send the jitters back to the Source, which is like a giant recycling center for energy. Energy transformation.

I was getting to the root of the problem. It was coming down to one thing: believing in the wrong reality. The societal norm is a construct, and so was the version of me I had been living. I knew of my inner strength and intelligence, but I was surrounded by people who didn't.

Motherhood sent me down a rabbit hole of information prompting me to question what is "natural." A strong sense of intuition sparked during that time, an intuition that had been buried under years of social conditioning, in school, at home, at work, all over the place. The primal instinct in me began to awaken. The animal who had been put in captivity paced until she reached a trance like state. She needed to block out the over-stimulation of constant onlookers, and see past the bars prohibiting her from running free. There comes a time when the tiger remembers she is a tiger. Isolate an animal in a small cage and it will bite itself or start losing chunks of hair. I'm no different. Cultural conditioning has promoted an environmentally-in-duced illnesses, and I wanted out of that loop. Love and connection is my natural state of being.

Triptych III:

Dreamscape

Remembering

I found science to be a gateway to spirituality. Many get caught up in the surface concepts of science, but I experience it as an astounding map to connect the dots. If you delve deeper, you arrive at string theory, multiple dimensions, and the holographic universe. It all blows up and warps into a magnificent space-time continuum riddle. Mom told me most scientists were atheists. As a middle school Science teacher, I couldn't agree with that. I had the tendency to dissect facts and test truths. Before I was a seeker of truth, I was a seeker of proof. Atheism didn't ring true for me. It felt cynical and vacuous. I knew there was more.

Science shifted perceptions of spirituality. Labels like a hippy, flake, or mentally ill were planted. It's a misfired program I accepted when I was younger. Another boyfriend said, "people preaching about spiritual enlightenment are some of the most broken humans I've ever met." His words buzz in my head like an annoying gnat I want to smash with my swatter. I can't help anyone who doesn't know how to find Source within themselves. He just didn't see it. I was forced to reconcile the truth that we are all on our own separate journeys with an array of purposes. In his resistance, there was a lesson for my own acceptance.

I don't want to fall into the "let's start a cult" category. But wait, starting a cult sounds kinda fun and kinda cool. We could all wear robes like Gustav Klimt, or just be naked. I'm sure someone will have something to say about my spiritual naked church.

The first time I felt the presence of a spirit from the other side was when I had two infected wisdom teeth. My experience with synchronicities gave a nod to the poignancy of an inflamed tooth of wisdom, pulsing with a fire to be felt, and dharma to be recognized. It was labor-day weekend, my surgery to remove my wisdom teeth was resulting in dual dry socket infections, and I sat there sleepless without painkillers. I felt like someone had bashed my skull repeatedly with a lead pipe. The pain was becoming unendurable. I lay there helpless, as each second was lasting a midnight eternity.

When the moonlight began to blend with the rising sun I felt my grandparents' presence. I was hardly close with this side of the family, but there they were. I felt a hand on each of my shoulders. I knew one was on each side of me. I felt a neutralizing comfort wash over me. I was still in discomfort, but it was not nearly as acute. An undeniable sensation of love cloaked me with the message, "it will be okay." This can easily be explained away as chemical reactions in my brain to cope with pain, lack of sleep, and fear. I realize that. Logic agrees, but my intuition does not.

The experience left me with a knowing and a sense of peace. Even with the grains of skepticism that danced in my thoughts I knew my grandparents were watching over me, and to my surprise, they were able to pierce my reality and alleviate some of my physical aching. I know they used their ability to transmit the potent vibration of love over me and around me, like an electric blanket of relief.

I didn't have another experience as intense as that for quite some time. My days are sprinkled with the deja vu experiences of already knowing someone, or all of them actually *being* me. I am somehow looking at myself at a different stage in my evolution throughout the time-space continuum of existence.

The next clear-as-day afterlife happening I witnessed involved my cat. Ghostie was the U-Haul cat. She pissed on everything for years and left me with a scar on my face. My beloved. She was almost twenty years old, miserable, physically shutting down, but refused to die. I was eight months pregnant. Another life was about to enter this world, and poor Ghostie...it was her time to go. Sobbing, I took her in to meet her maker. Yes, I Kevorkianed her. I felt like a hypocrite, growing one life inside me as I snuffed out another. Ghostie was a bundle of anxiety. Her quality of life grossly diminished. In my heart I know I showed her mercy. I loved her turquoise eyes paired with a Russian blue coat, even when she was hissing "fuck you" two inches from my face each morning. When confiding in others that knew her, they replied, "I would have put her down years ago."

After the deed was done, I wrapped her in a blue blanket and put her in a cardboard box, to be buried at home in our yard. The drive back to the house was a quiet five-mile ride in the mountains. I left the radio off and tried to calm my saddened heart. That's when I heard something. A purring. Despite her catty clawing bitchiness, she had one of the most calming, radiating purrs. *Okay, this can't be what I'm hearing. That cat is dead. I'm turning on the radio.*

I arrived at home on the cold night in early November. It was too late in the evening to bury her. Instead, I brought the box into the garage so it wouldn't stink up my car. I lowered the garage door and crouched down to say a final goodbye, before I went inside. I closed my eyes, and there it was. The purring. My eyes popped wide open, like I'd heard a ghost...a Ghostie...a fucking dead cat purring at me. *This is nut job city.* But I was so sure and so freaked out, I uncovered her face and body, wondering, "Did they not one-hundred percent kill her? Is this cat still alive?"

I unwrapped her face. Dead. Yet, as I stared at her cold eyes and their lifeless glare, with rigor mortis setting in, I kept hearing the purring, plain as day. My Ghostie's soul was lingering. I felt like she was saying thank you. She was no longer in pain, and I was probably the only person who was nice to her (other than the murder part). I excused myself to enter the house, feeling confident she would cross over if I left her to rest. The following morning Kane buried her in the woods of our front yard. Living in the mountains, we had to immediately adapt to the savagery of nature. Poor Ghostie's body was dragged from her grave, and into the center of the front yard twice that month, visible through the family room window. At least I knew her soul was no longer inhabiting her body. I could cope with the breakfast cat carcass on the front lawn. Mountain life, not for the faint of heart.

The more I lean into spirituality, whether it be through meditation, reading, or listening to binaural beats, the more spirit leans into me. I like being in tune with elements of Consciousness. It's a teacher from the other side, sometimes in the form of angels or guides. It's difficult to acknowledge these realms without feeling hokey, but I'm not into backing down. I'm into peering over the edge. Isn't that what I was doing when I tried to get as close to intentional death as possible? I was ready to drop the fear and find my purpose.

It took a few years to fully wake up. About thirty-nine to be exact. I found, after spending numerous years contemplating the end of my existence, and taking the end for a test drive, waking up was inevitable. When your days have been doused in crimson bloodletting, leading you closer to an unavoidable death, you are stopped in your tracks when a ray of light shines down upon you. The blood dries on the pavement and turns into a petroglyph.

My main goal became not drifting back to sleep. I began to do things to sustain my new awareness. It's like waking from a dream you do not want to forget. I wrote things down and skipped the mood-fogging substances. I began doing things to stay centered and poised for growth. Intentions became crystal clear, and doubt began to fall to the wayside. This time around, I didn't care if spirituality came off as cliché. I'm not a recovering addict. I'm a recovered soul.

I've died over and over, like ground hog day. I feel glimmers of gratitude for getting through it. My future Self resides in me. I keep reviewing my life, and I'm convinced I can hop back down and do it right this time. I vow to remember where I came from. The message I keep hearing in the back of my head is, "Do not play it safe this time. Make your dreams come true. Go all in. Hang on and be your true Self."

It's like a panel is cheering me on from above. I've made it past more check points than previous attempts. In some way, I feel the panel of supporters and watchers, are me. They are different lifetimes of me shouting down to me, like my swim coach and fellow swimmers used to scream and yell through the water at me during meets. I received it as a muffled sound of familiar voices. What were they saying? I think they sound happy…I think they want me to keep going. I must almost be to the finish line. Breast stroke. Butterfly. Freestyle. This time it's a relay.

My lessons are absorbed with a drop of saltwater sanity. Epiphanies seem to come after consecutive days of spiritual focus. I had been meditating twice a day for over a week. It put me in a completely different headspace. Somewhere deep in my sub-conscience I was still asking for a sign. Was I on the right path or making a huge mistake. I settled into bed, as I watched the night fall through the window. My little one was next to me, and the dogs sprawled out at the foot of the bed. I had been sleeping so deeply, my dreams were becoming quite vivid again, similar to when I was a child. With groggy eyes, I rested my head on the pillow, welcoming a good long slumber.

BAM! BAM! BAM! BAM! BAM! BAM! BAM!

A gasp of air cranked my jaws open and filled my lungs to capacity. What the heck was that noise?! I was certain my house was being burgled. Or maybe it's our friend. We had rented out the bottom room in our house to a young man we knew over the last few months. Maybe he locked himself out. Why was he banging on the door like that though? Is he drunk? Oh no, maybe it's one of those mountain men that's come out of the woodwork to rape and pillage. It still happens, so I hear. There are people tucked in the cracks up there. Men who wanted to leave society. I quickly peeked out the back window, where the knocking would have been on the door from our friend. But no one was out there. I crept back into my bed and lay still, listening for movement. But no one came. I glanced at the clock. It was 2:12 AM. I took notice of my dogs, still fast asleep. "Well that was weird," I thought to myself. The dogs can hear a coyote or a rabbit an acre away in the yard of our mountain home. They go nuts when they smell a bear at 3:00 AM. But tonight…nothing. I was too tired to analyze it, so I cuddled up further under the covers and went back to sleep.

When I woke up in the morning, I chalked it up to one of those dreams you have where you fall off a cliff and are shocked into waking up. It must have been something like that. I texted our friend and he replied he was no where in the area. He had stayed at a friend's house near a 14er he was going to hit. I didn't elaborate too much. Then I was whisked away by the duties of motherhood for the next 15 hours. I had all but forgotten the incident by the time I went to bed. Toddlers have a way of extracting memories. They filled my day with countless questions and trillions of mini-stories of their magical lifetime within a day. It's quite beautiful, and by the time story time rolls around, I'm ready to be tucked in too. I recently finished weaning my littlest daughter, so she is sleeping with daddy. My older daughter is next to me. Night time is her time to catch up on quality time with mom. The dogs were hogging the foot of the bed once again, but I didn't mind. I liked the way they kept my feet warm with their solid stature. After another reading of *Goodnight Moon*, I nodded off with them.

BAM! BAM! BAM! BAM! BAM! BAM! BAM!

"Gaaaasp..oh my god. Not again," I thought upon this rude awakening. A panic hit my heart as it exploded with rapid beating. "This is it. I really did hear that sound last night. But they must have chickened out. Now they are back, whoever they are."

Surely I was about to hear clinging decor and drawers being ripped open. Soon I would hear the footsteps of whomever had just been rapping on the door. This time I was scared. This was no joke. I tucked my daughter's head under the blankets with me. Maybe they wouldn't see us in here. Maybe they would just grab the checkbooks on the kitchen counter or something else of value. I lay under my sheets, just like a child afraid of a shadow in the night. I tried to recall where Kane put the baseball bat for intruders. But no one came. After my heart beats began to calm, I peered from under the blanket. The dogs were still fast asleep. What the hell was going on around here? I looked at the clock. 2:12 AM. It sent shivers up my forearms and goosebumps down my neck. Someone was here. I couldn't see them, but I sensed it. It was all around me.

As I laid in my bed, I watched the moon glow past the 60 foot Pine tree swaying outside my window. I was overcome by a stillness that filled the room. I felt the warmth of the love frequency, like a pink cloud of cotton softening every molecule of air in my bedroom. The stillness had words floating through it. I couldn't see them, but I could feel them. A message. Words dropped down as thoughts. It was a knowing. I was waking up to my purpose. There was no one standing in my room with me, but I felt something. It reminded me of a place I had been before. It was that same stream of peace I floated on beyond the hexagon-tiled floor. The same divine presence enveloped me. An intelligence of love. If the sound of a thought could expand to fill a room, that is how the message was transferred. It washed over my body, like a warm sunny wave from the Na'Pali Coast.

"You are never alone. You never were, and you never will be," it said, like a crystalline echo filling up the room. It knew me, whatever this was, and it was answering my lifelong question to the Universe. I was wrapped in a feeling of peace. A peace so calming, I drifted back to sleep.

Over the last decade, I had explained away my previous near death experience as a effect of the concoction of drugs I was on. My atheist mind of science-insisting logic pushed away any other possibilities. But this incident provided clarity and validation. It unified things. What I experienced years ago was real. The realms I went to were the same. Once when intoxicated and near death, and the other while completely sober and aware. Spirit hit me from both angles, until the connection was clear and I could receive the message.

"You're not psychic, Katie," grumbled Kane. *Damn, I'm not trying to read your mind but thanks for the vote of confidence.* I reserve my right to exercise skepticism, but my open heart and mind told me *this is truth.* I have suspended my belief system to allow for other possibilities and perspectives. Childbirth put me into direct connection with intuition. There are other ways to align, but this was mine.

I began to have extraordinary expansion happenings. After one session with my acupuncturist, I thought I must be dizzy from the treatment. As she moved about the room, I could see a fuzzy soft purple glow around her. It moved with her and spanned about three inches around her silhouette.

I checked other objects in the room to see if the halo fuzz was covering everything. It wasn't. There must be a smudge on my contact. So I blinked a few times. But her halo was still there, like a luminescent glow of lavender.

I have heard of people who can see auras, but I had never experienced it firsthand. It always seemed like a fantasy super-power, like wishing you could fly or become invisible. A tiny little part of me always thought those people were making it up. In that moment, I became one of "those people." I shifted from being the doubter to the doubted. Although I didn't have proof someone wouldn't believe me because I didn't talk about it to anyone.

I was still settling in to the idea that I had a right to experience my own reality. I knew what I saw, and it was mesmerizing, captivating, peace-inducing, and it gave me a certain confidence in myself. For once, I didn't need to confirm what I was experiencing with anyone else. I didn't need validation. I confirmed it with myself, and that was enough. In hindsight, this was a huge transition in trusting my Self.

As enchanting as the experience was, I didn't know if I would ever be able to see an aura again. Maybe I needed to keep myself in a state that was induced by the acupuncture. Budget would prevent that for some time. I didn't see another aura for almost two years. I attended a seminar in Boulder, when it happened. About halfway through the speech, there it was. I moved to other areas of the room, certain it was an effect of the lighting on stage. Without warning, the speaker became surrounded by a glowing translucent aura. Once viewed, I was unable to continue my disbelief. It became a deeper part of my knowing. *Yeah, sometimes I see things.* Apparently, that's who I am now. My imagination has shifted into an ability. Much like any skill, it takes a little practice and focus to tap into. For some, it appears effortlessly.

I'm tantalized by unraveling the bigger picture. Intense introspection begs for expansion. The anxiety, depression, and madness I experienced in the past is lifting. Not without waves of resistance, but ultimately, things are transitioning. I have reframed those symptoms. Perhaps I have always been a different expression of human. One they did not have a word or term for when I was younger. One that is largely misunderstood. The stuck energy in my nervous system is getting a chance to escape and return to its authentic form. By telling my truth, I am discovering Truth.

Rocky Mountain High

"What do you think about open marriages?" I asked Kane, as we stood in the kitchen, knowing he'd be cool with it. Before he met me, he was having threesomes with his two female roommates. I knew he was open to this type of discussion. We weren't the typical married couple and I think we prided ourselves on refusing to fully conform to tradition.

"They're cool. Why? Do you want a girlfriend?" he delivered with a sly grin, as he leaned towards the crack in the back door, blowing the smoke from his one hitter outside. He always liked the idea of me with another woman. I knew that, so his response didn't surprise me.

"Maybe, but what if I was curious about other men?" his face washed over with a restrained wave of *I'm about to lose her*. And he was right. My question wasn't about wanting variety. It wasn't about exploration. It wasn't about becoming swingers. It was about getting permission to connect with passion and love. Love that had slipped through my fingers and drifted from my heart years ago. I didn't want to die without love. Nor did I want to live without it. I missed sex with love. Soul-bearing sex. That's what I wanted before I died. And I was done trying to find it in him. I didn't feel safe with Kane. He couldn't see me, and I wanted to give him permission to get his needs met with someone else. If Kane chose this path with me, I might be able to find out what presence during sex was like. Just not with him. Cheating was not an option for me. As it turns out, neither was marriage.

"Sure. I'm not possessive or jealous. You know that," he responded, swallowing any recognition of pain. A cockiness feathered over him. A cloak that protected him in life.

I heard, *you have the freedom to meet other people and be sexual again*. And I took it.

"It could be kind of like Polyamory, where we are completely open about who we meet and are considering? Be absolutely open and honest?

This would go for you and other women too. It might be good for us. What do you think?" I clarified, while bending over our pristine marbled granite countertop in the kitchen. It had shades of the sunset washed into it. I loved it for its beauty. And I would miss it. The decisions being made over its flawless surface were filled with sledgehammers of truth.

"You really want to try this? To spice things up? I'm okay with it. You need to be safe though. We can alternate a date night or something, if it goes that far," he suggested, starting to absorb a notion of some of the benefits. "No crazy people. No one comes to the house."

"Agreed," I delivered, confirming the beginning of the end. That day we exchanged vows, I forgot to tell him…I'm not marriage material. That is, I can't be bought.

Housewives and stay-at-home moms all around me were using sex to barter marital agreements. People have joked about it my whole life. When I felt my marriage shifting in this direction, I felt disgusting. I won't be a prostitute. My gut told me I was supposed to be turned on by my husband. I was to desire physical connection with him. But I didn't. I didn't want him touching me. I was convinced I had a hormonal imbalance rendering me incapable of getting aroused. Then it happened. My sacral began to feel, but not for him. There was nothing wrong with my body. There was something wrong with the depth of connection. I want an exchange of love and pleasure.

"Kane, it hurts," I said as I stopped him once again.

"Fine. It always hurts with you. You never like sex with me," he said defensively.

"It's not you, it just feels like broken glass inside me. I don't know why it hurts so much," I replied.

"Well, we could use more lube if that's the problem," he suggested.

But I knew the issue was beyond that. Ever since my second was born, sex was excruciating. No one seemed to have an answer. It took me peeing blood for me to demand I go to the doctor. Kane was annoyed.

"Seriously? You have a bladder infection again?" Kane asked.

"I don't know. I guess. Something is wrong, My body hurts so bad. I need to drive to the emergency clinic and get medicine or something," I pleaded.

"Katie, it's 1:00AM. Is this really necessary?" He asked.

"I'm going," I told him.

"Fine, be back by the time I have to start work in the garage. I can't watch the kids all day. You want this to be your job, then do it," he reported.

Over the next month I had numerous visits to the ER—alone, and a couple trips to my gynecologist. They almost had me going in for bladder surgery, when I decided to get a third opinion by a naturopath. She simply asked, have you tried going off birth control pills? It had never occurred to me. But she said the "broken glass" sensation and combined with blood is a sign of inflammation. Inflammation that can be caused by synthetically induced menopausal symptoms from tweaking my system with progesterone. I detoxed. I went off birth control pills. The pain went away, and my moods stabilized in a way I could hardly identify. They had been tampered with for so long.

"Great, I guess we are back to condoms," offered Kane. In reality, we were back to nothing. Pregnancy terrified me now.

A month later a new friend, Hans, texted me a quote from one of his third grade poems. My life has great timing. The irony fills me with gratitude. This is how my day starts at 7:17AM. If I tapped out years ago, I never would have had mornings sprouting with:

"Mary wore tortoise shell glasses
she made straight A's in all her classes
she had the school beat
she likes to cheat
she never gets caught
and always passes."

Oh Hans, your third-grade poetry fancies me. Up until now, he had been my virtual friend, exchanging memes and playing linguistic cat and mouse. I shot him a text, "I want to meet you in person. Today. Noon."

He responded with his classic neurosis, "That's in like ten minutes!" (It's not. It's in two hours.) "I'm hung over, my eyes are bloodshot, and I'm shiny with alcohol sweat," he whined.

"Get over it, Hans! Today is the day. Pull yourself together," I insisted. He caved and agreed to meet me at a local park. As I pulled up behind his black 4Runner, I was exhilarated by this little rendezvous. I hopped out of my Subaru and climbed the hill about twenty yards. I saw him towering above me, so I waved at my previously incognito pen pal. We hugged, like long lost friends do, and sat at a picnic table. The cool air gave me a jitter and I confessed I had never been to this park.

He replied, "Oh…I think this is the sort of location people meet up to do shady things, like deal drugs, and meet strangers under a myriad of questionable circumstances." He gave me the lowdown on his charmed upbringing, which he flung himself through as the black sheep. Well done, Hans. After he was satisfied that I posed no risk, he suggested we go to his place, as he needed some hair of the dog, and my teeth were noticeably chattering from the cool air setting in at altitude.

Hans had a way of harmonizing with my moments of intimacy. Three nights ago, I tried to watch a session of Erika Lust porn with Kane, to try and revive even a spark of passion. With a cosmonaut's precision, at precisely 11:48PM, in the middle of the fifteen-minute video, Hans sent me a "Big Tiddy" moth meme. His teenaged son had shared it with him. I heard the ping on my phone and couldn't resist. I knew the text had a better chance of extending pleasure to me than my efforts to induce arousal for my spouse through porn. Porn yes. Husband no.

But what does it mean? It means Hans and I exist on a moronic molecular plane of immaturity and empathy. Synced in sadness. He's a forty-seven year old vodka drinking, sativa smoking, neurotic ball of piss, vinegar, Jerry Garcia, Photoshop, and the Oxford English Dictionary. He speaks with private school pretension and the quirkiness of Jeff Goldblum. He boasts of his impeccable morals, while trolling his counterparts online, patting himself on the back every time he wins a battle of words and whit.

I discovered Hans could be rendered speechless in person. Especially if you dance around in yoga pants, after toking some Blue Dream. An overflow of kitchen items haphazardly spewed out of open cabinets and into cardboard boxes. My neighbor, an ambitious mountain woman with a horse, was in the middle of a move. I thought it would be fun to invite Hans by for a beer and a chat while I squatted at her house, which so happened to be right next door to mine. I ducked out here, from time to time when I needed to clear my head.

As Hans approached the home, I quickly waved him into the front door. He paused with caution and asked, "Are you sure this is cool? Feels a bit shady. What happens if your husband comes to the front door? Is he gonna freak that we are hanging out?"

"Of course not. You're fine," I hastily consoled, knowing this looked sketchy. But I've been known to take a calculated risk or two, especially when the reward is to feel alive again.

It was a hazy, cicada-singing, star-twinkling summer night, and for the next three hours, we smoked herb, babbling until we laughed ourselves into hysterical fits of tears. I haven't felt this free in a long time. Hans positions himself in front of a window with plain view of my house. He says, "I want to make sure he has a clear shot, if he so chooses." I assure him my husband has guns but wouldn't shoot anyone.

"Yeah, no one wants to kill anyone…until they do. That's how it works," Hans mumbles, nervous Kane might shoot him through the kitchen window at any moment, but not quite fearful enough to stop our high school style smoke fest in a dimly lit, partially abandoned house. Hans leans in, maybe at the opportunity for someone else to pull the trigger.

I'm infatuated with this feeling, but Hans skipped out before we crossed a line. He fumbled through his mental thesaurus, and came up with, "You smell like a girl," as he awkwardly made a mad dash for the door. Any closer than arm's length, and he got jumpy. The next day, we could barely remember what had us laughing so hard, but it didn't matter. It felt good to get lost in laughter. That much is tangible.

I was feeling some zest for life again. Hans doused my fire with a quote from Macbeth referencing the meaninglessness of life. As much as I adored his recitation, I disagreed with its sentiment. Life is not without meaning or purpose. His un-emotional demeanor is familiar. I've been married to it for a decade. I continue to poke around his barricaded blood blister of a heart, trying to make it bleed like mine. Hans needs my display of uninhibited passion, as much as I need his loyal indifference. It's a pattern of attachment we both know. He is a safe stranger, the perfect witness to my unraveling.

If I am to make any sense of this, let me be alone with my thoughts. Let me sink into some Pretty Lights. Let me let go of all their stories about how life *should* be, and sift into the appreciation of what it *gets* to be. My life shifts into a favorite summer song I play a thousand times. My soul can't get enough of that sound. My heart is insatiable for this vibration. Hit replay. Hit replay. Hit replay.

I wasn't ready to let go of my endless summer sunsets. I sunk into the kitchen table and cried. The leaves rustled with a brisk change as the wind blew through them. Kane looked at me with dismay and rolled his eyes. He was numb to my emotions. It's coming. I'll be forced to change. I'm asking for it, but I'll resist it.

Although I have trouble with transitions, I miss the seasons when I can't see and feel them. The beauty is hard to perceive without the shift. Life is a paradox. I need the earthly reminder of my coordinates throughout my trip around the sun. The somber sound of crisp aspen leaves indicated a change of season that I was not yet ready for, but desperately needed. Would I ever really be ready? I feel it. All I have is Now.

Tasting a little death makes life more palpable. There are varying levels in which this can be achieved. For some, watching an action movie might suffice. For others, doing something invigorating, like skydiving or kayaking with whales off the coast of Alaska may be what it takes Exploring what helps me taste life in a way that reminds me of its potency and its poetry became my endeavor. I need my heart to race until the endorphin dump is achieved. Nature's speedball. My daily vitamin.

This urge to see what's beyond, took me just far enough to receive the message. Acknowledging my past mistakes, understanding them at face value, and then letting go became most important. I will no longer be the carrier of my family conditioning. I am breaking the pattern. It isn't easy, perfect, or final. It's an ongoing process that starts with noticing. I will not continue to imitate the negative traits I have unconsciously absorbed. I will consciously say, "Those are not my thoughts. Those are not my traits. That doesn't have to be me, and it isn't me." I create new mantras. My lineage got me this far, and now, as a unique, empowered spirit, I can take it from here. I will thank them for passing the torch to me. I knew it was a relay, but I now understand it's not a race.

I have gotten good at overcoming obstacles. But I can stop manifesting obstacles for the sake of overcoming them. I get to learn new habits. I get to enjoy the habit of living in the moment. There's still a flamethrower in the back of my head that wants to get lit at times. I hush it like it's an angry baby who's missing her nap. *Nite, nite baby flamethrower...shushhhhh.*

I was changing. When faced with frustrating incidents I began to ask myself, "What am I supposed to learn from this?" I tried not to think of unfortunate situations as happening *to* me, but rather *for* me. I no longer thought of karma as coming to get me or as punishment. I also challenged myself not to use perturbing experiences as opportunities to judge others.

I flip it, and the wounds become lessons that help me evolve on my journey. The pain softens. It sounds good on paper. It looks good on a meme with a beachy background, or a mountaintop destination, with eclectic cursive writing that says, "Explore More!" It sounds amazing, like the jump I need. But to actually do it is quite another thing. Diving deep is terrifying. I'd have to push past the fear. Jump into that lake of icy water on New Year's Day. Now do it every day. That's Waking Up: Stage One.

My need to be saved was lifting. I didn't need a knight in shining armor on a white horse. I am the white horse. Untamed, galloping, grunting, and bucking. The helicopters have been so loud, I couldn't hear the pounding of my hooves. I run wild, just for the sake of feeling the wind, the power, the freedom.

I was trapped in a rabbit hole of anguish for a while and it took time for me to tunnel my way out. In fact, I never expected the level of guilt I would feel for finding my way out of the dirt. My relationships have shifted. I realized some people needed me to stay lost.

"Go back to the way you were," Kane said.

"Laying in bed, depressed and suicidal?" I questioned. *Fuck no.* I could have never predicted how it would feel to let others down by pulling myself up. It's contradictory and baffling. I've been warned not to bite the hand that feeds. But I told myself, "Quit reaching for the hand of your oppressors to lift you up. Lift yourself up. It's not only possible, it's the only way."

From my experience, Oneness felt lonely at first. I reminded myself, it's my turn to let my light shine. I craved the freedom to be authentic and help others in the best way I could. What do I have to lose? My reputation? Ha, that was a thin sheet to begin with. At times the process felt like someone took my guts out and hung them on a grappling hook. *Nothing to see here.* Gurgles blood. *Just keep moving.*

I started to have faith in my journey. But when did I begin to believe I possessed a light within a spectrum perceivable to others? Hans. He dropped down from the macrocosm to bear witness to my vulnerability.

After our first meeting, Hans led me up the stairway of his house. I followed and scouted the place out, like I was entering the vacation home of someone's rich uncle. We were innocent, and yet it felt mischievous. He poured us tiny bar glasses of grapefruit juice as he unfolded the rest of his life story. I could tell Hans had gleefully told the story of his woes many times. He had all the punch lines perfected. The story as he enjoyed telling it, not as he suffered experiencing it. That much he had a choice over.

I intended to read Hans' body language in person. I had created an image in my mind, but I needed to know if it was accurate. There was something freeing about meeting a stranger in person, and being able to say whatever comes to mind, knowing you can go back to life, as if none of it ever happened. No loss. Courage gained. I wanted to ask him something bold to his face. This was one of those opportunities.

"If I wasn't married, would you be interested in me?" I asked, while staring him in the eyes. I sought validation on multiple levels. But this wasn't just about validation, it was about being unabashedly vulnerable and exposed in truth.

Hans squirmed from the other side of his bachelor sized bar, uncomfortably conversed with himself out loud, and outwardly yearned for the safety of his computer. I'm not giving him time and privacy to orchestrate a response.

After a few long moments, Hans said, "You are beautiful." Seeing me shifting in my seat he clarified, "Your mind is beautiful."

My eyes welled. For a person who had been beaten down to accept a constructed label, and manipulated to identify with the concept of mental illness, these words were profoundly healing. I had needed to hear those four words for a lifetime. Anyone can call me pretty, or desire a warm body next to them, but to notice my mind and admire it above all else? This is the recognition I have longed for. This is what Kane didn't see. My heart ached and healed at the same time.

ABRACADABRA!

As a lifeguard, I learned to scan the water. A thrashing victim, about to drown, can look as innocent as a person playfully splashing and bobbing in the water with friends. The desperate cries and attempts for life are muffled by the sounds of perpetual laughter, chatter, and slushing water. Human turmoil can be misinterpreted, or overlooked altogether. The company I've been keeping hasn't learned how to scan. I must learn to be my own buoy. I listen to the water whisper to me. I scope out my vital signs.

I sent out an S.O.S. in the form of lipstick smeared mirrors and pills rattling in plastic containers. It came back to me, tenfold. The Universe delivered. All I had to do was ask, and believe it was possible, not with my mind, but in my heart. A person can understand something intellectually, *I've read all the books,* but it must be internalized and embodied to swirl through the cosmos.

I braced myself for a colossal shift. I felt a gate being opened. It was my third eye. A path was being laid to accelerate my journey. I asked the Universe to show me what else was out there. How could I get out of this mess? To my astonishment, I started receiving alternative ways to heal. Traditional therapy was put on the back burner. I hit a plateau with it, and it was time to move on. A spiritual quest had been awakened. Opportunities fell into my lap like the magical gifts of childhood once did.

Over the summer, I had a passing conversation about a mysterious entheogen. Plant medicine had come onto my radar. I had no desire to be under the influence for entertainment or escapism at this stage in my life, but something about diving inward interested me. The subject disappeared, unregistered with my mind for a few months. Then the Universe boomeranged my curiosity. I signed up to attend an ambiguous "lightworker workshop," addressing metaphysics, metacognition, purpose, energy hacks, and attunements. The woman hosting appeared to be something of a mystic and kept blerping on my sonar. She was living off grid in a yurt, one of those extremists truly walking the walk. Maybe she had something interesting to say. Surely it would be better than watching another mindless sitcom at home.

The event host trotted into a cubicle of a room, located in a plaza building. She flowered the air with her English accent and Downton Abbey poise. Her tact and prudence was balanced by a decorative blue headscarf and dream catcher earrings that flowed in white feathers down the sides of her neck. Her deep brown eyes twinkled with the secrets of a gypsy. I was officially intrigued.

Our charismatic instructor engaged us in a evening of quantum consciousness and balancing the biofield. Some of the information might have been difficult to absorb had I not taken some classes in Subtle Energy. My days teaching middle school Science and reading articles on quantum physics while the kiddos viewed BrainPop videos on the human body systems provided prior knowledge.

As I settled into the workshop, a tall blonde swooped into the room, adorned in a mini skirt—despite the frigid weather, fringed bag, and beach-combed hair. Carmen was another beacon of light. She looked nothing of an executive from the corporate world she described herself as coming from. Acting as a messenger of divinity, she shared stories of her astounding healing. She spoke of plant medicine from the Amazon and a little green frog that helped her clear mold poisoning and Lyme disease. A slight scarring of pink dots adorned her ankle from her treatments. As I contemplated her words, she invited me to her Land Rover, where she shared a medicinal snuff, known as hapé, made from a mixture of tree ash, tobacco, herbs, spices, bark, roots and flowers.

"This will clear your energy. The indigenous tribes use it to ground themselves," she shared.

Is this what CEO's are up to these days?

"Breathe in, then hold your breath as I blow this up your nose. Focus on opening your heart," she instructed. I didn't expect those words to come out of this tall-blonde-suburbanite- turned-bohemian looking woman. With the punch of an earthy smelling salt, a stinging burn quickly ignited my senses. My fingers fumbled to find the crest of my nose, as I blinked my eyes and allowed her to do the second nasal passage. After a minute, I began to salivate, my body anticipating a vomitous purge. A nasal drain of medicinal herbs mixed with tobacco slowly dripped down the back of my throat, and I began to spit into a Kleenex.

I closed my eyes while we listened to instrumental music, and an intense inner visual entered like a dream. Hapé is not a hallucinogen, but it is powerful. I witnessed my heart beginning to glow from the inside. Rays of light shone through all of the cracks, and the light filled up my heart until the fractured outer layer burst and existed no more. Hands reached in and massaged my blood pump, giving light to the glowing ball. I thought of all the people I had love for, and little spheres of light came out of my heart and merged with theirs. My heart was opening, healing, and expanding.

"It's normal to feel a little dizzy or nauseous with the hapé. It really stirs things up that have been stuck. Plus this Columbian batch is potent," my mentor warned. She later explained, "Okay, I didn't realize this batch was like they actually sent a Columbian to punch you in the stomach."

I exited the car to breathe in the cold November mountain air. Here I was, sitting with a stranger, under a starlit sky, consuming substances I'd never heard of. I have found the seekers of truth again. It had been too long. I continued to spit as my mouth salivated. As I reopened the car door, I looked into the fierce eyes of my new friend, and confessed to her, "my life is changing, and I need it to."

She peered back at me with a deep understanding in her eyes that said, "I know…me too."

We exchanged stories of recent synchronicities and other oddities we were experiencing. "I keep seeing the numbers 11:11 and 4:44 when I look at the clock. It's almost comical at this point," I told Carmen.

"It happens to me too. Divination." she replied.

I shared my recent meditation practices with her, "I learned a visualization that involves filling up my body with a healing golden light. Each time I do this, I close my eyes and imagine a sparkly vapor filling up the inside of my body. I start with my toes, feet, legs, and up to each organ in my pelvis, abdominal area, chest, and so on."

"That's amazing. I've been doing a lot of deep meditation too," Carmen softly spoke to the air in front of her.

"But the last time I did this routine, I couldn't visualize any of my organs. It's as if I had been gutted. No intestines, no stomach, no heart. I couldn't locate them. It felt empty," I revealed.

"Maybe you are," she droned without a flinch.

She was right. The old me was being ripped out, rung out, and something new was being put in. I didn't know what it would be. This was part of my path.

"Do you want to go deeper? To find out what it is? I know a local woman who facilitates transcendental meditation through Shamanic Healing. She's amazing. It's like a decade of therapy in four hours," she pumped out, with the enthusiasm of a teenager who just discovered live music.

I was curious what *deeper* meditation might be. I thought meditation was about letting your mind go blank. To observe your thoughts without judgement and let them pass. To experience the absence of clutter and enjoy the peace of silence. But this sounded like more.

"I have to get home. Be well my friend," Carmen wished as we parted ways.

As I sat in my car, assessing if I was ready to drive home, another wave of nausea rolled over me. I opened the car door and felt a geyser of liquid come up my throat. I purged a deep maroon liquid. It was baffling, as I hadn't consumed anything of this color or texture. I stared at the gloomy mess on the pavement that hurled out of my body, wondering what it was. As I studied it, I had a knowing. The red river streaming down the parking lot was a portion of the sickness festering in my heart. The hape´ was extracting disease. I looked at it like it was a frog that had inexplicably dropped from the starry sky. It was a strange occurrence, but I felt relief.

A pitch-black sky swaddled me as I drove home. A crackling fireplace met me with warmth when I opened my home's doors. I tip-toed up the stairs, promptly slid under my blankets, and curled into the fetal position. I met a deep restful sleep.

As my eyes detected daylight, I rolled out of bed feeling lighter. I took three steps into my bathroom and gazed into the mirror. Countless mornings I've paused at the mirror to find a sad, blank, glassy-eyed vessel with a missing soul reflecting back at me. Yet this was not the empty glare of a hangover. My eyes were clear, bright, and full of depth. The hapé had a cleansing effect on me.

Without any unnecessary analyzation, I thought, "I need to be doing more things like this." I was shedding weight and building muscle in Cross-Fit, which felt incredible. But what about the emotional weight and spiritual muscle? My voyage in life was leading me to knowledge about how to keep those parts of myself healthy and happy as well.

In the following weeks I researched the shamanic facilitator. I read her bio over and over. Should I trust her? Carmen said her session went four hours long and was the best therapy session she ever had. Surely it was worth a shot.

The shaman offered other modalities such as Reiki Chakra Balancing, Quantum Biofeedback, a Photon Sound Beam Machine and Astrology readings. The healing session took the client into a deep meditative state through a series of rituals, then raised the person into a realm of higher consciousness. She was the facilitator, not the interpreter of meditative journeys. *Not FDA verifiable, well duh.*

Now that I was clear of alcohol and pharmaceuticals, I felt clarity and purity of mind and body. I was intent to keep up the new habit. It wasn't about avoiding pain this time, it was about feeling present, whole, and self-actualized.

As I pulled my car into an inconspicuous parking spot in a dank empty lot, I questioned my sanity. I was flooded with old programs suggesting I was being irresponsible or immature. They were in need of deactivation. Have I become so desperate that I trust non-certified, underground healers? Kane wouldn't approve, but I was making my own decisions again.

Upon entering the office, I was greeted by an enormous sound-bending gong and burnt sage. It was well beyond Pier One Imports. A woman with long brunette hair appeared with a wide smile and a warm, yet witchy demeanor.

"Welcome. I'm Victoria," she spoke with a coy air, while motioning me to sit down in an adjacent leather chair.

She leaned in, "Katie, why are you here?" She invited me to share my background, all the key relationships throughout my life, my experience as a human, and where I'm at now. She listened with unbroken eyes and a discerning ear, only interjecting to relate connections from her own life.

After our initial intake, Victoria dove into an Astrology reading based on my birth chart. She included a Synastry reading, which is designed to compare two or more birth charts together to determine the dynamics of compatibility in the relationship. This gave me insights into my marriage. It confirmed things I already saw, but didn't want to acknowledge. Previously, I thought of horoscopes as entertainment from the back of a magazine, but some of this information rung eerily true. I put it in the side pocket of my mind for future contemplation.

An hour passed by the time we finished our consultation. The candle in the room flickered with rhythm, and the room synthesized with energy. Victoria grinned, "It's time to start your Shamanic session." She rambled about a few other details, but I wasn't comprehending her words in this moment. I was enthralled by her face, as I saw shadow-like brush marks begin to breathe over parts of her profile. My head tilted with astonishment as the silhouette of a crow-like bird appeared over her forehead, wrapping around her eye and feathering out into warrior-like stripes across her cheek.

I blinked my eyes and did a double take, like the times I'd seen auras. Her face was still morphed into a painted indigenous medicine woman as she began to conjure up her own guiding spirits to assist me on this journey. For a split second, I mentally rehashed opening my water, remembering it had a seal. *No one drugged me, right?* No, they didn't. Apparently, this is just the kind of thing that happens to me now. I'm beginning to accept it. This woman had a gift. I knew because the healing spirit within her revealed itself in the form of a hovering shadow upon her face.

I climbed onto her massage table and let the drips of a water feature relax me into submission. I closed my eyes as she began her work. An earthy smudge of sage filled my nostrils as it whisked over my body. I felt a cool stone placed and balanced on the center of my forehead. The chime of a tuning fork woke up my ear with a vibration that rippled through my body like it was recalibrating each individual cell. A calming melodic voice took me through a guided visualization and into a deep state of meditation. I was open to guidance but not overt suggestion.

After she took me to an underworld of relaxation, she redirected the journey to one of elevation. "Now you will ascend, effortlessly, and weight-lessly," her voice rung like a singing bowl. I visualized my body becoming lighter and raising up into the sky, floating past the clouds, through the atmosphere, above the stars, and into a higher realm. I walked onto an onyx plane and moved forward, amazed at how quickly my mind adapted to the concept of being weightless.

I arrived at a threshold, where humanoid light beings became visible on the horizon. *What is going on. Fuck it, I'll just roll with it.*

"I can't put all of this into words. There aren't words that come close to what I'm seeing," I relayed to Victoria. "One of the beings stands out to me, like I know it."

"I understand. Walk towards it. Who is it?" she posed with a tone of neutrality.

Despite my lack of experience with this concept, I knew it was my Higher Self. I thought the being would come close and talk to me, but instead it floated *into* me. I described what was happening to the healer.

She reworded, "You have integrated with your Higher Self." It was like a motherly presence rejoining and nurturing me at the same time.

"What is happening now?" she asked.

"A group of light beings is surrounding me. I'm sorry I keep calling them that. I don't know how else to describe them. They are guiding a ball of white light into my throat," I told her.

The beings put their hands just over the skin on my trachea. It felt like a warm healing light. My eyes welled up with more tears. My throat felt tender, like a freshly healing wound. My voice had been functioning with reactive anger. It was out of balance and they were trying to help, like tuning an old piano. My true voice had been repressed for centuries. They were soothing its ability to express with calmness and clarity.

After the throat healers were done, the shaman led the visualization to a pond. Again, the hazy mists shaped like humans, but translucent, absent of facial features, and emanating a pulsing intelligence appeared.

"I see another being," I said.

"Sit next to it. Ask it what it has to show you," she guided. The spirit guide stood up and took me for a walk into the void. The being stopped and we sat facing each other, surrounded by the absence of light. Then, an "earth" was created around us, with grassy meadows, sparkling streams, blue skies, and fluffy clouds.

"She created nature around us," I shared with awe.

All images appeared in my mind's eye, while I was awake. I watched it and experienced it as if I was in a game of virtual reality. The shaman's meditation ritual served as my transcendental goggles. On this earth that materialized, a house appeared. I was happy to see something else familiar. However, the roof was promptly ripped off. Startled, I imagined what a missing roof would do to the safety and security of the house. Just then, the spirit guide abruptly pushed the house aside, quickly folded in its walls, and flung it like a Frisbee. Except, the spirit didn't use its hands. It used its mind—what I understood to be the force of intention. I was scared when the being made the house disappear. There was an emptiness.

During this journey, the spirit guides I encountered spoke with ESP. At times I understood a guide as "they" because they seemed to hold multiple consciousnesses in one body.

Through the darkness I heard, "Home is not a house. A house is just a box. You must be at peace wherever you are." I wondered what other meanings this walk had, so I asked with my mind.

They replied, "I had to show you it is possible to create something out of nothing, because you didn't believe it could be true."

Tears poured down my face as I was reminded of how stuck my creation space had been. They were trying to crack open my perception of reality, and for that I was grateful.

We went back into the darkness, but this time I wasn't afraid. The guide began to playfully skip along, then stopped and hugged me. They shifted from seeming like a female to a distinct male energy.

Words echoed between the sound waves, "I had to present myself as female first because otherwise you wouldn't have followed me."

It's true. I would not have trusted a male. Because of my ill experiences with men, I would have assumed him an evil spirit. I'm glad he demonstrated I would have been wrong. In spirit, we are all a perfect balance of masculine and feminine. This being scanned their hands over my body and emitted healing energy, similar to reiki.

"Things will be different now," they said with gentle strength.

Then we walked into the blackness of pre-creation again. I waited to see what would happen. The more I trusted, the more appeared. A deep velvety curtain enveloped us and then dropped into the void. The being began walking briskly, and I rushed to keep up. I was confused why he was doing this, but I felt the urge to follow. Then he stopped suddenly as he pointed to his third eye, that point between where his eyebrows would be, and then up into the air. From his fingertip a pink light lit up like a band of neon Christmas lights and reeled up into the sky. I followed the fuchsia rope with my hand, floating swiftly up into a space-like sky using the power of flight. I waved down to the guide, "bon voyage."

Next, I arrived at a new level of sorts. Victoria suggested, "Look for a door or passage." A tunnel arose, so I got inside.

"I see a green orb inside this tunnel," I detailed out loud.

"Move towards it, as sometimes beings can appear as orbs of light," Victoria informed.

As I did this, I sensed intelligence. I told it, "I feel like I'm suffocating in this tunnel."

To my surprise, it chimed back, "Then quit making it a tunnel."

The tunnel immediately dissipated. Without warning or discomfort, the orb went straight into my chest and lit me up. It circulated my inner cavity, then came out through my fingers and reappeared as a luminescent green silhouette in the form of a human.

The green being was vibrating quickly and tried to communicate with me. "I think it's trying to talk, but it's so fast, it's just a buzzing speedy sound," I relayed to the shaman. It was like a recording that had been turned up to hyper speed and I couldn't tell what it was saying. The language was undetectable.

"Ask it to slow down, so you can understand its words," she suggested.

As the vibration calmed, I heard them drop another mind stream, "Slow down, so you can hear. Meditate." It continued, "You are one of us. You are Light. Your soul's purpose is to shine. We have messages, but you have not been listening. You must meditate to connect with us." Waves of tears washed over me as I felt this profound message grace my heart.

Then the orb turned into an angel and showed me guardian angels protecting my children at all times. It showed me a picture from my grand-mother's house of an angel watching over two children as they crossed a bridge. *Oh yeah, I remember that painting.* I continued to feel a salty recognition on my cheeks, as I understood the message. They are always with us. I can exhale. I do not have to panic myself with the immense responsibilities of motherhood. I can trust and feel comforted, knowing a greater power is watching over all of us.

Previously, I believed in angels as a phenomenon that could exist, but never really put any trust into them. I especially wasn't willing to put that kind of ethereal trust when it came to something as tangible as my children. However, after this communion, I had a renewed sense of knowing towards eternal beings. I could believe in miracles again.

The green light being and I dropped down, like an elevator shaft, into the kitchen of my house in the mountains. I was overwhelmed with a thick, dense air. Pressure surrounded me, as the air resembled a tank of water 10,000 leagues beneath the sea. I didn't like the feel of this place. Is it always this uncomfortable here? I asked the being, "Is there anything you can tell me about my marriage?"

It replied, "You are not ready to know yet." Instead of marital insights, it relayed, "Hold space for yourself. This is not selfish, but helpful and neutral." Then the green being wanted to go up again because the air in the kitchen was too heavy. As we ascended, I felt things drop from me. I was relieved when we rose beyond the weight of my house, and of the earth. The being said, "I needed to take you higher so you could let things go."

Before the journey was over, I asked a final question, "Am I ready for plant medicine?"

I was informed via knowing that I must journey one more time. I needed to practice meditating so I could hear their guidance.

"They are showing me something," I told Victoria.

"What is it?" she asked with curiosity.

"They are showing me a positioning for your hands," I guided her.

"Ah, wonderful. Sometimes I receive guidance as well," she shared. As she placed her hand on me, with fingers over my third eye and thumbs on my crown, an intense flow of energy rushed through my head. I knew of chakras, but never put much weight towards their efficacy. However, my skepticism was being blown away as my sixth and seventh chakras opened. I felt fused with cosmic energy. I wondered if that gaping hole on the top of my head would close up before I drove home.

They spoke, "remember how this feels, especially when you're meditating. This is what being open and connected to the Universe feels like."

I made it through the holidays, despite my disintegrating marriage. Kane and I were online dating. I met Riley, and Kane had numerous overnight dates to even the score. Riley helped me pass the time by encouraging me to express my sexuality. He was curious about my alternative healing journey, and I suppose it gave me someone to bestow my new found enlightenment onto. He was non-threatening and quite a bit younger. He breathed life into a very closed part of my soul because his station was set on "play" at all times.

In the middle of the day I would be at a playdate, or talking to another mom at the grocery store, and my phone would ping. A picture.

"Do you think my dick looks big?" Riley requested, as I presume he was crunching out his work day.

I had to tilt the phone so I wouldn't be charged with indecent exposure from his photo message. It made me smile a secret titillating grin that fulfilled me for the moment. Flipping through the pics on my iPhone had become like opening a spread of Penthouse magazine. I could almost hear the other moms whispering at the playdate, "What kind of vagabonds is she hanging out with these days? I hear she's been Tindering twenty-nine year olds." Meanwhile, I made sure the volume on my phone was turned down, just in case the video named "sex tape #1" accidentally started playing.

I'd entice him, "Yes! It's perfect. So big, show me more."

"Thanks babe, but like white guy big, or like porno Pringles can big?" he pressed on.

"It's huge. Any bigger and it would hurt and we wouldn't be able to have marathon sex in every position like we do now. Show me another angle."

My phone pinged again. This time a video with a text, "How about this one? Do you wanna see me cum?" Oh my, this young man isn't getting any work done in the office today. Our naughty secrets energized my day and distracted me from the shit storm my life had become.

"Send it," I typed, as the voice of a fellow mama drowned out amidst my surge of endorphins. It's like a crystal ball delivered Riley into my lap. Quite literally.

"Please send me some of you. You're so hot and sexy. I wanna lick you until you can't stand it anymore," he'd text back. *Dear lord, I adore this filthy-mouthed young man.* He was twenty-nine. He didn't fit in with his peers, and at the moment, neither did I. Sex was where we met in the middle. This is how we were perfectly matched, for now.

A month later, I felt the urge to call upon the healer for my second shamanic journey. The first journey was pretty fantastical, there couldn't possibly be more. Oh, but I was far from figuring it out. I have since learned to forgo rationalizing the supernatural. When you feel into the energy, it guides you. That is all that matters.

Victoria rounded the door with a smile. She brewed with anticipation for the lessons about to take place. The butterflies awoke and tickled my previously stagnant belly. She laid me down on her transcendental massage table. With the cling of a bell, my second session began.

"I'm standing in a dark abyss of outer space. I'm beyond the realm of stars," I described to her. Looking down upon myself, I noticed I was a powder blue humanoid. My hair cascaded in periwinkle waves, with the distinct patterning of a woodcut print. As I walked to the edge of my visual field, I began to see a canvas wrapped around the perimeter with grassy hills.

"I see a rainbow," I continued. I walked towards the rainbow and asked what it was. The rainbow reached out to me, bending its prism of colors.

"What's happening now?" Victoria asked.

"It turned into a small triangle." I intuitively knew to reach into the dark metallic shape, despite its size fitting the palm of my hand. As I reached, my body shrunk to squeeze through it and then returned to its regular size. Like a celestial Alice in Wonderland, I welcomed the beyond.

Gravity pulled back my head as I whisked away on a stream of fast flowing water. I clenched my knees as I rafted through a series of colorless walls. Each door was camouflaged with the jet black sky. They opened and shut as I went through them. I could only detect slight changes, as if feeling my way to the bathroom in a midnight hallway, too dim for a hint of a shadow to emerge. My stomach sensed a subtle drop as the river gushed into the form of a waterfall.

I landed in an emerald lagoon without so much as a drop of moisture getting onto my hair. I walked effortlessly out of the pool of water to discover a mirror-like reflection of myself along the ground. As I crouched to look closer, it appeared to be a fluid glass window. I peered into another world.

"I see another place," I documented, while viewing a bright land with lime green grass and a white fluffy castle, sparkling like an angelic Taj Mahal. *What is that world? I must know.* "I'm headed to the castle."

I reached through the water-like glass and descended to the other world. The heavenly castle allured me to its steps. I curiously wandered into the building. Arches upon arches lined numerous hallways. Like an adolescent trespassing through an abandoned building, I proceeded with caution. My feet landed without a "clack" on these floors. I reached the center of the building where it opened to a magnificent garden courtyard overflowing with lavender and other botanicals.

Concerned, I told the shaman, "There's no one here. It's just a garden."

"Can you talk to it? Remember, everything in this realm is consciousness," she guided.

With the magical mindset of a child, I allowed the possibilities to open. It felt silly, but I took her advice and asked the flowers what this place was. The bed of flowers swayed and their petals jittered in response to my acknowledgment. I was amazed by the infinite ways consciousness presented itself. As I felt the unmistakable warmth of being home, glowing figures appeared from each of the arches surrounding the courtyard.

This sublime realm was exponentially far from Earth. I am grateful I journeyed to the upper realm before the concept was explained to me. When exploring consciousness, I found it validating to discover something on my own time, and in my own way. Therefore I didn't get stuck wondering if my mind created it based on prior suggestion, or if it truly presented itself organically. Fluffy light beings inside a glowing palace were never a part of my drunken conversations as a bar fly—I would have remembered that.

I had been drifting through reality in a state of amnesia. It was time I was reminded of the boundless existence I was already a part of. I learned to hold my hands out with my palms up when I meditate so I can receive renewing energy. My depletion was unnecessary. All I have to do is be still and ask for the eternal Source.

"Why have I felt so disconnected?" I asked.

They transmitted, "You've forgotten your true nature."

I gained a sense of my original mission, my calling. To discover my own luminosity, connect, and feel the unconditional love of creation.

We are woven together in this tapestry of existence.

I saw how some people were vibed into my life to bring up wounds that needed more opportunities to heal. Some people were of extreme light, but didn't realize it. They buried their light because it made them feel different. This had been true for myself as well.

Finally, I asked about the nausea I was feeling. For the past month, I was experiencing debilitating nausea. Sure, I could blame it on personal problems, stress, etcetera. Those issues were on the surface, but I wanted to know what was at the core. It felt like pregnancy nausea, so much so that I took an at-home pregnancy test. But it was negative.

"A rebirth is taking place," they dropped in a sonic wave. I realized the sickness I felt was part of this metamorphosis.

An ache fell over my heart when it became time to say goodbye to my soul's home. I had to carry the profound messages with me, but I did not want to leave this realm of weightless love and joy.

The whispers of nature spoke to me with magic, when I was a child. A monarch butterfly rested on my elbow, or a feather gently landed in the center of my path on a hike, and I would feel the connection. The mystical messages didn't go away, I became numb to them. It had been decades, but I was beginning to feel again. The Universe was using symbols as a medium to transcend the barrier between the seen and the unseen. They reached my heart amongst this scattered and chaotic world.

A soft blue light projected from the hands of my spirit guides to the core of my heart. This was their parting gift of love. When I returned to my body and opened my eyes, the last wisps of blue light gently returned into the shaman's heart center, like smoke through a vent between worlds.

I was overwhelmed with a sense of beauty and yet experienced a resistance to it. *What is this world I've been shown?* It is magnificent beyond measure, and yet requires me to release all preconceived notions of concrete reality. The other side is phenomenal. Who will believe this? I'm not even sure if I do. But I want to allow myself to, because it is pure love. It is Source. Somehow I don't need convincing of that.

Flower of Life

I stared at my notes scribbled on a tiny piece of paper I'd torn from the "grocery list" notepad hanging from my refrigerator. I breathed in a stream of hope shadowed by desperation. How many times have I fixated on a list of wants and needs, goals and aspirations, attitudes of gratitude, pros and cons, must haves and deal-breakers? Every endless list I've started has nudged me along the way, chipped at the hardened personal crust, filed down the rigid programs, shone light on unconscious habits, and kept a fire of transformation smoldering. Though something was different about this list. It felt raw compared to the others. I was finally getting to the nitty-gritty. My previous compilations were focused on outside connections, things *out there* that I thought I needed, but today I was looking at a list that spiraled like a staircase into my core. It led inside the belly of the beast.

The only control I have is control over myself and how I react to the world. My personal state of being is influencing what experiences I draw into my life and I'm making choices based on those experiences. My state of mind sends a direct request, and this list is every howl of grief I've called out to the universe staring back at me. Yes, it is me who needs to heal. The rest of the world is not to blame. Not Kane. Not my parents, my bosses, my co-workers, my doctors, my lovers, my friends, foes, strangers, or even my path. They will respond in their own time to the songs of truth singing to them, whether as a feather, numbers or whatever their language is. I keep hearing this message, "When you discover your light, you help illuminate others. This is how we heal the world." It starts from within and ripples out. The everlasting echo of divinity.

My inner darkness rumbles from the paper. I haven't escaped the pits of the human condition. Is all of that mine? Yes, it is. *It's time to own your shit.* Of course, the programming of the current world, as well as my parents, contributed to its creation, but consciously or unconsciously, I chose to take it in and make it mine. It is now my responsibility to look at it and process it back out. The words sit patiently in erasable ink, ready to be rewritten.

Need to heal:

The incessant need for outside validation
Loneliness and fear of abandonment
Hatred of waiting in uncertainty
Intolerance for feeling ignored
Anger & explosive reactivity
Fear of the unknown
The need to control
Self-punishment
Low self-worth
Self-judgment
Self-hatred
Self-doubt
Insecurity
Anxiety
Guilt

Wow. No wonder people get stuck in a downward spiral. I was familiar with self-affirmations: the art of stating a positive intention, with emotion, and wording it in present time. I was happy to balance the shadow work with light. I invoked a courage within and allowed myself to ask the Universe for help. I permitted myself to believe I was worthy to receive messages of transformation. I allowed myself to trust that connection existed.
Intentions:

I ask to heal my heart
I ask to ignite my voice
I ask, who have I become?
I allow confidence and clarity
I ask to be shown my authentic self
I ask to be reconnected with my soul
I am open to connection with my guides
I am open to heart-soul-love connections
I ask for confirmation of my soul's purpose

Before I went on the spiritual retreat, I called up advice from a couple friends who had journeyed into transformation in the same way. My first confidant, Jordan, met me for dinner to share his heart on the mysterious and healing plant medicine he'd sat with. Our dinner date was a meeting of kindred spirits. We were not bonded in a romantic connection, we were aligned in a soul evolution, the deepest kind of friendship there is.

As I waltzed into the bistro, I noticed we were both wearing vintage khaki green Army jackets. I hadn't worn mine in years, but today I had been compelled to throw it on. I was on a mission, and something told me I was about to meet a person of revolutionary mind.

"Ah, lovely jacket," Jordan charmed.

"Thanks! Same. It belonged to my uncle. He was in Vietnam." It had been passed down to my mother, and now to me.

"It's buzzing with energy. Mine is from a local thrift store," he spoke, paying honor to the original owner of his jacket, its seams kept together with unknown tales of a fellow man.

Jordan had a grin that lit up a radius covering four tables, maybe more. His eyes sparkled with youth, or was that enlightenment, with a steady glow of anointed wisdom. My bellowing laugh ricocheted through the exposed vents in the ceiling, as he shared his stories of trial and triumph as a stand-up comic. Sometimes, when I meet someone new, subjects of secrecy pour onto the table, as if an abandoned stream channel has just discovered it is an estuary. Jordan, my ocean. Of consciousness. I trickle back into the knowing. This time the undertow is a welcoming force of warmth that leads me to the Mother.

"I feel like I want to experience psychedelics again. I need change. I feel out of touch with something I once had," I confessed.

"What else are you looking for? Healing?" Jordan asked with serious, and deeply caring eyes.

"Yes. For depression, anxiety..and a break through I guess. I want to see the beyond *and* the core," I admitted.

"She might you that. Illness can manifest through unhealed emotional wounds," he said. "I've had medicine that can heal. It's very powerful...not what I would call a recreational plant."

Our tabletop turned into the canopy of the jungle. We chattered like exotic birds. But what is below? *I must climb down the vine of the soul, into the ferns. She is with us. She has been summoned. Ayahuasca...ayahuasca...ayahuasca. Without yet knowing her name, I've been asking for her. She has found me.*

It dawned on me where I had read this word before. Aya-hua-sca. I remember reading it, but never knowing how to pronounce it. When I was 19 and rummaging through a natural food store in Illinois, I came across it. I was trying to find natural solutions to cure asthma, anxiety, and depression. Western medicine had failed me and I was looking for alternative options. It was way back then, that I had gotten into organic foods, filtering water, and questioning Western medicine. A number of books I came across had chapters on vaccines, in relation to asthma, inflammation, and the immune system. And the books on severe depression spoke of a tea made in the Amazon that had miraculous effects on people. They shifted their lives completely and were never the same. Ah, but in the time before iPhones, how was I ever going to figure out how to get there? I thought, "I don't think I know the right people. I don't know how to arrange that kind of voyage. My crowd stays in walking distance to the bar." But I was curious. Her seed was planted.

After a few hours of exchanging enchanting tales, we made our way to the door. This was a synthesized discussion, condensing our sagas into an introductory meeting over a delectable roasted beet salad. My astral ally leaned in for a familial hug. I've felt this embrace before. Solid, trusting, home. He scrubbed the side of my cheek with his unkempt beard and tucked me into his shoulder. I was on the right track. These stones are stacked with intentional symmetry. A high country cairn. True North ahead.

Still, I sat with fear for a few weeks, tossing it back and forth in my head. Is this irresponsible? No, the pills were worse. I know that. But everyone keeps telling me those are good, and this other stuff, this plant medicine, is questionable behavior for a mother. Okay—no one told me that, but I was aware of the societal rules. They were still being duped by the war on drugs. Sponsored by: the people who make drugs. And Kane thought I was nuts anyways. So who cares. I went with my gut. *I want to change. This is the only way it's going to happen.* Deep within, beyond the fear, I know this.

A couple of months passed since my dinner with Jordan. During this time, I made the decision to go. To taste the vine. Suprisingly, Kane tried to be supportive. He offered to put the girls to bed while I was gone overnight. He knew I was searching, and I could tell it made him uneasy.

"Every time you go somewhere, I feel you slipping further and further away from me. I don't know what I'm supposed to say. But go, if it's what you want to try, then do it," he uttered with half-committed support.

As I prepped for my trip, I longed for Jordan's shoulder once more. I needed parting words of wisdom to ease my mind and fuel my resolve on this voyage. He gladly responded with a series of detailed texts.

"This is divine medicine. She can heal DNA through time. Once you learn that, the gratitude for the opportunity we have to heal ourselves, and help the people around us, will make your heart explode. You can shift a genetic code that exists in the past, present, and future. It's beautiful," He commented, "As we heal ourselves, we heal each other."

"I'm setting an intention to let go of unhealthy patterns that have been stuck in my familial line," I expressed to him.

"Ask that the Mother present herself to help you with that intention. But understand, she will show you what you need to know, and not always what you ask to know," he taught.

"But what if I purge?" I asked, shuddering at the memory of that fountain of dark blood evacuating from the depths of my belly. The anxiety was already churning up my thoughts and threatening my determination to heal. Puking is vulnerable. You can't defend yourself when you're doubled over, vomiting demons.

"Purging is a true manifestation of releasing energy," he spoke. "It releases so hard it actually takes physical form. You might feel wrung out by the Universe, but in a way that leaves you feeling cleansed." Jordan was a friend of my soul. He turned up to help guide me on this path of renewal. A short time ago, he was a perfect stranger. Now he has taken the time to thoughtfully compose a message to gently send me on my way into uncharted territory. In order to be found, I must first get lost. Intentionally.

As I headed into the bush of my mind, I accepted parts of me would return to the dirt of Mother Earth, and parts of me that were yet to be discovered, would emerge. Letting go will lead me back to myself. My Darwinian mind, I challenge you. Show me what parts are ready to evolve.

My second confidante was Carmen, the blue-eyed bohemian, who was well-traveled on retreats of deep meditation. She had acquired plant knowledge and witnessed my soul peering over the edge, just as hers had been. I was grateful she reached out her hand.

"This way," her spirit whispered. She had the gift of unconditional love and the ability to lend soft but poignant advice. "Trust the process. When you're feeling 'sick', know that she is healing you. Send her gratitude and it will change how you feel. Also, remember whatever is coming up for you has already been inside you, and is now leaving you. So even if it's scary, go through it and trust her. If you are throwing up resistance, ask her to show you how to trust her." This was the counsel of a serious spiritual warrior. One who acknowledges fear but understands how to push through it. Another who has fought for her life.

Carmen continued, "On a recent retreat to Costa Rica, I learned your soul splits from you when you're a child. It won't reenter you, until it knows you have released your issues."

A disconnected soul. This makes sense to me. Why else would I be soul-searching, had my own soul not drifted outside me. The missing puzzle piece is me. On some level, I believe we are all part of the same soul, fragmented through birth so we can fit into a small body to experience life. Maybe that's why we don't feel complete. One day we will all merge back into ourself. If that is the longing for oneness we all seek, I wonder, is there a way to feel connected now? If so, how can I understand beyond the clockwork intellectual comprehension of the concept. Take me off autopilot. I want to feel it. I came here to live. I will go on this journey, to see if I can remember how.

Finally, she added, "Ask the shaman to clear your energy for you when you're struggling. You are supported. Someone will help you if you need it." This is what I needed to hear to feel equipped. I was ready now.

I was instructed to follow a modified "dieta" that week. No sex, no masturbation, no meat, cheese, processed food, alcohol, or marijuana. In order to get into deeper states of meditation, the body must be as pure as possible. This begins to clear the energy field and allow for realignment. The journey would take me light years away, beginning with a step outside my door, and back into myself.

Vertigo set in as my world turned with a velocity of rotation. My parched mouth struggled to swallow a mental Dramamine, but this vessel was as dry as an urn. When the plant is dehydrated, the water runs straight through the pot. I needed to churn the soil, replenish nutrients, and enrich the roots.

After much traversing, I arrived at a remote location. Like a hike into the back country, others arrived with quiet focus. We trekked through the mud, through a garden of wildflowers, and into the cocoon of a small structure. We unpacked our belongings and set up camp inside a globe-shaped room. Barely a word was spoken. People brought the bare essentials needed for survival and transcendence. Sleeping bags, a yoga mat, pillows, glasses, contacts, crystals, notebooks, and a change of white ceremonial clothing.

Assistants greeted each person and smudged their body with sage. The room filled with a smoky aroma of this earthy dried leaf. A man with a glowing smile and peaceful presence bowed to me as he held his burning sage, propelled by the large feather of a hawk. He was in service of the evening's ceremony, and the gift of selflessness emanated through his being.

Two shaman, Hannah and Cisco, facilitated the group. This was the beginning of setting a ceremonial space. Healing doesn't take place without it.

"Please circle up. We are ready to begin. Our intention is to hold space for you," Hannah shared, "Our hearts are open for you."

"We understand you all come here seeking something. We must care for one another, especially during ceremony. They key is to surrender. Grandma will show us," Cisco spoke, with his hand over his heart.

Then, each person in the circle shared their intention for attending. People from all walks of life were searching for answers to all the things the human condition presents. There were about twenty of us. We were a circle of strangers who began sharing, and were transformed with honesty by the time the last person spoke their most intimate burdens.

Hannah, the shaman with gentle folds of translucent skin lining her face like a map of astrological wisdom, offered me a rose petal from a wooden box. The scent was sweet and alluring, a reminder of the soft guidance in my presence. Cisco placed a metal bowl of fire in the center of the ring of people. Its flames danced like spirits of rage and forgiveness.

Lights were dimmed, as the ceremony space was created. One at a time, each person took a petal and dropped it into the fire, blessing it with an intention to release, as the flames climbed over the soft surface of each flower.

"Letting go of holding on," one girl spoke with eyes of grief.

Cisco said when a group circles up with a spiritual purpose, they have energetically synced up beforehand. Their paths, challenges, and messages will overlap. The young girl's intention resonated with me with a sobering realization that I too needed to loosen my grip on the past. I was here to shed layers. To let go of what I thought was real. To learn what it is to dissolve the old identity. To create space for something new, I must crack myself wide open.

After setting an intention to release, we returned to our yoga mats and settled into our individual spaces. Our mats were circled around an alter in the middle, devoted to various deities, roses, and a few meditation mats to kneel on. The sun had set and the moon shone with a welcoming glow, through the windows of a hexagon-shaped ceiling. My stomach was already nervous. *What would the tea taste like? Would I feel anything? Would I feel too much?*

The room filled with the silent anticipation of an omnipresence. When it was my turn, I walked to the alter and knelt on the pillow in front of the shamans and their assistants. Warm faces of compassion smiled at me, as prayers of love and protection were spoken over my cup of Ayahuasca. Two hands reached out to meet mine, offering the earthy brown tea. I received one ounce of the room-temperature medicine, swallowing it quickly, yet absorbing its unmistakable pungent flavor of powdery licorice, which left my taste buds stewing with a bitter after taste. I fought to breathe through the strong sensation, and not allow it to take me to a place of nausea. We were instructed to try to keep the medicine in for 30 minutes.

"Give Grandma enough time to arrive with her wisdom. Be patient. Breathe," encouraged Cisco.

I sat with my eyes closed, and waited. The room was filled with stillness. Longing. Fear. Readiness. In the room, as dark as a deep mossy forest, I allowed myself to turn inward. I began to see familiar geometric shapes, like when I was a child, tightly closing my eyes at bedtime. I watched as the medicine began to flow. Then the image of microscopic liquid blurbs pumped through small channels. *What was this I was seeing?* It reminded me of something I've viewed before. It was a magnified cell. A living cell, where DNA was located. I was witnessing the plant medicine working on a cellular level. She was showing me the science behind her magic.

As I continued to settle into the first deep meditation, my eyeballs felt tender. Darkness again. Then, an energetic finger reached into my eye sockets, plucked them out, and set them aside into the air. I felt no pain as I felt into the darkness of my empty eye sockets. Her voice dropped down and echoed, "You will not need these to see where you are going. You will look through your third eye."

I accepted this, as a warm pressure grew in the center of my forehead.

My skin flushed with heat and grew itchy, like a rash. I sat with my legs crossed and my arms folded in my lap. My eyes were closed as I faced my lap. The shaman came close to me and gently squeezed my shoulders and arms. "What is all this tension? You don't have to hold it all together. You can let go," Hannah said as she rubbed my back with the sweep of her comforting hand. I wanted to feel the tenderness of her consoling. Yet I sat rigid.

"What is inside that you are holding onto? Is it guilt? Is it blame? What is it? Look deeper, Katie..." She floated away from me, as her soft voice, with its Eastern European accent, echoed in the halls of my mind. Her voice. I knew it from eons ago. Through the stars, the galaxies, the infinite string of eternities. Like waking from a fainting, her voice, my teacher, guiding my soul back to Self, as I wake up out of the dream.

A flood of grief surprised me, washing ashore my awareness like a collection of every tear I never properly shed for friends I have lost. Friends I grew up with who joined me early on, in a quest to find themselves. All my trippy friends. Friends who dove outside the box or turned it into a ship to surf the currents of life. Friends whose soul paths were never far from mine, and yet of this plane they were no more. I had no idea I had been harboring such grief, such deep and sorrowful loss. I was so wrapped up in life the past ten years, I never flew to my hometown to attend their funerals. I was busy. Too busy to grieve. Too busy to feel. Too busy to remember our precious piece of life together.

I got onto my hands and knees as I watched a black ocean of sorrow gush from my guts to the floor, like a waterfall of sadness. This was not a purge, but a cascade of energy flowing directly out of my chest like Niagara Falls. I remained motionless as gravity and a rolling discomfort allowed the darkness of my unrecognized loss to depart my vessel. This dense energy was a deep black and eager to escape my body. *Thank you for showing me what needed to be seen in order to be healed.*

I breathed and drank my water. I had more work to do. I felt weak from the first round of processing old energy. *What the hell did I sign up for?* And yet, I felt relief. I paused and braced for more. A stream of thoughts rushed over my head like a river of every conversation I've ever had.

Resistance was building. I didn't want to let go. An intense emotional pain was surfacing. I didn't want to feel it. I was afraid. What if I let go and I never came back? What if I couldn't handle the intensity of the feeling and was washed away forever? I sat with my legs tucked under me on a turquoise meditation cushion, and begged, "Please, Mother, show me how to look at this and let go." A wave of nausea surged from deep in my belly. It was the same nausea I have been feeling for the past month, the same anxious ball of purge ready to strike like a cobra through my gullet.

"What are you?" I asked into the darkness.

The urge to harm yourself, it responded in a tar-like whisper. *Self-hatred.*

Terrified to look at the shape of this demon, I breathed slowly and deeply before letting my inner eye truly study its flesh. It was made of resistance. My white-knuckled fist to being my true Self and letting my light shine with an open heart. I purged a deep hurt from the harm I had imposed on my body and from betraying my soul. Suicidal ideation was an attempt to relieve an unfathomable agony. That option comforted me, that one day, whenever I chose, I could be done with the pain. It served as a promise of relief. But that is not what it created. It grew into a festering ball of hurt weighing me down and slowing my vibration into a murky mud puddle. The relief I needed would only come through expressions of courage. *Show me how to forgive myself.* I purged a violent stream of liquid muck. It was an eviction of pain. A release of self-judgment.

I felt like a cork that was being tossed about during a tsunami. An assistant sat next to me. He didn't try to hug me, but sat close, about one and a half feet away. I held my hand up in shame, "Don't. Don't look at me," as I cowered over my bucket in tears. I didn't want to be noticed in this pitiful state. But he sat and held space. Slowly, I softened my resistance to his presence and felt the relief of his acceptance. The healing of a witness. This was new for me. To trust a sacred space.

Exhausted, the room came back into my awareness. I couldn't tell how much time had passed. It felt like a lifetime. The center of the room began to stir. "Second cup, for those who feel called. Come to receive," announced Hannah. She had a motherly presence, emanating a caring embrace. I watched some people sift to the alter. After assessing my senses, I determined the medicine had calmed in me. I decided to go for another round. Once again, blessings, attentive eyes, and a patient heart.

I settled into the second round of deep meditation. The montage of a romantic drama movie flickered onto the screen of my heart. *Kane.* Breaths of love against my neck, glistening smiles exchanged in the lake, sparkling eyes of innocent hope, and the feverish delirium of new love. My resentment towards him softened. He wasn't growing along the same path as me, but that was suddenly okay. The Mother showed me it's okay to dissolve the wall my ego has built against him.

I felt the sand beneath my feet at our "secret beach" by the lake in Texas. I watched his kind and curious soul as he held up the crawfish who had visited us in our peaceful hideaway. "Look, Katie, don't let his claw git ya! He likes these warm shallow waters. Don't worry, I'll set him free. I just wanted you to get to see him. Isn't he cool?" his voice, so different back then. Gentle. Open. Loving. These long forgotten lazy days by the water, where did they go? Like an intangible dream. Kane…our bubble in time. I wasn't prepared for it to end so soon. I thought it would last forever. How had these moments of true bliss been washed away? The layers of pain strangled our love. The face of my oldest daughter looked at me, held up a dandelion and blew. In creation, there is also destruction. The lessons are intense at this level. The seeds were clouds whirling around me, angel kisses that permeated my skin and settled into my field. I remember. We chose this. How brave were we. We chose to dive down and learn this massive lesson together. That was our soul contract. To feel the paradise of our deep love, to expose one another's shadows, to experience the immense pain of loss, grief, and the death of a marriage. To suffer is to learn compassion without judgment. I was taught to judge others as selfish and weak to throw away a marriage. This is not the easy road, to break free is the hardest path. In my suffering, I learn humility.

"Thank you, ego, for trying to protect me, but I can be strong now, without being harsh. I can accept Kane for who he is and be grateful for the path we have shared. I can be brave enough to welcome wherever it leads next, even if continues to lead us apart," I conversed with myself.

I was shown that our—Kane's and my—other greatest purpose for uniting was to bring our girls into the world. Grandma sent me advice: "Do not to judge or shame your children into submission. That is not love. Cultivate a new way and demonstrate patience, despite the torrid currents of your present moment in life. You are both to shift things for your family lines."

I kept breathing and drank my water. The emotional density was dissipating, and I sat with gratitude for its release. I hung my head and curled into a ball on my knees. I rested, until the next wave washed over me. I could hardly lift my head up. I began moving through a portal. I was sucked through a vortex at the speed of light. I lifted my hand to brace myself and feel into the force of gravitational pull. *Where am I going now?* The room filled with the highest vibration I had ever experienced. It shook the room, and I could barely hear a thing except reverberating sound. It reminded me of the green light being I'd met before, the frequency of Love in motion.

I travelled to another realm. It's almighty in the center, and that's where I landed. Everything appeared in particles. There were microcosmic dots of reality, just like in the Science lessons I taught my students. Elements broken down into molecules, broken down into atoms, broken down into electrical charges. This was the frequency of creation. The space beyond string theory. Quantum structure. Evidence of a world where realities morph, depending on who is gazing at them, and with what intentions they set. I could see how it worked. My body was the shell of a vessel, and it sat there, like an abandoned automobile, as I floated in the room as sparkling consciousness.

I watched in awe as my arm separated into particles of light, a suspended cloud of golden mist, mixed with the dusty blue space of this infinite field around me. I could not tell the difference between solid and air. It was an illusion. I was just a thought. A mind. A soul. A spirit. Consciousness.

I was safely nestled in a globe of sacred geometry, a bud of the flower of life, translated in fractals. This is what some refer to as "the grid," or "the veil." It was like a peek into a sci-fi movie. I observed the vibrating nature of a dimension of the space-time continuum. *It is malleable*, I realized. I am witnessing consciousness. Flowing, changing, breathing, creating, everlasting.

The magnitude of emptiness existing outside our creation swallowed me in an upsurge of awe. I was overwhelmed as a river carried me on currents through heavy emotional states before I settled in a sense of peace and knowing that nothing can be lost or gained. It will always continue to exist. I internalized: All is connected by a cosmic stream of consciousness. Love is everything. It is the highest vibration. The highest octave. It is the energy of creation. We can let go of the fear of the unknown because the unknown is where creation lives. We are all different expressions of the same One. Our daily lives are far removed from the root of creation. The core of Self. But we can allow it in. We can allow it to flow. We can allow our understanding to transcend the different cages of reality we've been collecting. A deluge is only destructive if we value the qualities it is destroying. Otherwise, it is cleansing, nourishing, welcomed with ease.

Master plant medicines can be a gateway to the Light. But they must be respected. They must be kept sacred. And the timing must be right. This gateway led me to clarity and reassured me to be transparent about what has helped heal me along the way. I had to be open, willing, and prepared to look at myself, even the scary parts. However, I am convinced I would not have been able to receive any lessons, insights, visions, or healing, had I not first explored and gained an understanding of energy work. This deeply connected medicine work began with an embodied knowledge of energy. Healing can come in the form of purging, laughing, crying, or silence. Healing has as many forms as there are souls seeking it. Sound healing, breath work, meditation, subtle energetic body knowledge, and intuition development. There are many keyholes.

At first, I struggled with purging in front of a room full of people. Some cultures are free from reservations about bodily functions. It is seen as cleansing, a healthy and accepted process of being human. It felt liberating to allow others to watch my sadness, my shame, my release. I learned my display of vulnerability gave them strength to know they were not alone. In an energetic sense, you purge for each other. This circle of people was individually and collectively processing darkness to arrive at the Light. The seekers. They show up. My tribe.

Now we rest.

Rays of the morning's first light streamed through the skylights. We awakened with slow, intentional movement. Our circle convened and we shared our insights.

One man shared, "I didn't really feel anything or see anything. I guess I fell asleep." *Holy shit…did we drink the same tea?*

Exhausted and humbled, we communed over a modest breakfast of organic fruit, toast, and Rose Hip tea. "Be gentle with yourself today, and for the next few days," cautioned Hannah. "Your soul is tender. Take time to integrate. Spend time in nature. Nourish your body with healthy food and supplements. Let the lessons flow. Let the energy continue to release."

Cisco teared up, his heart filled with love and joy. "You do so much work here. I see all of you. You step up. I see reflections of myself in you. We are one," he spoke holding his heart. They were sending us home reborn, and a bit timid towards reintegrating into a turbulent world of manifest form.

After working with Ayahuasca, a person is softened. I felt stronger, yet more vulnerable. It can be a challenge to foster the lessons learned and maintain this renewed perspective. Ego wants to return to what it knows, and the current world has a knack for sucking up the Light. It is filled with density, a by-product of unconsciousness.

As I reenter my realm of society, things are unfamiliar. I feel uncomfortable and sometimes lost. I'm evolving and my surroundings don't match up. The depression was a symptom of being stuck and paralyzed by the fear of doing something new, and the disapproval it might render. I was introduced to alcohol as a young child, normalized by getting Dad a beer from the cooler during a summer cook out. When I didn't like their way of life, they normalized medicating my instincts. This was the dead end of the matrix life. 40 hour work weeks, bottled emotions, and substances to cope. Choosing to opt out of that life had the power to release me and allow my life to expand. This Earth Medicine. This is what heals, because it allows me to see. I've put in the order, now the Universe is sending it back with a resounding echo of change.

Insights and epiphanies continued to unfold as I stepped foot by foot into my days at home. I left the jungle of the Underworld, but the Mother came with me. I went slowly like a sloth, with intention, and I listened. I began to understand the disruptions in my memory file. The trauma I felt as a child was so subtle it was disguised as insignificant. My seedling identity grew into what I was now. The programs I accepted as a child shaped how I viewed and experienced the world around me.

During that time, I had been terrified of my father and allowed anger to protect me from his overbearing and emotionally disconnected demeanor. Dad...the fear became raw again, memories and visions of his rage, the rage I wanted to release and not pass along to my daughters. I was reminded of the sharp crack of skin on skin as he slapped me, the pitiful wailing of Mom as she rolled on the floor in anguish over the lipstick footprint on the crap-colored carpet in my childhood bedroom. She ignored my pleas for help, too disillusioned by her own fear of my father to answer my desperate yearning for acceptance and protection.

That little girl felt abandoned and victimized, and I kept up the habit of treating her that way. I developed a mentality that no one cared about me and no one would help me. Anger, fear, love, and disconnection became bound in a neurological synapse. I was not possessed by a demon. Rather, a thought pattern had tricked me. This mirage of a message swindled me until now.

I received a new message: it is safe to have an open heart. Mom and Dad are afraid too. They do not want to be alone or forgotten. This is the human experience. These are the lessons our souls came to learn. Mom is afraid she did a bad job. As I grew up, I was mean to her. It was the only way I knew how to be strong. I had to face my fear and judgment of weakness. She wasn't weak. She did her best. She sat with me when I cried as a child. She was a good mother. A loving mother. A brave mother. A human mother. A perfect mother to launch me on this journey.

The insights appeal to my scientific mind: this is a time of Secondary Succession. Things need to burn off, for the forest to survive. This is the natural flow of healing on the Earthly plane. Some lifetimes are an exercise in Primary Succession. Tundra doesn't flaunt extravagance, but it is sturdy to the frigid wind and blistering sun. It happens amid solitude, is exquisite in its delicate beauty, and fragile to human trekking. It honors a path of observation and stillness. It is laying a new foundation. It takes time, and that's okay. There is so much of it.

I am filled with blessings of wisdom. It is common to feel an urge to share this knowledge with listeners. I interpreted the curious mind and lost soul of my lover as an invitation to share.

"I wish you could go," I texted Riley one morning when he was at work. I was leaning in, hoping with the eagerness of my newly reborn self that he might. "You'd meet new people and see what Aya shows you."

Ayahuasca is a teacher. After a while, I realized I knew some of this all along. I saw how life got distracting and over time I fell out of touch with my connection. The program of the human experience is so complex, it is hard to wake up out of. My soul's journey. The memory of divinity. The connection to Source. My path. The Light. Spirit. So many dimensions. I was in awe.

"Yeah? You think I could handle it?" Riley questioned with hesitance.

I continued to share with Riley, "When you go into journey, you can see yourself in the conscious form you were in before you were born. You experience the infiniteness of the Universe. It shows you that you chose your specific life, your parents, your challenges—*everything*, to help your soul evolve. But once you have absorbed the lessons from the challenging experiences, you have to let them go to make room for better things."

I shared everything with my young lover, my fingers tapping the phone like a typewriter, in my eagerness to tell him about the truth. It was like purging again, but this time it was in love and hope, a tea I wished he might sip.

My phone beeped with a message from him. I'd touched something in his heart. "It's interesting," his message read. "Do you think everyone has this experience with the medicine? Do you really think I could handle it? I've tried everything...I want to feel better." The immense light at his core burst through his heart center, transcending the phone screen, prompting me to share more.

"You have to release things when you get stuck in a negative feedback loop," I continued. "Your life will expand when you let go. When you welcome the wisdom of the plant, you see that your thinking truly creates all that exists in your life. The Universe *does* work this way. So if you worry and relive thinking patterns of loss, then you will keep attracting what you worry about. If you are guided by fear, then more things to fear will come to you. But if you can allow yourself to be guided by love, then more love and ease of life will come to you. The journey starts with loving yourself. It also starts with trusting that everything is here to help you. It will all lead to a greater connection to your higher purpose in life, if you can go with the flow. And maybe that purpose is as simple as learning how to be happy and to share that happiness with others. I mean, I think that's kind of the point of life, to be happy, love and be loved. Have you ever had an experience where you were in touch with the Source of all creation and were filled with nothing but the infinite bliss of love? I've had it when I did a solo hike in the back country, and at other unsuspecting times. This is what it can bring you back into connection with. What do you think?"

It was too much for him. My phone went blank without a return text message. Sometimes a person may ask for truth, but not be ready to hear it. Riley turned his radio off. If the frequency of truth does not match the frequency someone is currently operating on, the message will not be received. It is hard to consider you have not only attracted the positive things in your life, but are energetically responsible for attracting the negative ones as well.

Like a magnet turned the opposite direction, the message will repel or bounce off a person's field. They may hear it later in a soul's whisper, calling them back home. It's not up to me at this point. Riley may have asked me to crack the door open so he could catch a glimpse, but it's up to each individual to cross the threshold. It may take years…lifetimes. This is not of my concern. I move at my pace. They will move at theirs. All are perfect.In this interaction I received a message of my own. It is time to move beyond the limitations of others. I recognize the imbalance of our vibrations more readily, but releasing the cord between his world and mine was not easy. I couldn't force someone to rise to my frequency, and I couldn't let myself get sucked down to match theirs. Inevitably the latter would happen if I continued to share space with Riley or Kane. That wouldn't do any of us any good. If I am no longer in alignment with them, then I will be alone. This thought terrified me. It is a threshold I have feared crossing. But now I am in the thick of it and there is no turning back. In my deepest of knowing, I remember the message from the middle of the night: you are never alone. You never were, and you never will be.

When the dawn of a new day broke, my brain popped with a recollection of a series of classes being offered by a local clairvoyant. Subtle Energy Awareness. Who knows if those classes are even still available. This is what Aya does. It nudges. I think I need to see about signing up for that class. As it turns out, the series is only offered once per year, and it just so happens to be starting its yearly session next week. This is how it works. When you are ready, things fall into place. A discount appears. A house sells. Money arrives. A schedule opens up. Your journey continues uninhibited by the density of Earth. It flows.

Zap the Motherboard

Disease stays dormant in the nervous system, until one day there's an outbreak. It's been spreading without your knowledge, but had your subconscious consent. This is the program that's been implanted. It starts out a microscopic seed. It grows, and poisons from the inside. I wondered what was wrong with me. I said I would never be like them, like the ones that hurt me. But their disease was contagious. That's the only virus I'm concerned about. The one that is spread by abuse and a lack of consciousness.

I felt like the seed was planted without my consent, but that's how it works. There's a massive social grooming for lower frequencies. Then we don't know who started the game, but somehow we are all playing. This disease disrupted my DNA. It left me buzzing with a vibrational match for abuse, and until I softened and transmuted it, I kept attracting the same pattern. That's why I went to therapy. That's why I welcomed my spiritual quest. I wanted to remove the seed of hurt. I wanted to remove the program. And there was more than one. It's hard work to dig it all up. But this is the only way I could find the core of who I am under all of these layers, patterns, paradigms, and programs.

Sometimes Ego needs a pinch collar, sometimes it needs a treat. It is a tool for experience, and not the essence. I will thank this voice for protecting me, but now I am asking to hear from another source. The pain was in the resistance. I heard this phrase fifteen years ago, and I now understand it on a spiritual level. *Attitude of gratitude, you got me AA*. Messages of enlightenment snuck into a 12-step meeting. If only people in AA recovery could shift from operating from a program of dependence and desperation to self-trust and self-empowerment. That program was hi-jacked too. The real transcendence of it's founders was discovered through psychedelics. A steady stream of wine and sitcoms and I would have never woken up. And that's what I came here to do. Much like a first chiropractic adjustment, the correction doesn't "hold" the first time. The muscles are not relaxed into the spine's new position yet. It takes some effort and consistent practice to maintain a healthy new positioning in life. I've been in a victim-predator feedback loop for quite some time. I released the codependence of my mind from the construct. I wanted to be free there too.

I was one of those spirited kids who needed "more", and when I didn't get more, I interpreted it as my being less. My parents had a perception of me being an extension of themselves, but I didn't fit their mold. Because there isn't a mold. I am not blaming myself anymore. My soul is not to blame. The faulty programs of Ego were on autopilot. I was taught to obey, especially in public school. Not to think for myself. The system was more important than the living organisms. The souls. That much was clear to me. As I got older and what felt natural to me fell outside the walls of the main-stream box, I was forced to conform. This put me further into dis-ease. Not a mental illness. Dis-ease with the structures. Dis-ease with what the masses were doing. What is accepted socially, medically, and purposefully ranges from culture to culture, country to country, and from time period to time period. For me, the current box was causing me mental, spiritual, emotional, and soulful dis-ease. I was at dis-ease with a small, inflexible box.

Just how dark did I need it to get before I could acknowledge my own light? It was time to zap the motherboard. Time to upgrade. Anything was possible when I staid clear and trusted my innate intelligence. I had to remember how it felt to be in a fog, asleep, terrified to believe, scared of being alone, and unaware of this powerful connection. I had to remember how it felt before and after. To wake up on the other side, of the other side, of the other side. There are no sides. That is the illusion.

Frog Medicine

"**D**o you know people have died from that shit?" Kane offered as a gentle conversation starter, as we sat down to watch his favorite television show. He was dropping a ton of fear on me for considering Kambo. I found it ironic he never blinked an eye at my medicine cabinet full of pharmaceuticals. No one was scared I would die, kill, or kill myself as a side effect of a plethora of lab rat pills.

"Is that supposed to be a helpful insight? Just what is your point?" I asked him, disgruntled on our khaki cushioned couch.

"My point is, do you think before you do anything?" he poked at me. Kane landed on a recent episode of an Alaskan survival show. "You could never survive out there," he switched up the conversation. "I bet you'd break down in tears if you had to face the elements like these people. I'd have to carry the weight for you, or leave you behind and hope you could hang on until I could come back for you," he confessed with bitter pity.

The previous night we were watching a documentary about a hiker who got his arm stuck under a boulder. He was out of cell phone range. The young man had to drink his own urine to survive and considered ways to sever his arm to freedom. Curious about the effects of drinking your own urine, I sat next to Kane, Googling facts about urine consumption. He hated when I got on my phone during tv time. But I got bored and wanted to expound on the information. Apparently, many yogis used this practice to assist the body in its purification process. They rinse their face and hair with their own urine. Sounds primal. I'm in.

As Kane drifted into a self-satisfied coma of envisioned survival elitism, I snuck into the bathroom and locked it. I reached for the glass drinking cup I used to rinse my mouth after brushing my teeth. The sounds of the television blared outside, and the flashing lights from the programming blinked at me from the crack under the door. I squatted above the toilet and held the cup between my legs like I was testing for an unwanted pregnancy. A light golden stream quickly filled my glass and splashed on my fingers. I set the cup on the counter as I wiped myself and waited to flush the toilet. I stood and stared at myself in the mirror. My eyes pierced back at me with a fierce determination. I lifted the cup and smelled it. Earthy—like a solo hike in the woods, when you piss on yourself and say *fuck it*, it's me among the animals.

Luckily I drank a lot of water, and was on a mostly vegetarian diet at the time. This decreases the pungency of urine. *Pee is sterile,* I said to myself. People piss on open wounds from jellyfish. I touched the liquid with my fingertip, then touched my finger to my lips. It was smooth, like the consistency of water with a touch of heated gelatin running through it. I took a sip. Salty. Then another. Not so bad. Then a gulp, as I refrained from breathing in through my nose.

I poured the rest of the cup into my palms and splashed the warm, marking substance on my face. I felt my skin tighten as it dripped from my eyelashes, nose, and the wisps of hair around my face. I smiled with pride at my reflection in the mirror. I could survive anything. Little did Kane know of my inner strength. Almost ten years of marriage and he didn't know shit about me. The piss test. The ultimate test of lost survivors in the wild. I had proven to myself I could survive anything, in the case of an unexpected apocalypse.

I weighed the perceived risks when it came to pharmaceuticals, Kambo, plants medicine, and my health. The stigma of having delusions of grandeur if someone spoke of a profound purpose, intuition, or connection to God blocked me for awhile. Modern day labels of mental illness imply people can't trust themselves. This is the opposite of healing. I continued to seek balance and clarity on my journey. Kambo uses the secretion of the giant green monkey tree frog from the Amazon. I was intimidated by it, because a friend told me it hits like a freight train. He said, "there aren't any visions with it. It's just straight up energy purging."

I did more research on this modality, weighing the pros and cons. I learned it enters through the lymphatic system, which allows a rapid distribution to other bodily systems, perhaps recalibrating the brain's serotonergic systems, with peptides. I read articles of people who had autoimmune diseases, but were completely asymptomatic after working with Kambo. Indigenous tribes in the Amazon have used it for over three thousand years. One of the primary reasons was to clear panema, which is bad luck. Warriors used it to increase stamina, strength, and clarity. This sacred medicine is thought to bring about a deep healing. I was getting lighter. I wanted to stay this way. I was being called by this mysterious creature and its secretions. It's time. I signed up for an upcoming session. I reminded myself of the process for Kambo by reviewing the practitioner's email and guidelines listed on his website. I began a dry fast. The following morning, I drove to a local city. Parched with thirst, I parked my car in a gravel lot, alongside a modest yoga studio. As I walked into the square room, filled with the aroma of burnt sage, I noticed a circle of familiar faces. It was reassuring to see the smiles of my fearless companions. I may not know them out there, in the matrix of life, but in here, we held sacred space for one another's healing.

Ceremony began with the use of Sananga, which is a traditional eye medicine made from the shredded roots of a shrub. It clears negative energy and settles your body into a ceremony space. And it stings, like a hornet to the eyeball. After the Sananga, I had a visualization of me walking out of my body. I was left on the mat like an thick eggshell cracked open. My Higher Self knew this was a job for the body to complete. She would hold space for me as I dealt with these heavy earthly energies.

The practitioner, Todd, mentored us, "Meet the medicine half way. Let her do her work. It is amazing how much is accomplished through the breath. Pain is there for you to heal. Do not bypass and skip into bliss. Do the work. Learn to meet the pain, and work through the pain. Dig deep and uproot the old karma to be released. This will allow you to feel grounded and blissful on a daily basis, and experience less of the harsh mirroring out in the world. The more shadows you face and release, the less you have to see it out in the world. You may feel weak at first, like you cannot hold your body up, but once that passes and you sit up straight, the energy aligns in your chakras and is able to lift up and release with a purge."

His sharing was followed by an offering of hape´, breathing, and song. This is the way to unify our intentions. Todd spoke to me with discreet attentiveness to determine what I was working through, and where the portals should be placed. Then, small gates were created by burning the top layer of my skin with a tiny unscented Himalayan incense stick. I flinched as I watched this ritual performed on me. Yet again a brief notion of "what the hell have I've gotten myself into," washed over me. I have learned to push through the fear, or walk along side it. It doesn't stop me anymore. I was instructed to chug as much water as I could to assist in the process, which was about 1 liter. The frog secretion was carefully applied. I felt the warmth of its medicine creep up my leg.

I felt moved to do this, and yet, the possibility of my hands going numb or face swelling up was a bit troubling. I will trust the medicine. I will trust the skill of the practitioner. I will trust the calling. I want to be fully unstuck. There are more layers to expose and heal. I can feel it. I am not on maintenance mode just yet. I'm still in the thick of it. No going back.

A warm rush of tingling travelled up my legs, through my arms, hands, and fingertips, and into my neck and face. This is it. For a moment I thought, *take it off*—NOW. It's too much. What the hell did I just do?

I looked up at the assistant, "I'm afraid," I tell him, "My hands are numb." I felt my heart pounding in my throat and I felt as though my artery might burst through the flesh on my neck like a gory Japanimation scene.

"You're fighting it," he said, "what you're feeling is normal. You're safe, drink water, let go," he instructed me.

There was a giant ball of energy in my core that I thought would be impossible to get out. I feared I might get stuck with it. I could hardly hold myself up. My lips were feeling tingly and face swelled. The energy was stuck in my head and it ached. I felt discouraged that I couldn't withstand the surge of energy trying to escape my body. But I kept forcing myself to drink more water and allowing the purge. I positioned myself on yet another bucket, and let the nausea flood my system until my ability to hold it in became saturated. It induced a projectile purge. My teeth and jaw chattered uncontrollably, unlocking energy that has been clenched for years. I have ground down and smashed the enamel of my teeth, over the last few years, holding in the frustrations of my life. I've been sleeping with an unsexy night guard over my teeth, but wouldn't it be easier to let go? I'm trying.

I shook and quivered with an energetic uprising I have never experienced before. The practitioner and his assistants played traditional music that assisted the process. The less I thought, the more it flowed. They blew tobacco to clear my system and push the energy to the surface when I appeared stuck.

After the release, I experienced the most relief I've ever felt. Lightness. Happiness. Laughter. Elation. After twenty minutes of processing, the practitioner removed the medicine balls from the gates. I felt exhausted. I've had a masonry of emotions just below the surface and I was finally able to cry. I had not been allowed to feel for quite some time.

The healer consoled, "It is okay to feel your feelings. Sometimes the energy gets stuck in our face when we are stuck in our head. Too much thinking and analyzing. Just be present and allow." He shared that at other times the swelling can release and dissolve like the release of a mask, revealing a more authentic layer. This medicine will cleanse you, both physically, emotionally, and energetically.

"Your eyes are crystal clear blue," he shared as he gazed at me with a peaceful recognition. When I looked in the mirror I could see the clearness he was referring to. I can now decipher the subtlety of energy in my eyes. I know when I'm clouded and when the energy has been lifted and I am lighter, brighter, and pure. This purity of energy allows for greater connection to my Higher Self and love.

I lay on the floor and rested. Tears streamed down as I felt the gift of surrender. The release of deep seated pain. I felt like I'd run a marathon through a thundering rainstorm. Never had a hard wood floor felt so inviting. Someone placed a blanket over me, and sprayed rose water over my tender skin. "You did good. Rest," a voice whispered.

After another twenty minutes, an assistant brought me herbal tea and a bowl of fruit. She consoled me, "You are so strong, so brave. Be kind to yourself and know your strength out there in the world too." The circle of participants unified by sharing some insights from their experience. The practitioner listened intently to the tribe he had facilitated healing for. He shared a bit from his own healing, and extended his gratitude to those that had allowed him to assist in theirs.

After a few hours of rest, a connection came to me. In my younger years, I had the urge to "get it out of my system" when drinking. I was on some kind of mission to purge something. Except alcohol filled me with poison. Hangovers are culturally normalized. I realized the instinct to vomit negative energy has always been with me. I just didn't know about plant medicines of a higher frequency. Kambo is what I sought.

In closing, Todd added, "religion is filled with rituals to create a space for healing to take place. But organized religion can get cluttered up with rules and stringency. Keep the rituals simple and the prayers brief. The space created is presence. Presence allows the healing in."

During plant medicine ceremonies the singing, drumming, and blowing of tobacco smoke kept me out of my head. The more I was present in the moment, and allowed the process to take place without the blocks of my mind, the more I experienced the healing. Once the stuck energy was purged, the current could flow again. I could feel joy in the quiet still moments, or on a noisy city corner. I began to hear the quiet voice between channels. There she is. That's me. I understood *connected*.

The Kambo practitioner followed up with us via email. After a long nights sleep, I woke feeling detoxified and re-birthed yet again. A day ago I thought, I feel good, is it possible to feel even better? Yes. Yes it is. I had been weighed down with suffering and sickness for so long, I forgot what healthy felt like. I forgot just how good this life can feel. Kambo is a vital force.

Ceremony

"This is how to do it, Katie. Put the bowls facing inward," Kane instructed. I stood in the kitchen as he instructed me how to load the dishwasher his way..the "correct" way. I guess the open marriage wasn't enough for him, and I've better things to do than soap dishes for the zillionth time. I could feel my IQ lowering, as a brigade of Mohicans lined up along the loft above our dining area. I sent a secret glance through the forest of my mind. I gave them the silent "okay" and a thousand *woohips* flew through the air, piercing each and every one of Kane's perfectionist words, pinning them all over the walls of our family photos.

Kane's voice faded as I was whisked away by a daydream.

Today I'm reliving one of my sexual peaks. I'm convinced my lover, Cole, is a companion from another life. How else could he know me so well? All of his tastes are identical to mine. His tongue fits my mouth like a heavenly breath, caressing my soul into bliss.

"I'm stuck in the house with my roommate," Cole texted me.

"Is your roommate the spouse you're separated from? Because mine is," I confessed to him.

"Ha, well she's my ex-girlfriend. It sucks. I'm stressed, but we can't afford to move out separately yet," he shared. His relief traveled across the technical waves. Situations like ours don't translate well to happily coupled peers. And they were the unspoken choices of forced partnerships. In a dim lit room, with the neon glow of a phone, we had each other.

"All the more reason to work out our frustrations. The air is thick in here. I might take a drive soon. I have his car tonight," I texted back.

"Meet you at the trailhead? The one at our halfway point?" he replied with no hesitation.

"Really?" I asked, not sure if he was just being another fuckboy, fishing for phone sex.

"I'm serious. I wanna do you in your ex's car. Be there in fifteen," the ping echoed through my room.

I didn't have time to second guess. I had the evening open to run an errand and this became it. I gripped my boots on and started my car like I was ditching the country. As if this was my last chance. I needed to feel pleasure. I needed human connection. I needed the release.

I hopped in the car and sped down the mountain as the night welcomed my rendezvous. I navigated my Subaru like it was a Nordic longship constructed of old growth oaks. I led it through icy waters, guided by the dragon on my bow and stern, and a sail threaded with the silver strings of my heart. Minutes later I parked in a vacant dirt parking lot next to Cole's ship. Our floating islands briefly met. We locked eyes, like only lone warriors do, and are compelled to exchange a prolonged smile, words of breathtake, a soft embrace, and in this case…more.

To the West was the burnt orange of the Rocky Flats, and East the lights of Denver. I rolled down my window and Cole leaned in to kiss me. His wavelength filled me like a tide and I started to wonder if this might be the sweet mist that heralds another crashing wave of destruction.

"Hop in the back?" Cole asked permission.

As we stripped down like we were transitioning in a triathlon, I asked, "will you go down on me?"

"Of course. Tell me how you like it," he spoke softly as he touched between my thighs.

Kane thought my dirty talk was too chatty and bossy, but Cole thinks it's hot when a woman knows how she likes it. That's why Cole is the one going down on me now. And he does it with perfection. I can hardly feel my limbs. I'm disoriented-this is how I like it.

As Cole came up for air he whispered into my neck, "I wanna fuck your throat babe." My ears perked and senses woke up like a stay-at-home mom hearing a "50% discount" pitch at a Pampered Chef presentation.

We wrestled around the cramped back seat like it was an amateur UFC fight, breathing a play by play of our match to each other. Fighters like their egos stroked. Warriors root each other on. We knew how this worked. We knew what we liked. I bent over the back seat and grabbed a plastic handle bar, as I thought, *this is what these holds are meant for.* I braced myself as he held my hips.

"Be loud," he requested. I moaned in a primal release as he tugged my hair then placed his powerful hand carefully over my delicate neck and squeezed. I liked feeling my life in his hands. Trust is where the edge is found. Cole understood this. I allowed his hand to tame me, like a wild horse chooses who can grab her mane. We raced full speed to the brink of the cliff.

I was recalling our laughter of ecstasy echoing through the rocky mountain canyon, as the dust cloud settled and I was brought into the present moment. The kitchen. Kane's dish lecture. Get me out of here. I asked of the Universe. I've come to a fork in the road. This is what happens when you wake up one day and realize the face you've been staring at for the last ten years never really knew you.

Over the course of the next few months, I attended subtle energy awareness classes and began to have a more academic understanding of Awakening. Many of the happenings I have experienced are shared by those who are walking a similar path. It is a relief to learn this, and I feel supported by the seekers, empaths, and intuitives I sit amongst. To feel elated, possessing the urge to teach others, then flung into a state of apathy, or feeling overwhelmed and isolated, and at times arriving at blissful acceptance and connection, are all symptoms experienced during different and repeating stages of waking up.

The metaphysical knowledge I gained from class helped me interpret the messages I received during deep meditation. Ironically, I would have rejected much of the information if I didn't have a friend in college who was a Physics major. He was ex-military and told me ESP is not only possible, but proven. Picking his brain helped lay the foundation for some of this work. Subtle energy practices taught me how to find my center, securely ground myself, and listen to my intuition. This foundation taught me how to open up and allow the messages in, to understand which voice was that of my Ego and which was that of my Higher Self. Preparation defines any journey, and I have been studying like a Samurai.

I broadened my lightwork by taking a Reiki Level I course, which helped me understand the energy transference of light with a new perspective. The buzzing in my palms. The diversified approach to intuition. To call upon unconditional love and feel it flow through my body and into another in a healing surge. Each modality has a unique angle of gifts that support the whole.

Avenues to cleanse my system continued to connect. My chiropractor put me into touch with a local acupuncturist. It was time to revisit the meridian system of traditional Chinese medicine. As I gave the acupuncturist the lowdown of my current situations, she took an inventory of my pulses.

"The qi (vital energy) is stuck in your liver," she stated, "this is often a holding point for emotions, to block them from flowing into your heart and causing you pain. Your body is trying to protect you from grief, but the result is being stuck, which isn't good in the long run."

Once again, I'm faced with another angle of needing to let go. As she worked her prickly magic, I felt a gush. A sock to the gut. A wave of grief sucked the wind out of me and I begin sobbing. Streams of tears relentlessly cascaded down my face. How is it possible to have this many tears! And why did I wear mascara to this appointment? I didn't know this was going to happen. I didn't know how sad I was about ending my marriage. The open marriage seemed like a logical solution, but the reasons behind it were not playful at all. It was the result of a lost connection and severe dysfunction. I felt grief like when my grandmother died. A gravity of loss beyond words. This is what I didn't want to feel. A loss so painful. My heart squeezing and imploding like I'd been hit with the death touch.

I continued to sob as I struggled to see through blurry eyes, to sign my payment on the acupuncturist's iPad. While holding my soggy tissue, attempting to wipe the strings of snot coming from my nose, I apologized, "I'm sorry for crying so much. I think I feel better," I tried to assured her.

With caring eyes, the acupuncturist looked at me and relayed, "What you are feeling is good. You are processing stuck emotions." Feeling doesn't *feel* good, I thought to myself. "Your health will improve from this. Rest and drink water," she instructed. That night I continued to cry for about twelve straight hours. I slept intermittently throughout the night, waking only to realize my pain, take a gasp for air, and cry myself back to sleep again. The next morning my eyes were swollen, and I looked like I had been through yet another wringer. Around noon, something lifted. The tears dried up, I took a shower, and I felt lighter. Renewed. Another layer was stripped away, just in time for the Peruvian Shaman.

A text from my bohemian friend shifted my attention. "Katie, if you feel called to do this, it could be life changing. Only you know," Carmen insisted. "The money is insignificant. I'll lend it to you, and when your house sells, pay me back."

I sat with it and decided yes, I was being called to go on a three-day retreat with what I would consider an Amazonian traditionalist. I like triptychs. Three is the magic number. Beginning, middle, end. I was ready to dive deep. One weekend, three stages. I recalled the process of scuba diving. I didn't descend straight to the bottom. No, I lowered, acclimated, lowered, acclimated, lowered, acclimated, then observed my surroundings. That was the path to clarity. Only then did I reap the full reward of another aquatic dimension.

I was driving home from energy class, on what was normally a busy highway. As I reached the point where the mountains meet the flatlands, I saw flashing red lights. Stillness, on a starless overcast night, not a car besides mine in sight. The police officer sat in his squad car parked next to an enormous stag with magnificent antlers. He lay motionless, lifeless, defeated. I couldn't ignore this rarity. *What was an elk doing so low in altitude tonight? Where was his herd?* They don't migrate this route. I pondered the symbolism of an elk...a dead one. My spirit animals grace me with their wisdom.

This stoic giant symbolizes endurance and patience, and reflects on relationships. At any other time in my life, I would have bailed on my situation. I would have been driven by impulse to escape the pain. Relationship or job not working out? Fuck it. I'm gone. But now... life was not allowing for that. It doesn't fit. I've grown past that solution. The elk totem asked me to pace myself. I may not be the first to arrive, but I will get there without burning out.

A dead elk signifies I am not yet exemplifying the traits of endurance, patience, calculated measures, and stamina. *Slow down, Katie. Make your plan and sit with the discomfort of not having immediate gratification. The elk is urging you to pay attention. He is showing you how to traverse your new migration path.* I could choose to view the elk on the side of the road as a mishap of wildlife mingling too close to modern life. Or I could listen to my gut. I could listen to nature. No one else was in sight. This message was for me.

When I arrived at home I wondered, was that impossible elk even there? Did I just see that? A few weeks ago, I had asked to be shown what animal spirit guides might be connected to me. Owls and cougars kept presenting themselves in tarot cards, t-shirts, tattoos, and billboards. My helpers. I had invited them closer. Yes, in slow motion, with piercing antlers lying in defeat along the dark reflection of the asphalt, the Universe spoke. I chose to listen.

"I'm going next time. On my own," Kane announced as he sipped on his morning coffee.

"Where?" I asked.

"To take Ayahuasca," he replied with a somber tone in his voice.

"Do you really want to? Do you feel ready?" I wondered as I adjusted to the glare of morning shining past him in the window.

"As ready as I'm going to be. I've done plenty of hallucinogens, but not for a long time. And I know, I know..this stuff is different. I want to see what it is," Kane explained.

"I think that's great. Meditating beforehand helped get me in the right head space. If you want to know anything, just ask me," I opened to him.

"Thanks. I already made a couple phone calls. I'm good," he assured me as he set his mug into the sink. I wondered what lie ahead for us. This is not the path most married couples take. At least I can appreciate that.

The following week, I commuted to another distant location. Travelers from all directions carried bags into the house. Ceremony will be held upstairs, which is also where the men will sleep. The women will sleep downstairs. We began with a short introduction by the Peruvian Shaman, Cielo. He shared bits from his life story, his journey, and how he came to be here. This gained our trust, put our anxieties at ease, and set the tone for the retreat. He proceeded as a professional, having taken a thorough inventory of each individual prior to this weekend. He relayed expectations for the appropriateness of behavior by the group, and explained his process. Then he led the group in song together. Despite the lyrics being an unknown language, the repetition of sound harmonized us as a group. The circle was unified.

After Cielo's short talk, the group dispersed. He called us up one by one to ask more specific details about our history and what we were here to heal. He called it "doing your work." This wasn't a girl's glamping trip. This was serious transformation. The intention of his work is to assist people on their healing journey, and connect those in an awakening process to the Source, through nature's divine medicine.

The tools of his trade were laid out on a square woven mat. Among them, Florida water, a cologne used by shamans for cleansing and healing, tobacco leaves, some fresh flowers, and an array of drums, flutes, and rattles from South America.

Chirps of a symphony of exotic birds rang in the air, mingling with smells of soil and damp moss. The Underworld was near again, I could feel it. The air was cool and clear, early morning mist still hanging like a veil hinting at the gentle worlds that lay beyond. We were called to ceremony at seven o'clock that evening. Cielo began with another beautiful song accompanied by his assistants. They set a mood of peace and unity. His gravel voice was like a cave, encouraging us to look deep, be brave, and ask Mother Ayahuasca to show us how to heal.

"Do your work," he said. "Surrender." The room was smudged with sage and palo santo to ensure our space was energetically cleared and protected as we journeyed. "No more speaking. We must respect one another's healing space," Cielo instructed.

One at a time, we were called up for hape´, if we so chose, to get us into the ceremonial space. Then we were called up one at a time for an ounce-sized cup of tea, from a miniature bronze goblet. The tea was blessed by the shaman and his lineage. We sat on our mats, lights dimmed, and waited.

Time sifted into insignificance. Chirping, croaking...sounds of the jungle. Is that the shaman playing one of his instruments or am I already there? My eyes had been closed, my legs folded beneath me, my palms heavenward...waiting. I blinked my eyes open to peek at my surroundings. The room was hazy as the sun had set. Sounds of the breath increased around me. A few moans of release from members of my tribe. "The Mother is here now," the Cielo spoke, "thank her. Show her you are ready. Ask her to guide you. Surrender."

I began to plummet down a tunnel lined with Day of the Dead skeletons. The spirits of Incan wisdom came to meet me. Some of the faces appeared to be laughing at me. Their mouths opened and closed in a mechanical chomp. It was not unlike the descent of a rollercoaster enclosed in a dark shaft. I couldn't see when I hit the bottom and became parallel with a new level; I felt it. I became aware of a black blob in the pit of my stomach. Like a tar ball, it slowly thudded from side to side in my gut, aware I have detected its presence. Knowing I had more darkness within to face, I asked the Madre, "What is this?"

A whisper, "It is the need for acceptance, and the need to fit in," she said. "You have been feeding it, so now it has grown."

The darkness I was sensing inside, thinking I was somehow evil, or a mistake, was unrecognized light I let turn into a thick muck in the pit of my belly. I thought I let go of most of this already, but I had only scratched the surface. There are a multitude of layers, hidden hallways, and secret trap doors. This was in the cellar of my soul. I've felt it creaking beneath my navel, but like a child, afraid of the basement, I wasn't ready to descend into its cold musky dwelling. Until now.

The need for cleansing was so immediate, and the opportunity precise in that moment, that I forwent the cleaning gloves and grabbed the bucket.

Sometimes a mother reaches out and scoops up the filth with her bare hands. I can wash them later. It's an instinct I attained through child rearing. I cultivated a keen awareness for the look on a face when a release is on the brink, and a sixth sense when an arm needs to be grabbed and a body hurled to safety from a fall or a zooming car. I am the first to hear the twig snap in the forest.

It is time to be my own mother. The lump surged and I gave in to the process. I shed a layer of density that was smeared over the bulb of my inner light. This malignant mass, the same boggy color as my early childhood interior, was masquerading as my identity. By releasing the superficial needs of my Ego, I could illuminate the next layer. I saw how strict programming interfered with the flow of my life. The cluster fuck that had become my marriage was now on the forefront. I was fixated on what a family *should* look like. I would have to let go of that maladaptation too.

"Listen to the pleas of your children. Find a way to live in harmony," she guided me. It is the request of my children. Pachamama was showing me how to be a better mother. I am becoming a type of mother I have not yet known. This transition can be a slow unfolding and rebuilding. Seasons change subtly before your eyes, not harshly overnight. Be like nature, Aya teaches.

I looked up at the faces of the people in the room. They were painted skulls, floral yet harrowing. The Day of the Dead was in session. Their bodies shifted in flashes exposing their skeletons. The material is not real. It is borrowed equipment for our consciousness to navigate within. The bones are the hull of our ships, connected by a quilt of fleshy mass, and a web of zipping neurons. I saw energies in the room, soaring up, gushing down, and swirling through our circle of skeletal pods.

I can quit struggling to match up with what I told others is happening in my life. In the months preceding, I divulged details to friends of my rocky open marriage that was beginning to avalanche, in an effort to shed overwhelming emotions. Now I felt pressured to be consistent with my descriptions, although life was already shifting again. Perhaps the lesson is to allow people to witness my imperfections. It's okay to go through a rollercoaster with my partner. Growth happens and we can circle back and create a path that works for us, not just one that satisfies the preconceptions of marriage. Maybe our marriage is one of un-marriage. Perhaps we are soulmates of an unexpected definition.

I sat on my knees and placed my forehead onto the floor, resting my head in the crux of my elbow. My hair cascaded over my face as I nestled into my comforting cocoon. I continued to gestate. The Mother has a way of transforming her children into whatever is necessary to play out their lessons.

"Drink your water. Water is life," Cielo churned from the center of our circle. He broke into song, as if he knew one lesson had been realized. A celebration and transition to the next began.

I chewed on my necklace and enjoyed the sensation of putting my mouth on it. I blinked my eyes and discovered I was in the body of a child being scolded for chewing on her hair. My strands of hair were a soppy mess, but I felt a calming warmth wash through my body, as I caressed my face with this tickly paintbrush. At the same time I felt guilt and shame. I cowered, paralyzed in self-disgust and humiliation. The Mother Spirit consoled, "It's okay to feel pleasure. It is okay to have innocent playful secrets. It is okay to know yourself in this way, and to share yourself with someone in this way." This lesson was no longer about sucking on my hair in church or chewing on a pencil in school. She was showing me the root of a program that spread into a grove of maladaptation towards intimacy.

Consciousness was showing me my mis-wiring around shame and pleasure. The lesson pointed to my current relationships. I felt guilty for enjoying the pleasure of an open marriage.

I began to understand the connection with my extra-marital lover in a new way. This non-traditional path allowed me an opportunity to heal a deep wound. Others may have perceived my marital choice as consensual infidelity, but I experienced it in a much different way. My companion was playful and explored with me. After surviving sexual trauma, he showed me it was safe to feel pleasure and okay to be free. He was a healer to one of the most intimate and sacred layers of my Self.

I breathed into this lesson as the shaman began drumming. I felt the cosmic rhythm, the familiar ripples through my molecular body with every beat. The tribal waves of my youth embraced me with song once more. Cielo was in tune with the rhythms of our lessons. He rejoiced with us, then called for silence. "Keep listening. Dive deep. Listen to your body. Thank the Mother. You are safe. She is loving and kind, strong and wise. Do your work. Look inside," he guided with a voice weighted with the knowledge of a dusty ten pound book.

I swaddled myself with earthly arms as I sat upon my island. The Spirit of Ayahuasca is internal in many of her visuals and teachings. She opened my extrasensory perception. I felt a squeeze of hesitation, but deep down I know I was being called to this my whole life. I yearned for permission to be myself.

Self-acceptance is pivotal. This family of people are courageously seeking a path to healing, rather than numbing the surface. I am witness to them. Their sugar skull faces neighbor me, deep in meditations of their own. They excursion through death and rebirth.

Cielo came to each person in the circle with his Chakapa, a bundle of dried leaves used as a Shamanic tool to awaken medicinal power and support the cleansing of forces around us. We were releasing a fog of stagnant energy. The healer used his tool as a sword to dig out the stale energy and waft it away.

He shook the dried leaves on my head, behind my back, and under my neck. I felt Spirit working through him to clear the block in my throat. The leaves rustled and I felt the playfulness of the Universe, making me giggle like a toddler enthralled in the sounds and sensations of a new world.

As the ceremony neared its closing for the evening, Cielo and his accompanists began to hum a melody that banded the group. The music invited the soul of each wounded child in the circle. The silence hung in the air like a perfect note before the deep voice of a young man rolled out an aching song from lifetimes ago. *Let your burdens go, my children. Let them go.* A hymn from beyond time, channeling a divine compassion for the human condition, and a soothing message of transcendence and restoration. There were others who sang, but his voice was the Ohm that roved into the cavern of my heart.

As I slid into my sleeping bag, I typed the lessons from the evening into the "Notes" section of my phone. In the moment, I might have sworn I could never possibly forget these thoughts, but I knew better. Epiphanies can slip through my memory files. I would revisit the lessons in my notes, rather than repeat their mistakes in my life. I would stay aware.

The group slept in, then quietly grazed though the kitchen. Some helped cook a simple meal for the day, consisting of fruit, vegetables, and quinoa. Water and Jasmine tea were offered. We took turns using the shower to rinse off. After a night of radical introversion we all needed a form of rest, whether an afternoon nap, a walk in the forest, or convening with others about their discoveries. The second night of ceremony would begin again at seven o'clock.

The shaman opened by offering advice and insights on life. Then he continued, "last night you were gently cracked open and acquainted with the medicine. Tonight we dive deeper."

We went around the circle and briefly shared something we felt significant from the night before. It was amazing to hear from my fellow humans.

How raw and personal their struggles were, and yet how familiar. It was like hearing the cries of my brothers and sisters for the first time. I admired the men among the group, healing their father wounds, the suppressed emotions that prevented them from healthy unifications with women. They are leading the shift for other men to come out of the "mancave" and balance their feelings. I felt this heavy undertone in my heart, each time I heard my brothers being berated by adults and ridiculed by peers for crying as children. Our group became one with song, then welcomed the quiet of an impending voyage.

I meditated on letting go of unhealthy ancestral baggage. I wanted to know where the negativity inside me came from. The more I focused on it, the fatter it grew, twisting and sliding in my guts like an anaconda. Anger unrolled in me, as I heard yelling voices swirling around my body.

"Is this mine?" I cried. "I want it out of me!" I demanded of Aya.

Then I shifted to sadness. I sobbed, "I surrender to your way of showing me the answers to these questions. Please show me." My mind calmed with patience and presence. I breathed.

A timeline connected me to Nebraska. I was in the desolation of the Dakotas. Dad's family settled in North Dakota as farmers when they first came to the United States. I wondered if the yelling I heard was connected to a disruption on the land. She was showing me a lot of puzzle pieces, and I had to follow their lead. Sometimes, Aya shows you what you are most familiar with, like a game of charades, then circles back to the big picture.

My awareness shifts once more. I am a warrior. The screams become internal. Dad referred to me as a fighter, his voice either swollen with pride or frustration. I survive things, even when I'm brought to my knees. I find the strength to persevere.

Pachamama transfers thoughts into my forehead, "Anger and aggression are not true strength. A quiet, calm demeanor shows authentic fortitude."

I asked, "please help me understand this anger. Why does it exist?"

Then Spirit showed me a vision of hardship, poverty, being cold, hungry, and aching in agonizing physical pain. My gut told me I was forced to struggle to survive for many lifetimes. This has been the path for many humans. I felt tension as the stabbing bitter cold blew through uninsulated wooden plank walls. I was trying to sleep with the cramping of an empty stomach. I would do this over and over again, until I died. Earlier times offered a bleak existence. No wonder my disposition was coded with an edge.

I kneeled on my yoga mat and steadied myself on the purging pot. This is normally a comfortable position for me to sit in, but an acute pain sped up and down my knees like lightning. I shifted my weight, but the sensation of steel pins pierced my kneecaps from every angle. The crushing ache was becoming unbearable. *Dad.* He has knee pain. It is said to be a manifestation of pride. He couldn't let go of dysfunctional patterns because a stubborn sorrow wouldn't allow it. I would not let the vice of pride interfere with my growth in this way.

I heard Aya's words, "Humble yourself." And then an even more potent message, "You're no better than him. You are the teacher and the student, just as he is." I began to see a pain in my father's being, percolating through the decades that humanized him. Perhaps he has been one of the most poignant figures in the evolution of my soul. I have been a witness to his suffering, and this informs me of my own. He has been a father in the deepest meaning of the word. I am filled with reverence.

At the beginning of the evening I asked the Mother to show me how to go deeper. On a previous night, there was a lump of fear in my throat and I couldn't push myself to swallow any additional tea. Tonight was different. As I sat with my head hung, I asked, "Please give me clarity on my path in life. I surrender to what I need to be shown to heal and reconnect with my soul."

As I cushioned myself in child's pose the urge to allow my body to contort and crane took over. Cielo filled the room with a bewitching chant, quivering his voice, as he shook his rattles methodically. Another wave was being summoned. I raised my core to position myself on all fours. My vision was fuzzy as I observed my extremities, languidly combing the floor. Relaxation rose through my arms and into my head as I rolled my skull from side to side. I gazed at my hands and scanned their features, realizing they were paws.

The panther did not come to walk beside me in guidance. Aya transformed me *into* the big cat. I integrated the regal presence of the jaguar. I was consumed with tranquility in my new body of energy. Sitting on my knees and hands felt natural. The acute discomfort that was crippling me only minutes before had vanished. I was in two bodies at once, shape-shifting, layered in a cosmic unity of dual identity. I breathed slowly, as the ceremony space was set up for another round of tea. A candle flickered and a drum rolled, showing the path. I listened. The Mother spoke.

"When the cat is sick it knows to eat the plant to get the sickness out. It doesn't worry, it follows its instinct to heal itself. Be primal. Eat the plant. The jungle cat goes into a trance to find the plant and purge to clear its system of disease. You know what to do," she said. I crawled across the floor for a second cup. I had no apprehensions, no thoughts. I didn't fret over how the medicine might make me feel, or what it would taste like. I was on the hunt to heal my body. I went through the motions to complete my duty, then sauntered back to my place of rest to allow the medicine to do her work.

The Spirit of the Universe showed me answers by turning me into the big cat. She knew some lessons are best absorbed by transforming the pupil into a vehicle most attuned to the teaching. I began to understand. The jaguar is powerful, holding both masculine and feminine energy. The female jaguar does not have a title specification separate from her male counterpart. She is simply of the Panthera Genus, and Jaguar Species. To me this is meaningful because it reflects how she defies and transcends typical gender roles.

The big cat doesn't abandon its den. It always comes back to its hideout and cares for its cubs. This is instinct. The panther also goes out on solo explorations, and does not feel guilty. This is natural for some creatures. I am one of those creatures. The big cat doesn't feel ashamed. It can be both part of a family and independent. This is the natural balance for me as well. I desperately needed this understanding of myself. I thanked the Mother for helping me discover my constitution by placing me in the body of this animal spirit. I am reconnecting and realizing the essence of my Being.

After absorbing this transformative lesson the purge began to rise again. I dry heaved and didn't concern myself with how strange it looked or sounded. Cats do weird shit all the time, and they don't worry or feel ashamed. They just do what they do, follow their instincts, hack things up, or writhe in the tall grass until they feel right again. They know what makes them feel better. They are unapologetic for what others may consider bizarre behavior. They operate from a deep wisdom, and a playful acceptance of what feels satisfying. Sometimes the jaguar wants to feel flesh between her teeth, and sometimes she wants to be gripped by the nape of her neck. The panther savors the view from the perch of a tree branch. It offers her an elevated perspective.

I rest. I need time to absorb the messages and consider all the ways they manifest in my life. The jaguar's lesson is done for now. She dissipates from my human form. As I begin to think about my family, I sense a block prohibiting me from being able to be fully present and loving for my children. I feel like I do not have enough of me to give. What if I'm not enough for them.

The consciousness of the Mother communicated, "By rejecting yourself, you are in turn rejecting them." I saw with self-acceptance, I could be open, loving, and receptive to my children and all their miraculous beauty. I was enough, if I let myself be.

The last block relates to Kane. I still feel a brick in my throat. We are bonded by a supernatural contract in this lifetime. I need to see the path in which we are to move forward. I know what the answer is, but I am not allowing it into my vision. As I began to gag on this obstruction, Cielo came over to me with intuitive precision. He cleared my energy by blowing smoke, chanting in his native tongue, and using his Chakapa. My promised soulmate could not see my strength, and that has been a dagger to my heart. But he offered other gifts in this life. The first, the sacred present of unity. Then a house, a home, a family. Perhaps the most selfless gift of all was the permission to open the marriage and try things other couples were too afraid to explore. It was imploding, but we were trying. Kane didn't understand the need for my heart and soul to be free. But my soul knows, if he could, he would, because I am also a reflection of him.

My family has been going through a tunnel for some time now. It has been dark and noisy, scary and endless at times. We are struggling to connect, but my family is strong and we are brave. We are trailblazers. We chart new paths and do what others have not yet done. We are not afraid of the unknown. We forgo marital counseling and hop straight to the Soul of the Vine. We have the courage to see what's on the other side. What's at the other end of the tunnel—a new beginning. But not together. A Native American Shaman painting hangs on our family room wall. His face painted white with a deep dark stare, whispers to me when I pass it. Kane and I purchased it on impulse with our wedding money. We took it right off the wall from a dinky pulled-pork BBQ joint in rural East Texas. It was an omen that took years to unfold.

In our union, we uprooted our geographical family roots. We shook our ancestral patterns. We mobilized one another to facilitate change. We were meant to go through a huge shift. We were brought together, to lead each other to a fork in the road. The perfection of the path is lined with paradox. The shaman in the painting was watching over us, hanging from a nail on our dusty wall for the past ten years. He has been waiting…calling us into a space of transformation. Walking between worlds on a trek of death and rebirth, is part of our path.

He walked alongside us, as we uncovered our patterns of victimhood:
self pity
abandonment
conditional love
the need to prove ourselves
comparing how hard our lives have been
emotional imbalance: unavailable or overly active
convincing others to love us
competition and control
the need to be right
not good enough

We have been cruel to each other. Triggered by one another. Thank you for showing me where I have yet to heal. I learned, despite how hard we tried, we could not break the patterns without breaking the marriage. This was our lesson to bear. I accept it and release it with love.

A triptych's magnificence cannot be fully recognized without its third panel. I kneeled on my mat, content to tie the weekend together with a gentle closing. I had been in a state of transmutation, without comprehension of the byzantine nature of rebirth. The seat of my soul was muddied up with karma, waiting for the eye of dharma to open. I could not fathom how deep the base of my burdens resided. At first I covered my eyes with my hands, like a child trying to hide from the nightmare of their mind's creation. "No, no," I whimpered. Then the "no" shifted to "not anymore, I'm ready." I asked Mother Ayahuasca to help me have the courage to look at the darkness.

The muscular knot I had become accustomed to under my right shoulder blade welled up like a hardened ball of asphalt. This is where anger and frustration were stuck. The gob extricated from the healthy tissue and became mobile. It dredged along my spine as it travelled to my brain stem. A noxious tug pulled through the center of my body, and I knew it was corded to the bottom of my guts. With a convulsing surge I started to release. Staring into a bucket of obsidian, I asked, "What is this bottomless swirling abyss of black I see?"

As I gazed into the center of the black hole, it gazed back at me, and I feared I would be sucked into it. War cries drew closer from behind the shadowy silhouettes of my mind. An earthy moisture breathed into the pulp of my lungs and streamed up my nostrils with a calling for alertness. The screams besieged my bodily boundary, as I was bestowed an unyielding truth. Through this midnight mirror, she showed me I was the murderer.

I seeped into the subterranean labyrinth of the Underworld, where my deepest emotions burrowed. I entered the dimension of a past life. My bare feet sunk into the soft ground as I crept along a hillside, lit only by the glowing of a crescent moon, and the trembling light of a crackling fire. My heart pounded in my throat as the adrenaline in my arms helped me carry out my onus. I wiped the sweat from my palms, onto the chest of my tunic, before using my bare hands to snap their necks. Their powerful trunks went limp in my grip. I grabbed a shoulder as I leaned in to sink my knife into the thick flesh of a liver. With a sudden reflex I glared to my left and locked eyes with my fearful prey. This pause would break my rampage of survival. I disappeared into the darkness of the night, only hearing the sound of my thundering footsteps and panting breath, through the density of the forest.

I was a warrior, swamped with grief over the carnage I had to carry out. Alone, in a desolate woodland, I understood I had to kill or be killed. Watching myself from above, I witnessed a tender human and indomitable assailant breaking down from the weariness of her body, mind, and heart. As I returned to my body, I knelt on the damp soil and reached out, hoping to be lifted from my endless night. When no one was there to meet my hand, I collapsed. Tears merged with the downpour of rain that unleashed above me. There comes a point when the warrior becomes worn and tired of killing others, that it is time to sacrifice herself. A final bloodshed.

I wept over the loss of lives. I sobbed in wails and moans over my pre-destined solitude. Everyone fears the warrior. They despise the brutality of the fighter. They judge the cold-blooded austerity a survivor must be emboldened with. Onlookers do not know the depths of sorrow that match the strength of character a fighter must possess.

The persecution, whether it perceived or real, was devastating. I was afraid of myself. My jaw unhinged as the slaughter was disgorged into the bucket. When there was no more gore to be hosed out of me, I breathed out a dark vapor. With my mouth still unlocked and my tongue hanging with eviction, I exhaled the foggy spirit of death. I grunted up phlegm, patted my hands on the ground, and scratched at the floor to expel any final dregs of bloodletting. After the purging ceased, Consciousness told me, "It is time for the killer to become the healer." It is then I saw a male figure emerge from the shadows, dressed with arms of feathers spread out in a dance towards me.

Humbled by this experience, and sheathed with intuition, I whispered, "Are you here for my initiation?" I felt its presence swoop around me like a stately bird. I welled with a salty lake pooling in my eyes and asked Spirit, "but how can the murderer be the healer?"

She told me, "In order to offer healing, you must understand the pits of darkness."

At that moment, the pain and suffering I felt during my life from the butchery of suicidal ideation, became a gift. Instead, I understood I was granted an opportunity to bear an agony, in order to gain understanding, so I could use my wisdom for good. It was no longer a misfortune. It was an expansion. I was filled with gratitude, put my hands folded in prayer to my forehead and, with humility, thanked the Universe.

Then I needed to pee. The room continued to vibrate around me as I crawled to the bathroom and pulled myself up to look in the mirror. I observed an indigenous woman with a painted face, gripping a dagger. She held her arm poised to slice necks, hunt, and kill.

It was terrifying to be the warrior, always having to be on guard, petrified by gruesome tasks. I saw her saddened eyes, exposing the gravity of her challenges. I felt compassion for her. I raised my hand to the mirror and forgave her for her brutalities and said good-bye. It was time to let her go. Then I raised my arms and sparked an energy surge through my hands. Fields of particles and waves of light shifted as I healed the warrior. She shapeshifted from the nucleus out into a benevolent presence of Light. I watched the woman in the mirror soften and shift into the healer. I was freed in that moment, and took the deepest breath of oxygen I have ever been able to inhale. The most important healing was that of myself.

As I returned to my mat and settled into this epiphany, I was shown my current life is a shift from previous identities. I have been on a path of transformation for almost forty years, rubbing against the rocks, trying to shed the past to be reborn. Like the serpent, I molt my old itchy skin, and welcome the glow of new growth.

I was overwhelmed with gratitude for my parents, whom I didn't feel connected with, and sensed they never quite knew how to receive me. As a child, there was nothing more dehumanizing than to be told I was getting it all wrong because the things that fill me with life and purpose didn't match their agenda. For the longest time I thought a "good" child felt obligated to please their parents. I thought it was normal to feel guilty about who I was. In that moment, I understood their roles served an important mission. No others could fulfill this quest. I accepted that I chose them to birth me because they would be the catalysts I needed to rattle me into this metamorphosis.

This life is a portal from past lives. I no longer have to carry the weight of straining for my existence. I am learning how to soften. I viewed a timeline showing me how a vibration of violence resonated with Kane's family karma surrounding murder. Our love and our darkness were equally magnetized to one another. I saw that we were an energetic match necessary to shift each other out of this reincarnating pattern of brutality and violation.

I was filled with awe as I watched Cielo perform his rituals to clear our energy. He blew a smoky gust from hand-rolled tobacco leaves, and sprayed Florida water from his mouth, in a cleansing wash into the air. His blessings held space for us to connect with a divine knowledge, allowing us to heal ourselves. The power of the Universe is within. I understand these words now. They perplexed my mind as I dangled my five-year-old feet from a wooden pew, but now they rest in the soul of my knowing.

Centered in my ceremonial space, energy was clinging to my mortal body like a sticky film. I swept it off of my arms and threw it into the bucket. I flicked my hands like a bird shakes its feathers free of parasites. *Fwhoop-fwhoop*, birds rustled around me, using their beaks to help me clean my coat. My feet began to tingle with numbness as I sat criss-crossed.

"But what about my legs?" I asked into the stillness.

A soft voice, "you don't need those where you're going."

My body became weightless and I held my hands to the sky. The heavens of infinity opened up in an unfolding of sacred geometry, moving and restructuring miraculously before my eyes, showing me a fluid precision and incomprehensible perfection of the dance of Creation. I became a unified expression of peace, joy, happiness, and gratitude. I was One with the profound bliss of Consciousness. This is ascension. This is love.

Timelines

As I rinsed miniature dishes in the sink I heard the garage door open. Kane was home. A few weeks after my experience with the Peruvian Shaman, Kane left for the weekend to experience Grandmother for himself. The house was filled with barking dogs and squealing toddlers in his absence. The nights were free from the thick air of his silent treatment, yet weighted with uncertainty.

"Daddy!" Our two little girls cheered. As far as they knew, he had never spent a night away.

Kane shuffled up the staircase, with his bags in tow. He stopped on the landing and picked up a Matchbox car the girls had been launching off the edge of the top stair. He paused, then stared up at us. The baby gate blocked the girls and dogs from pummeling him with kisses. Tears welled in his eyes.

"Are you okay?" I asked him, concerned about the expression on his face.

"It's like a dream. All the timelines. All the good ones and bad ones. We can choose which ones we want to live. I asked how it all worked, and she showed me," he said as emotion poured out of his eyes and into mine. The tears began to overflow and stream down his face.

"Hug me! Hug me!" The girls cried out. Kane looked at them with his heart beaming with gratitude. He dropped his bags and stepped up the stairwell. Without bothering to fumble with the child lock, he leaned over and stretched both of his arms around our daughters. His eyes looked tired and I knew he needed sleep.

"It's a lot to absorb. We don't have to talk about it right now. I'll throw your stuff in the wash," I said gently to him. "Then I'll take the girls outside so you can rest."

"I don't know what this means for us, but I saw why you did this. Your life is different than mine. She showed me to let go," Kane shared. "I don't want to lose this. I want them to be happy. But I know this whole life is temporary," he said as he gazed at our girls.

"I want them to be happy too, more than anything. Raise them in the light of this knowledge, that we are all one," I offered with an aching in my heart. An ache from the powerful squeeze of love, that leaves it's tender mark on your soul.

"Okay, I love you," he worded as he reached his arms towards me. I leaned in to embrace him in a tight hug.

"I love you too," I sighed. "I'm glad you went. I know it's hard..to go deep. Ayahuasca is like nothing else. It is not a hallucinogen, it is a teacher."

"Let's stay in this vibe. Whatever this is, it feels better than where we were at," Kane said as he released his arms from me.

"I agree," I responded with compassion in my heart.

I suspected our marriage wasn't 'fixed', but we had a common vision that threaded our family together. Even if we divorced, we had a spiritual understanding. The trick is to stay in a place of remembering. To keep our egos on the sidelines, and our hearts in the center. A trick that will trick us many times over before our journey is done.

The ego can be a trickster, taking the reigns of a spiritual quest. Some people bypass the pain. As Kane and I split again, he fell out of alignment with our family's goals. He fired with projections, engaging us in the center of the matrix. I would ride this out with him again because divorce doesn't untether soul contracts. If narcissism was the first mirror, sociopathy was the next. The first is a victim program, and the next is pure evil. The family court system was full of them. A collective veil of systemic oppression was pulled for us as we spiraled into the dark vortex. It left us broke, battered, and fully surrendered. My lesson was to become sovereign, find forgiveness, and hold boundaries.

These systems. They aren't human. It's like the tale of Jesus talking to the devil. Jesus says, "What do you think? I've created a beautiful earth, with plants, flowers, water, and animals. The sun is shining and the land is nourished. The people are happy and well fed with shelter for all. The children are well-adjusted and families work together to enjoy this creation." And the devil says, "I think I'll create a system for it." And that is how the tale goes. Until Kali comes and helps them unveil the darkness. Destroy it all, and with that energy create something new. Something without these systems. The devil is in the details. The devil is the fine print. It's exploitation. If only we could stop believing the lie that we are the victim, we could override the system. Override the program. Because the system is a veil concealing the one true Consciousness. Us. The Collective. Source. God.

The Hummingbird

"What do you think of that!" Grandma burst with excitement. Her eyes sparkled as she grinned ear to ear. It was her seventieth birthday, and she came home with her first tattoo.

"It's so cool! I love it!" I exclaimed. She was my idol. I would catch her staring at me like she was trying to understand a younger version of herself.

"Oh dear, what's Mom done now," my own mother wondered out loud. "Your Grandma is always up to something," she rolled her eyes.

"I got it right on my wrist, so people can see it," Grandma clarified.

"Well, you can always roll down your sleeve if you don't want it shown," Mom advised with practicality.

"Oh no I won't," Grandma shot back at her. "In fact, I want you to roll up my sleeve when I die, so people can see it at my wake."

"Oh geez. Okay Mom, we promise to do that," Mom complied as she pursed her lips and rolled her eyes. I started to giggle. "You're just like her, you know that don't you," Mom shared with me as she squinted her nose.

"Come here, Katie. Look at all the details. I told him to use all the hues, to make it as colorful as possible," Grandma rejoiced as she showed off her beautiful hummingbird with a tropical flower. "He had lots of designs, but I knew this one was for me."

"Dad, I can't believe you took her to do that," Mom said to Grandpa.

With a doting look in his eyes, he softly replied, "It makes her happy."

"Grandma said she will take me when I'm old enough," I bragged to Mom.

"Oh Katie, you're the apple of her eye," she replied with a sigh, and a gentle smile.

"Where did you go to get it?" I asked Grandma.

"Grandpa and I took a drive out past Seneca, where I used to weld. It was near where that psychic I went to a long time ago used to be," she described.

"A psychic?" I responded with curiosity.

"Oh yes, she was the real thing, not like one of those fancy ones in the city. She had a small little shop way out in the country. That's how you knew she was good. She didn't need all that glitz and glamour," Grandma told with certainty.

"Mom, are you telling her stories again? It took me weeks to get the kids to stop asking me about the one your brother dreamed up last month. He told them he saw a cow that was born inside out!" Mom announced with fluster in her voice.

"Oh shush! My brother is silly. This is a real story," she hushed Mom.

"Did the psychic tell you your future, like a fortune teller?" I pried with a young inquisitive mind.

"Not exactly. But she told me a lot of things, and she was spot on," Grandma assured me. "Some people have a gift," she said with a lowered voice, as she squeezed my hand.

"Mom, is that true?" I asked, trying to get the facts straight.

"I don't know sweetie, Grandma won't tell anyone what they talked about," she replied with skepticism.

"That's because it's none of your business. But some of it came true, I'll tell you that much," Grandma rebuked. She gave me a wink and then gazed contently at her tattoo. "Come on Katie, let's go in my room and pick out some shirts that will go with this hummingbird." The hummingbird was speaking to me. I am thankful for the courage to acknowledge these ethereal signs. Her buzzing likeness followed me. Be playful, be light, be adaptable, look backwards, but fly upwards, have stamina, be infinite, notice the beauty of a fleeting moment, and drink from the nectar of life.

When I feel irritable, it is a sign I am not honoring my true Self. This feeling communicates I am not in alignment with my soul. It prompts me to reach inside and claim my sovereignty. When life is starting to crescendo, it's a part of the miraculous, breath-taking, heart-moving symphony of infinity I am a single note within.

Not all of my methods involve plant medicine, but I recognize I'm one of those people whose receptors don't get switched on unless the stimulant is fairly extraordinary. I'm not as extreme as a free-climber, but it takes me a hair more to get my reward system lit up. My need for healing was so deeply embedded it took radical measures to uproot my seeds of suffering and germinate new growth. It began with therapy, music, reading, and nature. Then expanded to meditation, acupuncture, essential oils, yoga, weightlifting, eating high vibrational food, connecting with community, plant medicine, sound frequency healing, intuitive readings, and practicing the daily use of energetic protection. I rewired my system. It was a reorganization of everything I knew. I allowed it to alchemize in the beautiful elixir of my life.

In this, I am the arch of change and the engineer of my own destiny. Connection through this variety of methods keeps me clear, reassures me of my path, and offers healing energy as my soul mounts through growing pains. There is no tidy ending. There is only Now. Things didn't turn out the way I thought they were going to, the way I wanted them to, or even the way I planned them to. That is the Present. I am a fractal of every soul I've ever met. Diversity is real, but separation is an illusion. We are all One. There is no ending, only transitions. It doesn't take away from the enjoyment of the ride. That IS the ride.

I discovered there is no reality to find—they're all real. The passionate, apathetic, unpredictable, and loyal Katie are all versions of the same Oneness that is continuously playing out in one life or another, like an eternal quantum switchboard. When others labeled me, I knew the Truth. The injury to my heart was unprovoked trauma. Much like a car crash, both injuries require rehabilitation of the body, mind, and spirit.

When I brush the hair of my daughters across their tender little foreheads, I feel my mother brushing mine as a child. Her gentle, soothing fingertip swept with intentions rooted in a deep love. She was a wonderful mother. She was *my* mother. Mom and Dad began their journey with intentions as pure as a newborn, and traversed their paths with the vigor, hope, and turmoil we each face in an experience of this magnitude. When I release the judgement, there is nothing but forgiveness and a love so limitless, it can heal the most woeful lows of any human story. Even ours.   I am a beloved expression of the Divine flowing through me. The people and places I tried to attach to, thinking they were the path, were just people, places, and things *along* the path. My path. And on this path, I am loved and supported by things unseen, beyond my wildest dreams. I chose to look at the core and heal at the root. Rewrite the code. Each stage was a stepping stone to get me to look into the pit of the volcano. In the crevasse of that inferno, my old identity disintegrated.

When everything and everyone seems to fall off-center, I can take it one journey-filled day at a time. I AM my experience in this life, and I AM the observer of my experiences in this life. The unknown is the ultimate freedom. I've reached a state of no-thing-ness, time and time again. The medicine speaks to me. She says, "You have to let go to be free."

In this perception, there is only one you, and there is only everyone. It's simple, yet beautifully complex in its duality. I shift from hope to trust. I gain an acceptance that if this was my last day, then I can allow it to be an amazing one. I can embrace an appreciation for the mortality of my body, while being filled with serenity in the knowledge that Consciousness is infinite. Soak up the love, gratitude, humor, and maybe even a dose of irresistible, seductively primal love-making. I can create a soundtrack desirable of hitting replay.

After continuous searching, I arrive at a place of stillness. This is where the answers are. I hear hypothetical voices in my head saying, "Katie, I am surprised you would do this." I tell those voices, "Well I guess you didn't really know me. Besides, I am not the same person I used to be."

ABOUT THE AUTHOR

Katie is a mother, artist, writer, psychic, energy healer, teacher, creator, and otherwise unsuspecting inhabitant of Earth. She enjoys sharing her journey beyond the falsehood of normalcy and into the flow of consciousness. Her intention is to serve as a clear vessel of Light and inspire seekers of the beyond to embrace their quest with an open heart. She holds multiple certificates in clairvoyance and has post-graduate studies in mindfulness-based transpersonal counseling. Katie is an advocate of plant medicine and the gates of consciousness they have the potential to open. When she is not navigating the matrix, she is immersed in discovering the beauty of Earth with her daughters and cuddling their Norwegian Forest cat, Alpine. She enjoys rock climbing, CrossFit, yoga, music of many genres, sunrises, sunsets, fresh water, wildflowers, clear night skies, laughter, deep eye gazing, the orchestra of nature, and losing sense of time.

www.ingramcontent.com/pod-product-compliance
Lightning Source LLC
Chambersburg PA
CBHW030407130626
46549CB00004B/1671